I GREET YOU AT THE BEGINNING
OF A GREAT CAREER

I GREET YOU AT THE BEGINNING

OF A GREAT CAREER

THE SELECTED CORRESPONDENCE OF

LAWRENCE FERLINGHETTI

AND **ALLEN GINSBERG**

1955–1997

Edited by Bill Morgan

City Lights Books | San Francisco

Copyright © 2015 by Bill Morgan
Letters of Allen Ginsberg © The Estate of Allen Ginsberg
Letters of Lawrence Ferlinghetti © 2015 by Lawrence Ferlinghetti
All Rights Reserved

Cover photo of Allen Ginsberg © 1959 by Chester Kessler
Cover photo of Lawrence Ferlinghetti © 1957 by Harry Redl
Book design by Linda Ronan

Library of Congress Cataloging-in-Publication Data
Ferlinghetti, Lawrence.
[Correspondence. Selections]
 I greet you at the beginning of a great career : the selected correspondence of Law-
rence Ferlinghetti and Allen Ginsberg, 1955-1997 / edited by Bill Morgan.
     pages cm
 ISBN 978-0-87286-686-7 (hardback)
 ISBN 978-0-87286-678-2 (trade paperback)
 1. Ferlinghetti, Lawrence—Correspondence. 2. Ginsberg, Allen, 1926-1997—
Correspondence. 3. Poets, American—20th century—Correspondence. 4. Authors
and publishers—United States—Correspondence. 5. Publishers and publishing—
United States—Correspondence. I. Ginsberg, Allen, 1926-1997. II. Morgan, Bill,
1949- editor.

PS3511.E557Z48 2015
811'.54—dc23
[B]

                             2015004113

City Lights Books are published at the City Lights Bookstore
261 Columbus Avenue, San Francisco, CA 94133
www.citylights.com

Contents

I GREET YOU AT THE BEGINNING
OF A GREAT CAREER

Introduction

One of the longest relationships between a publisher and a writer was that of Lawrence Ferlinghetti and Allen Ginsberg. Ginsberg's very first book, *Howl and Other Poems,* was published by Ferlinghetti's City Lights Books in 1956, and it was followed by a dozen more before Allen's death in 1997. Perhaps because of Ginsberg's action-packed life or Ferlinghetti's innate reluctance to talk about his work as an editor, biographers have not yet explored their author-editor relationship in depth. Their letters reveal the true nature of their lifelong friendship and working relationship. They show Ginsberg as a young man who initially lacks confidence in his own poetry and Ferlinghetti as a firm editor, strongly decisive about what is and is not appropriate for his new publishing house. Soon, however, Allen becomes more confident and opinionated and tries to exert pressure on Lawrence to publish the work of his growing legion of friends. Ferlinghetti remains steadfast in his decision not to publish what he doesn't like, and it is striking that the two manage to remain close friends for the next forty years despite their differences of editorial opinion.

The two poets first met each other in either 1954 or early 1955. The exact date is uncertain, because even though they both kept voluminous journals, neither one made note of their initial meeting. Ferlinghetti must have been immediately impressed with whatever poems Allen showed him, because by August 1955, Allen was writing to friends, telling them that City Lights was going to do a book of his poetry. On August 30, Ginsberg wrote to Jack Kerouac, "City Lights bookstore here putting out pamphlets—50 short pages—of local poets and one of William Carlos Williams reprint and one of [e.e.] cummings and will put out *Howl* (under that title) next year, one booklet for that poem, nothing else—it will fill a booklet." It is important to note the date, because Ginsberg had only completed the first draft of one section of the poem a few days earlier and the historic first reading of the poem at the Six Gallery was still more than a month away.

General Editorial Notes

Most of the letters in this volume are previously unpublished. Seven letters from Allen Ginsberg to Lawrence Ferlinghetti were published in Ginsberg's *The Letters of Allen Ginsberg* (DaCapo, 2008) and excerpts from a handful more appeared in *Howl on Trial* (City Lights, 2006). Ferlinghetti has always been reluctant to publish his own correspondence, so this volume marks a departure from that previous silence. It was only after repeated coaxing on the part of the editor that he agreed to allow their publication here.

The letters span the period from 1955 until Ginsberg's death in 1997 and end with Ferlinghetti's moving tribute to his old friend, "Allen Ginsberg Dying." The letters also document the passing away of the art and beauty of personal correspondence. In the 1950s, letters were the primary means of distant communication, but slowly the telephone encroached upon the written word. As the cost of long-distance communication dropped, Ginsberg and Ferlinghetti grew to depend more and more upon the telephone for domestic communication. By the 1990s, international telephone calls were cheap enough to make letters obsolete even for the most literate of people, and these poets were no exception. Allen himself wrote to Lawrence in 1969 that "alas telephone destroys letters!" As a result, the quantity, quality, and urgency of letters declined in their later years, but enough written documentation remains to give a true picture of the changes that were taking place in their relationship.

In general, footnotes are used only to supply important information that the reader needs to identify people and situations mentioned within the letters. Where notes are required, they are given the first time a person is mentioned in the book. Because the two poets were such close friends, they usually identified people only by their first names, such as Jack or Gregory, meaning Jack Kerouac and Gregory Corso. For purposes of clarity, these are identified as Jack [Kerouac], and so on, only when it appears that it would otherwise be unclear to the reader.

Spelling errors have been corrected in most cases unless it seemed that a playful spelling of a word was intentional, which was often the case with Lawrence Ferlinghetti. When material has been deleted from a letter by the editor, an ellipsis [. . .] is inserted to mark the missing text. If scholars need to study the excised passages, they may refer to the original letters preserved in the archives of Columbia, Stanford, and the University of California at Berkeley. It was a common practice for Ginsberg to send lists of names and addresses to Ferlinghetti, and those have generally been omitted throughout. Postscript statements that are unrelated to the text of letters are omitted without the use of an ellipsis. Allen frequently asked for copies of his books to be sent to him and friends, and those notes also have been omitted without note. In all other cases the standard three-dot ellipsis has been inserted within square brackets. In an effort to save space, repetitive dates and return addresses within letters have not been reproduced. The locations of the writer and the recipient are given when known. Most letters from Lawrence originated at the City Lights Bookstore on Columbus Avenue in San Francisco. All titles of poems, regardless of length, are given within quotation marks; titles of books are given in italics. Thus "Howl" refers to the poem of that name, whereas *Howl* refers to the book *Howl and Other Poems*.

Acknowledgments

Many people generously gave of their time to help compile this book. Without the interest and support of Lawrence Ferlinghetti, this volume would have been impossible. I have worked with Lawrence for more than forty years on a wide variety of projects and he has always proven himself to be unselfish, large-hearted, and supportive. This book affords me the opportunity to thank him for his friendship and encouragement, a gratitude I feel with all my heart, and I'm proud to have shared a bit of his life with him.

Although Allen Ginsberg has been gone for nearly two decades, he also must be thanked for writing such wonderful letters. During my years as his archivist, he was always helpful and generous to a fault, and I hope this work repays a small portion of that kindness. Most especially, thanks to Peter Hale, the secretary of the Allen Ginsberg Trust, who has always been ready to lend a helping hand. Without him, this work would be nothing more than a pamphlet. His associates at the Ginsberg Trust, friends Bob Rosenthal and Andrew Wylie, were also of considerable help, as they always are. It is a blessing that Allen's legacy has been placed in such capable hands.

The staffs of three libraries must be acknowledged for their care in preserving the papers of Lawrence Ferlinghetti and Allen Ginsberg and for their patience in helping me assemble this book. The bulk of the manuscript has been selected from their incredible collections. The Bancroft Library at the University of California at Berkeley; the Green Library at Stanford University; and the Butler Library at Columbia University are treasure troves for Beat scholars. Long may they remain the essential research facilities that they are.

In addition to benefiting from these institutions' collections, I was lucky to be able to pick the brains of many knowledgeable people, and I thank them all from afar. The efforts of Gordon Ball, Carolyn Cassady, Bill Gargan, Jack Hirschman, Bill Keogan, Nancy Peters, and Stephen Sandy are all appreciated and reflected in this work.

The exceptional staff at City Lights Books have made this book a pleasure to edit and they have given us a handsome volume to hold in our hands. Elaine Katzenberger at the helm of the publishing house saw the value of sharing these letters with the public. She and Bob Sharrard were early supporters of the project. Editor Matthew Gleeson saw it through many drafts with grace and intelligence. His suggestions were always spot on.

And final thanks must go to my loving and beloved wife, Judy. She is really the glue that holds all these Beat projects together, and I owe her more than I can ever express. I dedicate this work to her for a lifetime of help and never-failing encouragement.

I GREET YOU AT THE BEGINNING
OF A GREAT CAREER

◄ 1955 ►

On August 20, 1954, after Carolyn Cassady discovered Ginsberg in bed with her husband Neal, she drove Allen from their house in San Jose to San Francisco's North Beach neighborhood and dropped him off in front of the Marconi Hotel, a cheap flophouse near the intersection of Columbus, Broadway, and Grant Avenues. There, Allen took a room and reflected on a life that had brought him to that unhappy crossroads alone and penniless. The Marconi Hotel happened to be across the street from the tiny City Lights Pocket Bookshop owned by Lawrence Ferlinghetti. The following year, Allen moved into an apartment at the corner of Broadway and Montgomery, only a few blocks from the bookstore, and while living there he showed Ferlinghetti his poetry, provoking Lawrence's interest. Lawrence had just begun to publish small books of poetry as the "Pocket Poets Series," and so far had released his own Pictures of the Gone World and two other titles by the more established poets Kenneth Rexroth and Kenneth Patchen. By the time Allen took part in a reading at the Six Gallery on October 7, 1955, Ferlinghetti had already agreed in principle to publish a selection of his work, but the book hadn't yet taken shape. Ferlinghetti was in the audience on that momentous night and heard Allen read his great masterpiece "Howl" for the first time. Immediately he sent a telegram to Ginsberg, paraphrasing Emerson's famous note to Walt Whitman, which Whitman printed in the appendix to Leaves of Grass. Lawrence added his own postscript:

October 13, 1955: Telegram from Lawrence Ferlinghetti to Allen Ginsberg, both in San Francisco

I GREET YOU AT THE BEGINNING OF A GREAT CAREER [stop] WHEN DO I GET MANUSCRIPT OF "HOWL"? [stop] LAWRENCE (FERLINGHETTI) CITY LIGHTS BOOKSTORE

Because Ginsberg lived so close to City Lights, he and Ferlinghetti simply met in person to discuss the proposed book, Howl and Other Poems. *It wasn't until June 1956, when Ginsberg left San Francisco for a voyage to the Arctic with the Merchant Marines, that their long history of correspondence began. By this time the two were correcting the proofs for Ginsberg's book. Even at that late stage they reveal Ginsberg's lingering doubts about his own poetry, though his self-confidence would steadily grow in the coming years. Unfortunately, Ferlinghetti's letters to Ginsberg from this period have not survived, and his side of the correspondence will not appear until February 1957.*

◀ 1956 ▶

June 22, 1956: Allen Ginsberg on board the USNS *Sgt. Jack J. Pendleton* in Seattle to Lawrence Ferlinghetti in San Francisco

Dear Larry:

Well what news? I am in Seattle, will be here over weekend and thru next Friday, will return to San Francisco next weekend for a few days — arrive sometime Sunday I expect, around the 30th or 31st. If therefore you got or will get proofs hold on to them, I'll look them over myself.

Generally speaking the Greyhound poem ["In the Baggage Room at Greyhound"] stinks on ice, at least the end does — that won't last no 1000 years — I had a nightmare about it standing on the prow several days ago. I dunno what to do, haven't written anything better on it since leaving town. Maybe later.

If you call Kenneth by phone tell him I'll see him in few days, when return, Rexroth that is.

Spending much time gazing at the "misty vast nebulous and never-to-be-knowable clouds," and reading Shakespeare.

As ever,
Allen

Ginsberg discovered that Ferlinghetti's typesetter had not correctly followed his instructions for setting his long-line poems. Allen wanted the beginnings of the poetic lines in "Howl" justified on the left side, and continued with indentations whenever they ran on longer than a single line on the page. With some of the other poems, though, he used an entirely different scheme, indenting them like normal prose paragraphs. It proved to be confusing for the British typesetter, John Sankey, working for Villiers Press, and he charged them an extra $20 for all the revisions it necessitated.

Dear Larry:

This being my first book I want it right if can. Therefore I thought and decided this, about the justifications, of margins. (The reason for my being particular is that the poems are actually sloppy enough written, without sloppiness made worse by typographical arrangement. The one element of order and prearrangement I did pay care to was arrangement into prose-paragraph strophes: each one definite unified long line.[1] So any doubt about irregularity of right hand margin will be sure to confuse critical reader about intention of the prosody. Therefore I've got to change it so it's right.

It looks like the whole book will have to be reset practically. Find out how much it costs to reset the first proofs we received, which is my fault for not having followed precisely thru and made sure in advance it was understood. I will pay that no matter how much up to $200.00, which I guess it may well cost. [. . .]

This will be sure to delay things longer but the more I look at it the worse it seems, it's real bad this way, I mean you can't tell <u>what</u> I'm doing, it looks like just primitive random scribblings in pages. I had not intended the prosody to be <u>that</u> arbitrary. [. . .]

(My reason incidentally for the erratic is simple, most of it's prose but wherever it struck me as really poetic as I was writing I would indent all of a sudden.)

Allen

While on board the Sgt. Jack J. Pendleton, *Ginsberg had access to the ship's mimeo machine. He used it to print a small edition of a long poem he had written in Mexico in 1954 called "Siesta in Xbalba." Even this, his first*

---

1 Ginsberg wrote about the composition of "Howl" at great length in several places, including a letter to Richard Eberhart dated May 18, 1956, reprinted in *The Letters of Allen Ginsberg* (Philadelphia: DaCapo, 2008), pp. 130–139.

publication, Allen used as an opportunity to promote and support the work of friends.

August 4, 1956: Allen Ginsberg on board the USNS *Sgt. Jack J. Pendleton* near Wainwright, Alaska, to Lawrence Ferlinghetti in San Francisco

Dear Larry:

Enclosed find [. . .] thirteen copies of a mimeographed pamphlet of the Mexican poem I made up here on ship last weekend ["Siesta in Xbalba"]. Keep one yourself and put the other dozen on sale at 50¢ each if you think you can sell them. Give the proceeds to Mike Mc-Clure for use for *Moby Magazine*. You can advertise them as a charity type shot for *Moby*. I made up another forty and am keeping them or sending them out as whim strikes me. [. . .]

Reading [François] Villon for the first time in French thru Wyndham Lewis's biography which has a good selection of the poems and ponys for each.[2] Lament of *la belle Heaulmière* I dug the most, particularly the mad sensual stanza about *petiz tetins . . . ce sadinet assis sur grosses fermes cuisses* beautiful clear lament for her lost cunt, makes it so real.

Pass on any news of interest. Anchored presently near Eskimo town trading post of Wainwright but not allowed ashore as we might give them measles.

As ever,
Allen

At the beginning of August, Ferlinghetti received a few advance copies of the bound book Howl and Other Poems *and sent one of them to Ginsberg on board his ship near the Arctic Circle. Some of the poems that Allen had*

---

2 Ginsberg is referring to D.B. Wyndham-Lewis's book *François Villon* about the fifteenth-century French poet, which Coward-McCann had published in 1928.

submitted were not included in the final selection. Meanwhile, Allen's friend Gregory Corso had arrived in San Francisco unannounced, not knowing that Allen was away with the Merchant Marines. Awaiting Allen's return, Gregory introduced himself to Ferlinghetti and some of the other poets in the city. Before long, Lawrence would be making plans to publish a book of Corso's poetry.

ca. August 9, 1956: Allen Ginsberg on board the USNS *Sgt. Jack J. Pendleton* to Lawrence Ferlinghetti in San Francisco

Dear Larry

Received the copy of the book you sent me promptly — and was excited to see it. Everything worked out fine with the typography — it looks much better this way and it seems to have been real cheap to do — $20 is nuthin. I shuddered when I read the poetry tho, it all seems so jerry-built sloppy and egocentric, most of it. "Greyhound" looks fine, I'm glad you told me to put it in. Reading it all through I'm not sure it deserves all the care and work you've put into it and the encouragement you've given me, in fact to tell you the truth I am already embarrassed by half of it, but what the hell, thank you anyway for all your courtesy and I hope few people will see it with such jaded eyes as I do, tho I guess it's best the poems have a truthful fate than an over-sympathetic one. I wonder if we will actually sell the thousand copies.

Did Villiers send back the spare and extra manuscript? Hold on to them for me please — the poem's not printed. The choice is fine, tho since the "Dream Record" [June 8, 1955] poem is I think of early poems the best I wish it were there too.

[Philip] Whalen writes me that [Robert] LaVigne[3] sees [Gregory] Corso. I'm not sure what this means, but maybe it means that Corso is in town — if so maybe you can meet him around and get a manuscript? I didn't know he was on the West Coast. [. . .]

---

3 Robert LaVigne (1928–2014), a painter and illustrator who had introduced Ginsberg to his companion, Peter Orlovsky.

"Transcription of Organ Music" I still like, I'm not sorry. It's not revised so it's not bad "Art" like the rest of the writing. Its ineptness is its own and nature's not mine.

[unsigned]

Ginsberg returned from his voyage with the Merchant Marines in September, so for a while his communications with Lawrence took place in person. In November he spent two weeks in Mexico with Jack Kerouac, Gregory Corso, and Lafcadio and Peter Orlovsky. Afterwards everyone hitched a ride to New York City, except Gregory Corso, who planned to fly to Washington, D.C. at the invitation of the poet Randall Jarrell, who was the Poetry Consultant for the Library of Congress. Meanwhile, Ferlinghetti had decided to reprint 1,500 copies of Howl and Other Poems. *The reading that Ginsberg mentions in the following letter was one that eventually became something of a legend. During it Allen, a bit drunk, had stripped nude in order to shock a heckler. Later he began to tell people that he had done it to show that a poet had to be honest enough to reveal himself completely, nakedly. Eventually some would claim that Ginsberg disrobed at many readings, but in fact this was the one and only time he did so.*

December 7, 1956: Allen Ginsberg in New York City to Lawrence Ferlinghetti in San Francisco

Dear Larry:

Well, finally here in New York City. We left Gregory waiting for money order to arrive in Mexico City; it was sent the worst and slowest way possible, mail money order, several weeks ago, he was still waiting December 3. Money order from his girl so he could fly home fast, to [Randall] Jarrell's.

Reading we gave in Los Angeles was the most wild ever, I disrobed, finally, been wanting to onstage for years.

Peter, Lafcadio and Jack Kerouac and I came up here together.

Gregory by the way filled a whole huge Mexican notebook full of beautiful strange poems and silly pictures, writing more and better than ever. His book for you ought to be really great, individual and solid — he surprised me even by his great voluminousness and co-piousness and freedom of imagination all the way down on the trip, writing poems all over everywhere in bus stops and restaurants. His style developing looser and more far out toward an imaginative wop surrealism. He's as completely tough and original now as anyone I can think of. I was really kind of aghast and amazed how fertile and curi-ous everything he wrote seemed at the moment.

Well anyway, this letter from [James] Laughlin.[4] Open all letters you think necessary, personal or not, I don't care. I hope to give him something new, rather than reprint "Howl." So the reprint of 1500 *Howls* is safe. Grove Press has an *Evergreen Review* upcoming and they asked for reprint of "Howl" too, but I'll give them other material. Maybe later on if there's still demand, in a year or so, I don't know. Why 1500 copies?? Can you sell them? There are a number in the 8th St. Bookshop, buried under Rexroth's title [*Thirty Spanish Poems of Love and Exile*], but nobody I know in the Village has seen or bought it. So I don't imagine you'll dispose of many in the Village. Need some kind of advertising or distribution, but that's out of the question. [. . .]

Spent a long time talking with [William Carlos] Williams yes-terday, he heard [a] little about the San Francisco scene and was inter-ested. I read him some Gregory which he liked. Just spoke to Laughlin, told him to reprint "Sunflower [Sutra]," if he wanted, and will send him some new poems. I guess that would not harm book, might do it some good in fact.

Denise Levertov we stopped and saw,[5] she was nice to us, we liked her a lot. I was surprised how much a good Joe she was. [. . .] Levertov

---

4 The publisher of New Directions Books, James Laughlin, had written asking for some Ginsberg poems to publish.
5 While in Guadalajara, Mexico, the group had visited poet Denise Levertov and her husband, writer Mitchell Goodman.

is a good poetess, certainly, I read a lot of her work there. Regards, I'll write a clearer letter later.

Allen

Ginsberg continued to be a strong supporter of his friends' work throughout his life. In the following letter he promotes their writing to Ferlinghetti, but Lawrence had his own ideas about what he wanted to publish and did not always agree with Ginsberg's choices. Both poets had begun to make commercial recordings of their poetry at this point, too.

This letter also mentions that Knopf, a powerful New York–based publishing house, was showing interest in Ginsberg. At this point it was by no means certain that Ferlinghetti would publish a second book of Ginsberg's poetry or that Allen would stay with City Lights for the next thirty years as he did. In the years to come, publishers would repeatedly inquire about the possibility of publishing Ginsberg's work, but Allen's loyalty to City Lights was solidified in 1957 when Ferlinghetti defended the publication of Howl and Other Poems *in court.*

December 20, 1956: Allen Ginsberg in New York to Lawrence Ferlinghetti in San Francisco

Dear Larry:

[. . .] Did they play parts 1, 2 and 3 [of "Howl"] uncut on KPFA[6]? I didn't record the Footnote Holy part. Did they play Gregory's yet? Kerouac, off to Florida to visit his mother, stopping there tomorrow one day. Gregory working on your manuscript [*Gasoline*], you should hear from him soon. I read his first book and some new poems to William Carlos Williams, who dug them, would probably give you a publicity paragraph if needed, too. Also read him some Kerouac which he said was colossal. Also read him [Philip] Whalen's *Slop Barrel* which

---

6 KPFA, founded in 1946, is the first listener-supported non-commercial radio station in the U.S.

he liked, not understanding the Zen, but dug the art. He said you decided to reprint all *Kora in Hell* — is this true? If so, great. I have a call from Knopf, business, the girl said, will see them after Xmas. Don't know what they want, maybe to publish me, I doubt it. If so will give them book of poems, "Xbalba," "Green Auto," "Over Kansas," the poems you didn't want. Doubt they'd take them. I read them to William Carlos Williams too, who said they ("Over Kansas") he liked better than "Howl" and should publish. Well, whatever, I do want to publish them as a book, trimmed down to be twenty-five or thirty poems or less. I'll let you know what develops. [. . .]

Went to *New York Times* and bearded them for a review, got interviewed by Harvey Breit, and will, I think, get *Howl* reviewed there. Few stores carry City Lights, generally unobtainable unless you know where, but one review in *Times* or *Tribune* or *Saturday Review* could break the ice maybe.

Cambridge Review rejected Jack, Burroughs, Rexroth. You too? Gregory didn't say, when you write him ask. Accepted and dug Whalen and me. Some fellow from Grove, Don Allen, will be looking for San Francisco stuff thru Rexroth and [Robert] Duncan soon, for *Evergreen Review*. How was the reading with you and Philip [Whalen]?

[Jerry] Newman of Esoteric [Records] wants to set up a reading in his studio, maybe we will. Can you send copy of a recording? the KPFA? Please ask [Ruth] Witt-Diamant[7] to send me my tape, to this address, this week. A tape I loaned her. Lawrence Lipton[8] made a wild [one], the best tape yet, in Los Angeles and is trying to peddle to Caedmon or Esoteric, but that's impossible, the machine was a home one so the fidelity ain't right. Can get it on records thru Esoteric, if we make an engineered reading here, but haven't the heart to start all that over again, organizing a reading. Maybe before I leave.[9] Hard to

---

7 Ruth Witt-Diamant was the director of the San Francisco Poetry Center during the 1950s.
8 Lawrence Lipton (1898–1975), a journalist and the author of a 1959 book surveying the Beats called *The Holy Barbarians*.
9 The New York poets, Ginsberg, Orlovsky, Corso, and Kerouac were planning a trip to visit Burroughs in Morocco and then go on to Europe.

deliver, too self-conscious, a dramatic, really satisfying reading to order. In Los Angeles I got drunk and wailed. [. . .]

Viking publishing Kerouac [*On the Road*], pretty definite now, contracts maybe even already signed, and Grove taking novelette [*The Subterraneans*] for sure too. When he finishes editing his manuscript in about a month or so, we'll leave. Gregory is going — me, Jack, Gregory and Peter, who sends his regards. [. . .] Haven't written much, been busy peddling Whalen, Snyder, Corso manuscripts, a couple of weird short-line poems about being in Europe and dreaming of boys in Kansas. Will go see Knopf and find out what they want, I won't know what to do if they want a future book. *Howl* is safe where it is, at any rate. Doubt they'll be serious tho.

What happened at your reading, write? What's with the scene, anything new? How's Rexroth. Regards to Ron Loewinsohn if you see him, and John Ryan and [Jack] Spicer[10] if he's there. Did he give big queer reading at Six Gallery Thanksgiving as promised??

As ever,
Allen

---

10 Allen mentions several friends here: Ron Loewinsohn, a young poet and novelist; John Allen Ryan, a poet and painter who worked as a bartender at The Place in North Beach; and Jack Spicer, who was a poet and a founding member of the Six Gallery in San Francisco.

◀ 1957 ▶

ca. January 1957: Allen Ginsberg in New York to Lawrence Ferlinghetti in San Francisco

Dear Larry:
Glad to hear your reading so lively, I wish you'd write a more detailed description tho, who there and what kind of scene. Are there any other exciting readings planned yet, or available, I mean anyone else capable of giving something direct to audience? How did Whalen sound to you? I mean how did you like his poetry? I still wish you could publish him and Gary Snyder. Sooner or later they will be famous and salable [I] think. Gregory here in New York. We went to big [Richard] Eberhart party and corn holed [*sic:* button-holed] Arabelle Porter (*New World Writing*)[11] for an hour and a half, explaining. She wound up saying she ain't got any real power anyway. *Cambridge Review* came out, not much of ours in it. However there's a really live poem by Kenneth Koch. Since I've been here, I realize there's a similar movement to freedom in New York, on part of ex-Auden fairies and semi-fairies and non-fairies who been writing surrealist long lines. Koch's poem is good, read it thru, the end is really great, show it to Kenneth [Rexroth]. ("Fresh Air"). The three, Koch, O'Hara and Ashbery are friends and read Whitman and French poetry and seem to have independent spirit. Another, I visited Paul Goodman and read a lot of his poetry, I hadn't realized how much he's written. Never had a book of poetry out. If you are interested, ask him for a manuscript of a book. I was really amazed how good his poetry is. I'd seen a few pieces in *Poetry* occasionally. I don't dig his prose. But his poetry is straightforward intimate personal and factual and has bright eyes. Kenneth [Rexroth] must have his address. But if you are interested in at least looking at a manuscript let me know and I'll tell him or you drop him a card. [. . .]

---

11 Arabelle Porter was one of the editors of *New World Writing* during the 1950s.

Leave in a month I guess, when Jack [Kerouac] finished with Viking and Grove publication revisions and plans. Never did see Knopf yet. I am still trying to get *Howl* reviewed somewhere in New York, unsuccessfully. Grove man liked what he saw of Whalen and Corso and Snyder. Have you sent him any? Don Allen, for Grove's *Evergreen Review*. Will write Kenneth [Rexroth] today.

As ever,

Allen

8th St. Bookshop ran out — might check by postcard with others — all be out of *Howl* soon, sales picking up since I arrived.

Ginsberg had tried to honor his friend Lucien Carr by dedicating Howl and Other Poems *to "Lucien Carr, recently promoted to Night Bureau Manager of New York United Press." In the following letter, he mentions that Lucien was not pleased about this. In 1944 Carr had killed a man who was stalking him and since his release from jail he had been working for United Press, trying to put the past behind him. He always remained friendly with Ginsberg, Burroughs, and Kerouac, but he did not want his name associated with theirs.*

Once again Ginsberg mentions that Ferlinghetti turned down the chance to publish the poetry of Philip Whalen and Gary Snyder. At the time, Lawrence was more interested in poetry influenced by the European tradition than in the Buddhism-inspired verse of Whalen and Snyder. Also, as the beginning of this letter indicates, not all reviewers were kind to Allen's work.

January 15, 1957: Allen Ginsberg in New York to Lawrence Ferlinghetti in San Francisco

Dear Larry:

January 9 letter received, as well as clipping from [*San Francisco*] *Chronicle*. I was going to write [Norman K.] Dorn, the reviewer, a letter but I tried several, each a different tone and they all sounded goofy so I gave up. If you see him ever say we collectively rarely have lice, and I hope he drops dead of clap. No, wasn't really discouraged, just realized what a weird place New York book reviewing works like. [. . .]

What you say about Whalen is partly true, he is, despite straight speech, an esoteric, in subject matter, that is the Zen quietism; however he has excellent great funny grasp of his subject and deals with it straight and uniquely, that is, flat prose funny images and examples taken from real life, his, mixed with learning and doctrine. Williams, for instance, to whom I read Whalen, didn't understand what was at the center, but commented that each particular in the poem, the blocks, was real and clear. Whalen's center will be less impalpable, as he keeps writing in time. But these poems, now, do speak Jappy[12] to me, as do Snyder's. But perhaps you are right for your purposes you want something frenchy. You have enough to publish without; and Whalen will I hope be taken care of in New York. Don Allen liked him and *I.E.* [*The Cambridge Review*], so he'll have someplace to publish, sooner or later, which is what's important.

Listen, great tragedy. My friend Lucien Carr objects violently to using his name in dedication. His reasons are varied and personal and real enough for him — I had never asked his OK, and he has reasons why not. What can be done about omitting that line in the dedication in the second printing? Is it too late for immediate action?

It's my fuck up, but I have to straighten it out. Therefore if the whole thing is printed and bound already, have it done all over again and bill me for the second printing. It's about $100 more or less? Write them immediately and find out how far they've gone and to suspend operations, and what will it cost to eliminate the line, in toto. I dunno. Anyway I am bound by honor to DO something about it no matter how much it fucks everything up. So please write them and tell them send me carbon of answer, so can send you immediate cash or advice

---

12 In some ways Allen Ginsberg was a product of his times, and occasionally words such as wop, jap, and shade appeared in his letters and journals. Here he refers to the Japanese influence as "Jappy."

whatever necessary. I know this sounds crazy and probably it is but I have to. Please don't flip. I got the money so it won't screw you up.

What did you think of [Kenneth] Koch's poem "Fresh Air" in *I.E.* [*The Cambridge Review*]? I thought very good. Jack Kerouac, Peter Orlovsky and I went out to visit W.C. Williams who said he'd review the book — probably for *Times* I guess — so (this being Gregory's book *Gasoline*) with [Randall] Jarrell intro that ought to set up Gregory. Long funny afternoon we all got drunk and my father[13] drove us home here raving and weeping about St. Carlos. He dug Jack and his wife also. Gregory unmentioned above was there too, I forgot. He read mad silly poems to Williams and Williams loved him, but worried what he'd be like "in forty years." [. . .]

As ever,
Allen

February 5, 1957: Lawrence Ferlinghetti in San Francisco to Allen Ginsberg in New York

Dear Allen,
Howl will be delayed an extra two weeks due to deletion of Lucien Carr, and I have been completely out of [copies] for almost a month. However, it should be here in bulk by February 20 at the latest. I caught them in the last stage — the book had already been folded and gathered, but not stitched. Therefore, one section could still be taken out, reprinted, and regathered, etc . . . The total extra cost comes to $25, which I could use as soon as possible, to pay the bill. I have back orders from all over the country now — including big orders for Paper Editions. [Ted] Wilentz at the Eighth Street Bookshop in New York has ordered 100 copies. I sent him the last five I had. Gotham Book Mart has also put in a big standing order, and I sent them five of yours as a stop-gap. [. . .]

We all got photographed for *Life* Sunday night at a mass reading

---

13 Louis Ginsberg (1895–1976), Allen Ginsberg's father, was a poet and schoolteacher in New Jersey.

at Kenneth's [Rexroth] . . . I am sick of all these con operations, and I hope every photographer in the country crawls in a hole somewhere and drops dead. It all has nothing to do with poetry. I am not sending my poetry anywhere unsolicited, and frankly I don't give a good shit if they come and get it or not. I wasted enough post on *Partisan* twenty years ago . . . However, as for your book, I will continue to push and will send copy to Lisa Dyer at *Hudson Review* as soon as I get a copy to send. *Poetry* writes me that they will include it in a review early this summer . . . by [Frederick] Eckman [. . .]

> Best, regards, etc,
>
> Larry

Lawrence wrote an article criticizing a poetry reading given by Allen the previous fall in North Beach. The reading had been held in a cavernous auditorium that had a bad sound system, and Lawrence described Allen's performance as lackluster. Meanwhile, Grove Press asked to reprint "Howl" in a new periodical called Evergreen Review, *leading Ferlinghetti and Ginsberg to discuss whether or not this might impact sales of* Howl and Other Poems.

ca. mid-February 1957: Allen Ginsberg in New York to Lawrence Ferlinghetti in San Francisco

Dear Larry:

I saw that dirty review in *Intro [Bulletin]*[14] you cocksucker, but is it my fault the acoustics were bad and I was man enough to brave the storm and not read "Howl"? besides which having nothing worthwhile to read except "Sather Gate [Illumination]" poem I only read again to help make it with Gregory? and a lot of other excuses? Was it that bad? Other than that I rather agreed with what you had to say, it was a lousy reading.

---

14 *Intro Bulletin, A Literary Newspaper of the Arts*, vol. 2, no. 1 (Jan. 1957) issue.

Thank God you caught *Howl*, now the gods are appeased, send me the bill whatever it may be. Sorry the hassle and the delay and thanks for being so good about it.

Re, Grove. Don Allen says he would like to reprint "Howl" poem complete in *Evergreen Review*. I told him I had promised you no. He said he'd write you. I have various thoughts, but I leave it completely up to you, do whatever you think best for sale of City Lights edition and cause of Frisco publishing. It may be you can sell your edition enough before *Evergreen* comes out; it may be that reprint in *Evergreen* will help sell complete book; or it may be the converse that reprint will kill sales of *Howl* pocket book. Figure it out and make decision yourself. I'm not too personally eager yet to reprint like in *Evergreen*, since if I wait maybe someday I can sell it to *New World Writing* for some loot when I'm starving in Europe. On the other hand, Don Allen has been very hep with Kerouac, myself, Snyder, Whalen and the West Coast, and cooperated like a dream, liking everything and digging everybody — so I wish him well with *Evergreen* project and would like on principle to cooperate with his project. If you say yes to him it's OK by me; if you say no, equally OK. I told you originally I wouldn't fuck up your publishing with reprinting, so that is why I refuse to make decision now one way or the other and leave it in your hands. [. . .]

Kenneth Koch of "Fresh Air" is somewhere in Europe, has lots of manuscripts and never had a book. John Ashbery had two good poems in his New Yale series book, the rest of the book is chichi shit, but "Instruction Manual" and one other about teacher is good. Frank O'Hara will have a book out at Grove. They are three friends, all write similarly. [. . .]

As ever,
Allen

A good deal of discussion about copyright issues, which makes for dull reading, has been deleted here. But one significant complication came from the fact that Howl and Other Poems *had been originally printed in England before being printed in the U.S. Though Ginsberg makes the cavalier statement in the following letter that "it's all just a bunch of bureaucratic papers," from a business point of view it wasn't clear who owned the rights to "Howl."*

Meanwhile Ginsberg was planning a trip with Peter Orlovsky to visit William Burroughs in Tangier. By this time Jack Kerouac was already in Morocco helping Burroughs edit the chaotic manuscript that would become Naked Lunch. *Gregory Corso was on his way to Paris, where he intended to rendezvous with his girlfriend, Hope Savage. They all planned to reunite later in the year either in North Africa or Europe.*

March 3, 1957: Allen Ginsberg in New York to Lawrence Ferlinghetti in San Francisco

Dear Larry:

Have investigated but as far as I know, the book can't be copyrighted here because printed in England. If you know a way it can be, please do so in my name and send me bill for what it costs.

The best way, lacking possibility of U.S. copyright, is to copyright it in England. For that, Villiers would have to put I believe six copies on sale in England, and send it to certain prescribed British Libraries. If this is the best way, could you write and ask them to do that in my name and send me the bill?

If necessary, can copyright it in your name or City Lights or whoever, with the understanding that it's my copyright to use as I wish and get whatever loot I can. Though actually I guess no copyright is necessary and it's all just a bunch of bureaucratic papers so no point actually in doing anything, nobody has anything to steal except in paranoiac future lands. If it seems like too much trouble don't bother doing anything but if you know a simple way, please try it.

I finally leave here [New York], held up by getting Orlovsky brother out of madhouse[15] and tug/longshore strikes, March 8 via

---

15 Peter Orlovsky's brother, Julius, had been in a mental hospital for several years, and they hoped to help him gain his release before they went on their trip. They were not successful.

Yugoslav freighter name of *Hrvatska*. Nine days to Casablanca, one day stopover, another day to Tangiers, $185 fare, spacious accommodations and big picture of Tito in saloon mess hall. Jack left February 15, Gregory left a week ago on *America*, bound for Paris to meet great grandson of Shelley his girlfriend discovered (in Paris). [. . .] Gregory will work on his manuscript in Paris. Send me copies of any new books you put out please, would love to see them.

I wrote awhile back that Don Allen at Grove wants to reprint "Howl" in *Evergreen Review*, but I told him to consult you and take your decision. Let me know what you think, so I can give him something else if not. My guess is it wouldn't hinder sale of the book, but I don't know, so as I said I won't intrude on your business.

What's happening? I've now extricated myself from publicity work and am sitting quietly reading Blake and Mayakovsky — do you know the latter? — really the end, mad public prophetic style.

I hear [Charles] Olson[16] is there, what's he like and what's happening socially?

As ever,
Allen

Ferlinghetti wrote back just as breezily about contracts and copyrights. However, as Ginsberg's importance grew, this friendly handshake agreement would become more difficult to maintain.

ca. March 1957: Lawrence Ferlinghetti in San Francisco to Allen Ginsberg in New York

Dear Allen,
The hell with contracts — we will just tell them you have standing agreement with me and you can give me anything you feel like giv-

---

16 Charles Olson (1910–1970), an American modernist poet who taught at Black Mountain College.

ing me on reprints whenever you get back to States and sit in Poetry Chairs in hinterland CCNYs[17] and are rich and famous and fat and fucking your admirers and getting reprinted in all of seldenrod-man's anthologies,[18] until then, natch, the loot shud be yours since as you say I am getting famous as your publisher anyway. Do you want more *Howls* and other Pocket Poets sent now (which ones?) and charged against you? How many? . . . Am still reading Kerouac's poetry woiks and will be at it for some time yet . . . trouble is when I got back from New York I found about 100 manuscripts to read from all over . . . no exaggeration 100 . . . when do I get to see the Burroughs? after Grove and New Directions have refused or combed it . . . logically . . . Yes, New Directions is going to publish my *Coney Island of the Mind* with selections from *Gone World* and all the stuff on the Fantasy Record we made at the Cellar[19] which you never heard ("Junkman's Obbligato," etc.) . . . it is going to be a paperbound book only, to sell for one dollar or so — James Laughlin having taken a big liking to the format of the Pocket Poets series . . . The *Kora* is out[20] and have mailed you and Gregory each a copy . . . [William Carlos] Williams was here last week, by the way, and heard me at the Cellar [. . .] Max Weiss at Fantasy here is all ready to do "Howl" recording and knows lots of recording facilities in Paris and is going to write you or get me addresses and instructions for you very soon. Let him arrange it. He is great and honest. He will probably want contract and will send. (Re contracts, you see whut happens after one week in New York — I am talking just like all the other literary detectives there before I leave — contractscontractscontracts . . . well fuckem and fuck the *Partisan Review* whom I've never sent anything to and we'll make it here in San Francisco . . . I am going into publishing prose books and got printers lined up in east and have some really great ideas on reprints of long-

---

17 City College of New York.
18 Reference to Selden Rodman, who edited several mass-market collections of poetry, including the *New Anthology of Modern Poetry*.
19 The Cellar was a jazz nightclub at 576 Green Street in San Francisco that offered a combination of poetry and jazz during the 1950s.
20 Williams, William Carlos. *Kora in Hell: Improvisations*. (San Francisco: City Lights, 1957).

out-of-print authors and new authors, etc . . .) Sending copy to [Ray] Bremser in reformatory . . . as you request . . . Will soon send addition on *Howl* sales to-date. OK? G'bye . . .

larry

The letter from Lawrence Ferlinghetti written March 27 that Ginsberg refers to below has not been located. In it Ferlinghetti must have told Ginsberg some of the details about the seizure of copies of Howl and Other Poems *by the San Francisco office of the U.S. Customs Department. The Collector of Customs, Chester MacPhee, believed that the book was obscene and would not allow it to be imported from Ferlinghetti's British printer. Lawrence contacted the ACLU, which agreed to go to court to defend Ginsberg's book.*

April 3, 1957: Allen Ginsberg in Tangier, Morocco, to Lawrence Ferlinghetti in San Francisco

Dear Larry:

Received your letter of March 27 and was surprised by news of Customs' seizure. [. . .] Offhand I don't know what to say about MacPhee. I don't know what the laws are and what rights I got. Is it possible to get them in at New York post office and have them shipped on to you under other label or address? Transshipped from New York that is? Is it also possible to have any copies sent to me here from England? I suppose the publicity will be good — I have been here with Jack, Peter and Bill Burroughs all hung-up on private life and Bill's mad personality and writings and on digging the Arab quarter and taking majoun (hashish candy) and opium and drinking hot sweet delicious mint tea in Rembrandt dark cafes and long walks in lucid Mediterranean coast green grassy brilliant light North Africa that I haven't written any letters (this is the second in two weeks) or thought much about anything. I'll write to Grove to Don Allen and let him know, and he'll tell the lady from *Time-Life*. If you can mimeograph a letter and get some kind of statement from William Carlos Williams,

21

[Louise] Bogan, [Richard] Eberhart and send it around to magazines might get some publicity that way. Also let Harvey Breit at *New York Times* know for sure definitely — he'd probably run a story maybe. My brother is a lawyer and has recently done some research on the subject, I'll write him to get in touch with you and provide any legal aid — if any is useful from him in New York. I guess this puts you up shits creek financially. I didn't think it would really happen. I didn't know it was costing you $200 for reprint, I thought it was $80.00 each extra thousand. Sorry I am not there, we might talk and figure up some way for a U.S. edition, I guess that would be expensive tho. Be sure let the *Life* people in San Francisco know about situation, they might include it in story. The woman in New York is Rosalind Constable c/o *Time-Life*, Rockefeller Center. She is very simpatico and would immediately call it to attention of Peter Bunzell who is (I heard) writing up the story for *Life* in New York. Send story too to *Village Voice*, they've been digging the scene. By the way I heard there was a lukewarm review in *Partisan Review*, could you send it to me? Might let them know, too, as they took a poem of mine for later. I guess the best way publicity-wise is prepare some sort of outraged and idiotic but dignified statement, quoting the customs man, and Eberhart's article and Williams, and *Nation* review, mimeograph it up and send it out as a sort of manifesto publishable by magazines and/or news release. Send one to Lu Carr at United Press, too. If this is worthwhile. Also write, maybe, Jarrell, at Library of Congress and see if you can get his official intercession. I imagine these customs people have to obey orders of their superiors; and that superiors in Washington, D.C. might be informed and requested to intercede by some official in Library of Congress. Maybe I'll write my congressmen — is there a friendly congressman in San Francisco? This might be more rapid than a lawsuit. Copyright it under City Lights name — only thing is, if you ever make your money back and make some profit from all your trouble, and we go into a 4th or 17th edition, we divvy the loot. I don't think Grove book will knock out sales. They'll probably carry note about the full book.

Send me clippings of reviews — I haven't got anything besides the *Nation*, if anything comes through; also any further news of The Cellar, etc. sounds charming. Everybody must be having a ball. How's [Robert] Duncan. Regards to [Peter] DuPeru,[21] etc. *Ark III* out yet? Send one? I must say am more depressed than pleased, [more] disgusted than pleased, about customs shot, amusing as it is — the world is such a bottomless hole of boredom and poverty and paranoiac politics and diseased rags here *Howl* seems like a drop in the bucket-void and literary furor illusory — seems like it's happening in otherland — outside me, nothing to do with me or anything. Jack [Kerouac] has a room I move into next week, full of light on a hill a few blocks above the beach from whence I'm writing now, can look over the veranda redstone tile, huge patio, over the harbor, over the bay, across the very sunlit straits and see the blue coast of Spain and ancient parapets of Europe I haven't been to yet. Gibraltar small and faraway but there in brilliant blue water, and a huge clear solid cloudless blue sky   I never saw such serene light as this, big classical Mediterranean beauty-light over a small world. I'll write Señor MacPhee myself, ask him to let my copies go, big serious poignant sad letter.

Write me and I'll answer, let me know how things go, if there's anything you want me to do let me know and send along any clippings if you can. These aerogrammes are only 10¢ postage if there are no enclosures.

Thank Kenneth [Rexroth] for efforts and say I hope he enjoys the scene — it is pretty funny, almost a set-up, I imagine they can't bug us forever, and will have to give in. Let me know what the law is.

Rock and roll on all the jukeboxes here, just had a rock and roll riot at the movie house here a few weeks ago, and in fact before I left New York, me and Peter picked up on the historic stage show at the Paramount. I brought a few Little Richard and Fats Domino records here in fact.

---

21 Peter du Peru was a San Francisco con man and hustler whom Ginsberg knew and liked.

Only interesting person here besides Burroughs is Jane Bowles[22] whom I have only met with once.

As ever,
Allen Grebsnig
[Ginsberg spelled
backwards]

May 10, 1957: Allen Ginsberg in Tangier, Morocco, to Lawrence Ferlinghetti in San Francisco

Dear Larry:

Still here in Tangiers. Working on Burroughs manuscript with friend been in town a week name of Alan Ansen,[23] type in relays and sit and bullshit, story conferences, revisions, etc., hanging together huge 1000 page manuscript. Ran out of money and got grant of $200 from National Institute of Arts and Letters thru William Carlos Williams. Don't know how long that'll last, tho Peter now gets $50 a month from government for being mad.[24] Should be here in Tangiers another month. Quite an establishment we have here. Me and Peter upstairs with huge verandah and view of straits and bay, Burroughs downstairs with his majoun (hashish candy) and typewriter, Ansen on first floor — he an eight languaged ex-Harvard magna cum laude who used to be Auden's secretary and literary factotum, a large mad genius dilettante who helps edit and type Bill's work, and Paul Bowles arrived today in same rooming house from India, with his boyfriend painter an Arab primitive name of Ahmed Yacoubi. Haven't seen Bowles yet but Bill knows him well, so the scene ought to jump this week. Also since yesterday, Peter brought home a beautiful mannered deep voiced young Swede with rucksack and sleeping bag which he slept in on

---

22 Jane Bowles (1917–1973) and her husband Paul Bowles (1910–1999), mentioned later, were well-known American writers who lived as expatriates in Morocco.
23 Alan Ansen (1922-2006), a poet and editor who had once been W.H. Auden's secretary.
24 Peter Orlovsky received a small monthly disability check from the Veterans Administration.

our floor, sort of a luminous fellow who studied mathematics and got bored this year and they gave him a sleeping cure and shock in Sweden and now he's wandering around Europe with *Rouge and Noir*[25] in his pocket. [. . .]

I hope to God that new edition has Lucien Carr's name off it. Whalen wrote you hocked your back teeth to put it out, I hope you don't lose out on it — tho he said it was selling well San Francisco and New York. Thanks for so rapid action, I guess it will be alright and Grove won't do no harm, especially if customs story makes *Life*. Anyway what's new? How's ACLU doing? Have you got your money back on photocopy, and what cost was it? [. . .]

Jack Kerouac will be out in San Francisco in a few weeks if he isn't there now — he went on rapidly thru France and England and wants to settle his mother in Mill Valley. Has he showed up?

Spending all my time working on Bill's manuscript and writing nothing and won't I guess till I go off alone somewhere. Reading the Koran. Surah 55, but in new Pelican translation is a beautiful litany — rather like [Christopher] Smart. Have you been in touch with John Wieners who's starting new magazine *Measure*? I hear McClure shipped out. And also readings continue in Cellar. Regards to Kenneth, will write soon. I've been really busy, work all day typing and editing on Bill, and shop and cook for five people huge suppers nightly, Bill and Ansen supply money so everybody's happy. Peter reads French and I smoke a little T [marijuana] occasionally and drink a little Pernod and stay in evenings and afternoons. Today a big picnic on the beach tho. Write me if there's anything new, what's happening with the police customs and whatnot.

As ever,
Allen

Ferlinghetti printed a photo offset edition of Howl and Other Poems *within the U.S., a maneuver that took the matter out of the hands of the*

---

25 *Le Rouge et le Noir* (*The Red and the Black*) by Stendahl.

Customs Department, and the case against Howl *was dropped for the time being. Ginsberg refers to that American printing as a photocopy here.*

May 31, 1957: Allen Ginsberg in Tangier, Morocco, to Lawrence Ferlinghetti in San Francisco

Dear Larry:

Received photocopy of *Howl* here two days ago — mailed a month earlier, that's why I never wrote you about it, I only just got it. It looks fine, all the changes seem to be there and no screw-up on Lucien Carr deletion, what a sigh of relief I breathed over that. But changes in text are right as I indicated, thanks. Looks like a fine job of printing too, not suffer much from photo process at all. How are they selling now? Can you unload them? Seems there are now 5000 in print in all three editions, that's a remarkable lot. I hope the *Evergreen* "Howl" doesn't screw things up — I thought when I wrote you it might even help, but I don't know. What does it seem like from San Francisco? I hear *Evergreen* will copyright their magazine as a unit; and then turn copyright of "Howl" over to me by letter. Does that work in alright with ad interim arrangements you made? Have written nothing sizeable in Europe but have been occupied on Burroughs manuscript since arriving — it approaches termination, and I will be taking off for Spain maybe in two weeks and I feel the CALL coming so I may squeeze something out; if so will send you whatever manuscript comes up, whenever, but it will be some time. Anything from Corso? He doesn't answer my letters. Are you still in hock from the photocopy or have sales made up at all yet? I ran out of loot but William Carlos Williams came to rescue with $200 from [American] Academy Arts and Letters. That should get me to Paris or Venice, wherever it be. No plans yet. Mail for me will be forwarded. Did you write Villiers to send me some copies? How are court proceedings proceeding? And was there any reaction to your mimeographed bulletin?[26] I haven't seen anything in the *Times*, but I

---

26 Ferlinghetti circulated a statement on the case against *Howl*, which was published in

don't see *Times* regularly. Is anything going to happen with *Life* after all the fuss. May seems past and no story.

For the rest having a nice time, getting high with Paul Bowles and an Arab painter [Ahmed] Yacoubi and an English painter Francis Bacon and a French junky-bop-musician-disc jockey Bernard [Frechtman][27] and an English conman on the lam Paul Lund. Bacon, Bowles and Burroughs the only interesting expatriates around. Bowles very intelligent and courteous and wears nylon suits and spends evenings goofing with kief [cannabis] and listening to tape music, just came back from India. Though something empty somewhere with him, I dunno. He's rather nice looking. His wife Jane Bowles has a bad leg and is ill and reads Simone Weil and has a deeper nature and is very shy. [. . .]

I don't know what I'll be writing like but I suspect it be different from *Howl* book, tho how I can't say till I sit down if I sit down. Burroughs method quite beautiful — a sort of automatic recording of a stream of visual images. I sent a page of it to Phil Whalen — somewhat like a junky St. Perse — tho very American in imagery that passed before his mind's eye. Well write me what's new and what's fate of new edition.

Love, as ever,
Allen

Larry — also — is there anything I can or should do re court scene? I've been too occupied here to be in better touch. Recent nostalgia for quiet of Berkeley. Too many foreign fairies and Arab boys here and no women, an unhealthy scene. I wrote [Barney] Rosset asking what's happening with his record. Who's supposed to be on? Too many and the boat will sink. Would still like to see Levertov book and any other if it's out, please send.

P.S. Received also today your article in *San Francisco Chronicle*.

William Hogan's "Between the Lines" column in the *San Francisco Chronicle* on May 19, 1957.

27 Bernard Frechtman worked as a translator and as an editor for *Olympia* magazine.

Just got it before seeing this. No not too stuffy and thanks for all the kind words, and thank also [Robert] Duncan and [Ruth] Witt-Diamant for their kindness. Looks like a good move, if *Poetry* will carry a defense as you write and the *Nation*. Can you send me the *Poetry* and *Partisan* articles when they come? [John] Hollander's[28] particularly I'd like to see — your reference made me wonder. Who else did you hear from? Sure got lots of space — looks like things roll easier now than when we first started — glad also you quoted some of actual poem in your piece. Is there anyplace or anything you'd like me to write that would be useful? I've apparently been singularly removed and silent in all this, but if all these others can put their two cents in, maybe I should too, some kind of mad blab full of obscene vitriol. Reading *Typee* and *Israel Potter* and Melville letters lately. [. . .]

On June 3, 1957, two undercover San Francisco police inspectors arrested the manager of City Lights Bookstore, Shig Murao, for selling copies of Howl and Other Poems *and a magazine called* Miscellaneous Man. *Ferlinghetti was out of town at the time, so they issued a warrant for his arrest upon his return. Both Ferlinghetti and Murao were released on bail posted by the ACLU, pending a court decision on obscenity charges.*

June 10, 1957: Allen Ginsberg in Tangier, Morocco, to Lawrence Ferlinghetti in San Francisco

Dear Larry:
Received your June 4 letter today, with clipping. I guess this is more serious than the customs seizure since you can lose real money on this deal if they find you guilty. What does it look like? I guess with ACLU should be possible to beat — except this is local law — does that give

---

28 John Hollander (1929–2013), a poet and literary critic as well as a former Columbia College classmate of Ginsberg's.

police complete discretion to decide what's obscene? If so that may make it difficult.

Presumably a matter of local politics — therefore can anything be done to call off police through politicians at City Hall thru State College thru Poetry Center thru Witt-Diamant? If it is a matter of purely interpretive local law and juvenile bureau, perhaps somebody at Berkeley and State College know <u>somebody</u> at City Hall that can call a halt. — But arrest and formal charges have been filed already, so I guess open showdown is inevitable.

I remember your speaking of troubles with local police on Henry Miller — and not being able to beat the cops on that — is it possible also in this case? It was all funny before but could be very difficult, for you, you actually stand to risk so much, money. In any case if you get fined I'll try to help raise loot to pay it — you've put yourself out financially very far already.

Had awful fantasy of being in San Francisco and putting on big reading sponsored by State College at museum and inviting cops and ending in big riot scene. I wish I were there; we could really have a ball, and win out in the end inevitably.

There seems to be good ground for expecting to win out — but I haven't seen the *Miscellaneous Man* — if you can convince them my book is "Art," will you get hooked on *M.M.*? I wonder if that will prove a stumbling block — you didn't seem to think much of the *MM* story when you mentioned it sometime back. Does it make things harder or more confused with two separate issues to deal with?

Who or what is behind all this attention? It appears like customs were burned up when they had to let go and someone must have called juvenile police from customs, and asked them to take up and carry the ball from there.

Well these are just vague ramblings, I don't know the situation, you must have chewed it all over already.

One thing occurs to me — re *Evergreen Review*. They're carrying "Howl" complete and are due out soon if not now. Will they get carried in San Francisco bookstores? Will you be able to carry them? (Are you still selling *Howl* from the store)? And if Grove can't distribute

Evergreen in San Francisco for their special San Francisco issue, Grove will be in a hell of a spot and the police are likely to have the whole poetry population of San Francisco personally with all their mothers and aunts up in outraged arms. Well I guess the more the merrier. Really it's a ridiculous mess. Have you got in touch with Grove? Or maybe they can just slip thru unnoticed and not ask for trouble. Too bad Gregory Corso is not there to make an anonymous phone call to the juvenile authorities tipping them off that Paul Elder[29] is carrying same obscenity in *Evergreen* — infiltrating thru every channel — by the way is Elder selling *Howl* or any other store in town? — and what are they doing about it? — pulling their necks back in or continuing to sell? I'm really sorry I'm not there to take part in this latest development. I never thought I'd want to read "Howl" again but it would be a pleasure under these circumstances. It might give it a reality as "social protest" I always feared was lacking without armed bands of outraged Gestapo. Real solid prophetic lines about being dragged off the stage waving genitals and manuscripts, biting detectives in the neck, etc. . . . I wonder by the way if the communist propaganda in America will further confuse the issue, the police, the judges and even ACLU. I really had some such situation as this in mind when I put them in, sort of deliberately saying I am a communist to see what would happen . . . burning bridges (not Harry)[30] you might say. Well if they do send you to jail I'll make haste to return to San Francisco and wage war in person, join you in next cell. Poor Shig, after his motorcycle bust up to get busted on this kind of bum rap[31] . . . give him my thanks and apologies . . . I hope it was not grim. Strange to see his name in the paper.

I don't know what to suggest, I guess you already got testimonials from William Carlos Williams and *Poetry*, etc., judging from the article you sent me. Are local newspapers being sympathetic? I have a friend on the *Oakland Tribune*, named Jim Fitzpatrick, who is quite literate . . . might try calling him for some kind of local pressure pub-

---

29 Paul Elder was a well-known San Francisco book dealer.
30 Pun referring to Harry Bridges, the union organizer.
31 Shig Murao had just been injured in a motorcycle accident.

licity — give him a statement or something. Did Harvey Breit carry anything on the original customs seizure? He ought to be informed about this, I guess he'd write something and you might get in further angles there about what is Grove *Evergreen* going to do — and the fact that you've put out the [Denise] Levertov and [Marie] Ponsot[32] and are expecting Gregory next. As far as testimonials and official types, I imagine [Randall] Jarrell might be rung in and make himself useful. He don't approve of the dirty words in my book so I understand, but he is Poetry Consultant at Library of Congress and gets paid for it and he has visited your store and he did dig it as cultural center and he is interested in Gregory publication, so he should be conscience bound to make some kind of official Federal statement for you to use in court. With testimony from someone with his official title and ACLU backing you would have strong case, even if the judge had never heard of William Carlos Williams, Patchen, Jarrell or Rexroth or anyone since Ambrose Bierce. I'll write him; it might be good for you to get in touch with him and tell him what you need. Has *Village Voice*, who knew me and Greg in New York, followed the case?

Who else — man I got the greatest — get Josephine Miles[33] — no one can suspect her of any but most respectable judgment — to court in person — star witness. Well, I'm rambling.

I haven't received twenty-five copies yet, nor the Ponsot and Levertov (#5 and 6), and did get the single copy of photo offset edition. Yes, it looks excellent, as I wrote last note — I didn't think it could be done so neatly. What did it cost? Is that cheaper than Villiers reprint? You now have 5000 copies — 2500 distributed — will you be able to unload the rest or is it going to be a white elephant? Very relieved you caught Lucien [Carr] as per request.

Would like to see the Hollander review in *Partisan*. Any other reviews I don't know of, of interest?

---

32 City Lights had recently published Denise Levertov's *Here and Now* and Marie Ponsot's *True Minds*.
33 Josephine Miles was a poet and literary critic on the faculty of the University of California at Berkeley.

When you have time, do send out the varying other people I named some copies — usually it's people who can sell them by word of mouth anyway. I don't know who all I told you to — one kid in Brazil specially, and poet [Charles] Reznikoff, and also did you ever send to Tour De Feu? and other radical groups in France — Rexroth told me about them. Letter from Gregory the other day. Brought pistol back from Barcelona and waved it in existentialist cafe and got arrested as drunk and let out — screaming "Why did you all let me starve you bastards!" (to the existentialists) — and he said also he had completed his book for you and was sending it on, and was happy with it, it could be real great, I hope he includes a shorter revised "Power." He needs one long poem to establish solidity and scope, for a book. Essenin, Mayakovsky and Lorca who are like him, wrote big poems. He should too.

Have written very little but will sooner or later. When I have a manuscript I will send it to you to look at and publish if you can and want to; I won't go whoring around New York publishers I promise. The trouble is, what long writing I've done is more or less unpublishable lately — some autobiographical sexual history — send us all to jail. Burroughs influence has been to open up even more extreme areas and much more questionable taste, as far as subject . . . God knows where I'll end up, elegies in the asshole of some Istanbul hermaphrodite, odes to cocaine (the connection is finally coming tonite — had hash and tea and opium here but no coke till now) — anyway, I don't know what next — talking with Francis Bacon, a painter, a good one, interesting man, sort of an adventurer in regards to his painting (and won and lost 4000 at Monte Carlo and didn't paint till he was thirty) (and can always work as a cook) — and get idea of art as a funny sort of psychic gamble, an experiment with subjective areas and psychic material that can be dangerous personally — to say nothing of its publishability (its worth or its legal worth). This is somewhat romanticized, but I guess it could be also literally true — if you stumbled on some De Sade like or saintly absolutism in your own nature — or sexual compulsion or whatever — in the act of writing. Something like that happens on small scale with "Howl" which gives it power. Would like to develop that, tho it perhaps means sacrificing any foreseeable audience — which I see Burroughs has done — and to some extent Kerouac in his solitary vigils over notebook.

Expected to leave here today, so would have missed your letter, but Peter came down with the grippe, so remaining till tomorrow or perhaps another day — then off thru Spain several weeks to Venice and settle there awhile. [. . .]

I'd go to Paris but I have only 150 dollars and have to hole up with friend [Alan Ansen] in Venice cheap. Paris costs even more in summer. Don't know where the next loot comes from, but I guess things will work out alright, whatever happens. All mail previously sent to me here or Paterson will ultimately be forwarded to Venice — Burroughs remaining behind here a month more and will take care of that. I guess I'll receive the books (twenty-five copies) in Venice. Gave [Paul] Bowles my last copy. He's been very nice, dug the poetry, still follows little magazines when he can get them. Add him perhaps to your list — next time you send out a list of works. He isn't sinister; his life is safe and rather comfortable; but I suspect he would like to make it on wilder greater level. He reads William Carlos Williams and would maybe order *Kora in Hell*.

Will you ever be in position to print some pocket prose? The Burroughs manuscript is pretty great. It's more than the law will allow — as he commented, he'll probably wind up with the distinction of being banned not only U.S. but also France. Sooner or later we'll start circulating the publishable parts in U.S. If you're interested I'll send you a block of it to look at when we have copies. I sure would like to see a reading of this at 6 Gallery, Kerouac might do it if the police were barred. I don't think any court anywhere would uphold Burroughs. I can see ACLU reeling back aghast and audience staring in horror — and Burroughs leaning back laughing with a lushed up hashhead mad intelligent gleam in his Shakespearean eye.

Regards and thanks. Hope all works out well — keep in touch, mail will be forwarded wherever I am — write me and I'll pick up letter at American Express Madrid, in two weeks. If there's anything I can do tell me. What does Kenneth Rexroth say? Give him regards, I still have to write and will. Hello to jailbird Shig.

As ever,
Allen

July 10, 1957: Allen Ginsberg in Venice, Italy, to Lawrence Ferlinghetti in San Francisco

Dear Larry:
[. . .] Haven't heard from you since your letter describing arrest — that's over a month ago — have you been in jail? Am eager to hear what's happened. Please write fast aerogramme and say what's up — and I read of recent adverse-type supreme court decisions about obscene. I wrote Jarrell asking him give you official help but no reply has he got in touch with you? What's happening? [. . .]

Venice is beautiful; big heat wave all last first week; now great rain. Living with friend Ansen who has an apartment, and he threw a party when we came and invited Peggy Guggenheim[34] and Peter and I talked about T [marijuana] and masturbation and wiped our brows with big sweaty towel so she rushed away angry and didn't invite us to her big surrealist party that weekend. So I'm left alone in Venice to cook food and read about Fra Angelico and dig the great cathedral and row around in gondolas alas. But her house guest arrived this week is Nicolas Calas[35] a surrealist expert, who is secretly coming to supper in a few days — he and Ansen spent most of the evening reading parts of "Howl" aloud at the party we weren't invited to; and told Ansen he'd try [to] find a French translator for it and give it to [André] Breton, who he thought would be interested. If so, perhaps could get other books of the series translated and a French publisher. Will write more when I see Calas. I imagine Kenneth [Rexroth] knows him. I'm out

34 Peggy Guggenheim (1898–1979), a wealthy American art collector who opened her own museum of contemporary art in Venice..
35 Nicolas Calas (1907–1988), poet and art critic.

of money finally and living off Ansen's hospitality and Peter's $50 a month income. Where next I don't know, will stay here for the summer tho probably. Can't meanwhile get to Rome or Paris, where Gregory is up shit's creek (we sent him $5). He says he sent you his book [*Gasoline*], how is it? If relations with Guggenheim get any better will try to interest her in his cause, or mine, or both, or neither as the case may be. Meanwhile I'm set here awhile, so write me. I have no copies of my book — you sent them, or asked Villiers to? I haven't received them in any case. [. . .]

As ever,
Allen

August 21, 1957: Allen Ginsberg in Venice, Italy, to Lawrence Ferlinghetti in San Francisco

Dear Larry:
Not heard from you since July 17 letter — thought trial was due sometime round August 8 and so have been waiting on edge going down to American Express daily since the 13th hoping for news. I guess you must be pretty busy what with work at store and frazzle of law, but wish you'd let me know what's up as soon as you are able. I can't wait. Someone wrote me you had an extra good lawyer volunteer but beyond that haven't heard a thing.

I wrote Gregory if he wanted I'd write an introduction to his book [*Gasoline*], if he or you want — since I love his poetry it would be a pleasure. Haven't heard from him: tho earlier he said someone gave him an apartment for the summer and he'd met [Marlon] Brando and [Jean] Genet and wrote strange poem about Paris "Dollhouse of Mammal War." [. . .]

Been here all along except for wild trip with Orlovsky through Florence and Rome and we ran out of money and went to Assisi and were broke and happy and argued with monks and slept out at night, warm, on the lawn in front of their monastery and acted like wild Franciscans and begged food and talked about poetry and gave them a copy of *Evergreen Review*. Then hitched back to Venice and sneaked on trains. [. . .]

Writing a good deal of prose and some fragmentary poetry but nothing good. Vatican has fig leaves on all the statues — I almost flipped there. It is maddening after all the beautiful nakedness of David in Florence. Also been digging a lot of Giotto in Assisi and Padua and Fra Angelico in Florence and got high in the Forum and in the Vatican and have been having a fine time. I eat well because have kitchen and cook all meals in and so spend very little time in any kind of society except household or Ansen's guests. But been seeing a lot of different kinds of people. But for Christ's sake write me what's happening with the law, the trial, etc. Is there anything I should do? [. . .]

As ever,
Allen

Ferlinghetti's reply to the letter above has been lost, but he evidently had no news about the trial, which was still a month away from a verdict. Ginsberg's letter here includes an odd note about his friend Carl Solomon, who, like Lucien Carr, didn't want to be publicly associated with Allen and the Beats. It seems that Carl threatened to sue Ginsberg for using his name, but it proved to be a hollow threat and he remained one of Allen's close friends.

September 3, 1957: Allen Ginsberg in Venice, Italy, to Lawrence Ferlinghetti in San Francisco

Dear Larry:
Received your two letters of Aug. 28 and 29. Thanks for the check. I have been very broke — this gets me to Paris. Glad you are able to afford it. I had thought earlier you would use any profits to plough back into the City Lights series investment so could publish things like Gregory [Corso]. But I'm too broke to send it back now. Is there any possibility of any further money in several months if you're able to sell out the fourth magical printing? How many you printing by the way?

The *Time-Life* stories should maybe sell more too I guess, if they only mention your address in the story. Well things look fine. I got back here broke from ten day trip to Naples wondering what next and your check was the answer. Are you out of red really? [. . .]

But still wondering what happened to the trial?? Isn't it over yet? [. . .]

Listen — why not publish a book of Kerouac's poetry? It's really good — I think will be big famous book too someday. Have you seen it all? If you could follow up Gregory with a book of Jack's I think you'd have a really solid solid list — and with all *Time* publicity coming up on his new novel you couldn't possibly lose. You haven't seen all there is of his — an immense amount for you to dig. [John] Wieners also thinks it's great and took some for *Measure*. His agent, Sterling Lord, has about 500 poems. And Jack himself has more. I wish I were there to talk to you about it. If it's a financial matter — I be willing to apply any future royalties to help pay for it. [Malcolm] Cowley and Viking don't believe and won't publish it.

There is also the later problem of a whole mass of Burroughs material — some sections of which are complete in themselves. I have sent whole manuscript to Sterling Lord in New York City with instructions where to send printable parts — most is pornographically unpublishable in U.S., but large parts are possible. What Burroughs needs tho is something of his published at least as a sampler and City Lights would be perfect place — to put it in context with my work and others. If you're interested in this at all, same money deal applies. I will tell S. Lord, at any rate, to send you excerpts. You once mentioned possibility of Burroughs' South American letters section as a small City Lites prose book. That, maybe still. But we now have several hundred pages of newer wilder very more original almost surrealist but quite coherent straight almost prose poetry. Wieners also took small page of that for *Measure*.

I have started writing a lot and wrote a good new poem. Wieners has one about Seattle ["Afternoon Seattle"] which isn't so good, and *Evergreen* has another about Sather Gate ["Sather Gate Illumination"] which is better. It'll be another half year or year however before

I settle down and produce anything good enough for a book. However there's lots of time. I'm feeling fine, got enough loot now for a few more months and am going to Paris.

Please write me what the legal situation is tho up to date. Someone wrote me that Karl Shapiro [was] writing a favorable review for [*Prairie*] *Schooner* and there was a strange discussion in *London Times Supplement* August 16 that I saw. Maybe Shapiro be help on trial if it's not too late, and if he isn't the kiss of death.

Carl's [Solomon] letters — what's his address?? I had letter from him or family saying it was OK to use name — god it would be mad if he sued too.

If possible in 4th printing, there's still one typographical problem — which is, that on the dirty words we've replaced by dashes, some of the words have the first letter, and some don't. All should have the first letter, like: "who got f . . . in the a . . ." instead of total blank.

For that matter, if we win the trial — is it possible to put in the whole words now??? If so that would be worth doing, as far as I'm concerned. I never liked the blanks and think they actually weaken the effect and make it shocking where it should be powerfully hip. We put the blanks in to evade customs and protect Villiers — if we win have we green light? Or is this just making trouble when we got enough already. The book looks less "rebellious" and more poetic without the asterisks, in actual effect. Asterisks look like you're self-conscious and scared to say what you're saying.

Get more from Corso?? Says he sees Genet and had big argument with him about Gregory painting in oils on some friend's apartment walls — so Genet insulted American boors and Gregory called him a frog creep, or some such Gregorian scene.

Glad you wrote,
Allen

Dear Allen,

Got your last and guess you are now in Paris. I am working on Gregory's book right now, and he agrees with me that you should do introduction. You can write anything up to about 900 words, though just a couple of hundred will do if you want to keep it short . . . [. . .] The *Life* article on September 9, with your picture, is causing the national distributor to take two or three hundred copies [of *Howl and Other Poems*] a week . . . though this probably won't keep up indefinitely! *Time* article, on general scene here, is due out in another week . . . Have you seen any of the articles on the trial, except what I sent? Am saving clips, so you can go over them when you hit town again . . . Which brings up an interesting idea I have been toying with and have just now put up to Max Weiss at Fantasy Records — This is to get you to make a real sharp recording of "Howl," here in the Fantasy studios (I suppose you've not heard the very bad recording on Evergreen Record (Grove Press)[36] which you shouldn't have let them use, if you ask me) . . . Anyway, Fantasy would do a real professional job on this, both recording and distribution — both of which Grove did strictly on an amateur level. You would also get paid for recording, as well as small royalty on sales of record. I could send you some of this loot in advance, to get you back here — say this Spring, maybe — once we had it definitely set up. Fantasy is enthusiastic and definitely wants to arrange it, as the first in a Spoken Word Series, under the editorship of City Lights Books . . . So, anyway, please don't sign anything with Grove to give them rights to the "Spoken 'Howl'". (None of us have got paid for that recording — have you?????) What did they pay you for reprinting "Howl" in *Evergreen*? They never sent me anything for you . . . or for rights, to reprint . . . I trust you have signed nothing in the way of rights to "Howl" with Grove . . . When we get this set-up

---

36 Evergreen issued an LP record titled *San Francisco Poets* in 1958 which contained an early Ginsberg reading of "Howl."

with Fantasy you will have a regular contract with them . . . Let me know when and if you can make it here for this recording scene . . . (Of course you might make it over there, if you could make a studio recording.) [. . .] Trial is not over yet — we're in court again this Thursday . . . Yes, would like to see manuscripts by Kerouac, Burroughs . . . though can't promise anything at this stage . . . [. . .] Question of "Fucked in the Ass" not yet settled in court — so had to let that stand again [. . .]

later dad

Larry

In the following letter Ginsberg mentions George Whitman, who was an old friend of Ferlinghetti's in Paris. They had known each other since Lawrence's days as a student at the Sorbonne, and Whitman now owned the Mistral bookstore, which would eventually be renamed Shakespeare and Company. Allen also makes his first mention of a small pension on the Rue Git-le-Coeur, which would become famous in years to come as the Beat Hotel.

September 23, 1957: Allen Ginsberg in Paris to Lawrence Ferlinghetti in San Francisco

Dear Larry:

Received your letter today. Paris a great ball — later on that. Business — (ugh)

1. Gregory introduction: I'll leave here in a few days and see Gregory and sleep on his floor in Amsterdam and look at manuscript and your list of poems (if you sent it and it arrives) — and will send you a short introduction in time for you to use it — I hope. Plan to anyway. Back in Paris in two weeks.

2. Thanks for sending 4th printing *Howl* — surface mail is so slow, I won't see it for months though.

3. I haven't seen any articles on anything, except what's been in

Life so far and what you've sent me, I'm completely out of touch — but would like some details of what's gone on — can't you send me a few clips in chronological order covering the various trial days? — I won't be back there for awhile. Let me know what the final decision is with court.

4. Records — haven't heard Grove record. The record is probably a fuckup no doubt — they ignored my advice as to which recording and which part of "Howl" to print on record. However it was then too much effort to otherwise advise them, I tried by mail. But it doesn't make much difference, they're the only ones who'll be screwed. No, I didn't sign any exclusive contracts, nor any contracts for that matter — contracts are too hung-up and legal and if possible would prefer never signing any even if it means losing control over my own scribblings. Money: They gave me $40, six months ago and another $54 one month ago — I don't know whether for the record or for *Evergreen* reprint. In sum they've given me 94 dollars, but I'm not sure exactly what for. I asked them about pay for records and [Barney] Rosset wrote me they were paying per page on the review; per time or something equally divided on the record; and also that he'd sent Kenneth R. [Rexroth] $200 for expenses. Whether they actually did or not, or why or what for, I dunno.

At the time they reprinted "Howl," I hadn't made any other money (like from you) on the poem, and it wasn't much money anyhow, and I needed it, so I didn't assume they'd have to pay you for rights. Should they have? Too complicated — it wouldn't have been much anyway and no point worrying about it now. (In future you're welcome to any rights money anybody wants to give, so long as it isn't subtracted from any sum that would go into my starving pocket, and so long as it isn't unwilling payment on the part of some penniless entrepreneur who's not in the business to make money anyway.)

Re Fantasy record deal — that sounds fine, I will do anything anytime except maybe come back prematurely to U.S. Perhaps we can make decent recording here. Make whatever arrangements you think wise and by all means get me any money you can. I don't have specific plans, other than that I want to stay here for at least six months and dig

Paris and read and write — so I don't want to plan on coming to U.S. just to make another fucking recording of that fucking poem (which I'm positive was written two years ago in limbo by somebody else not me, maybe Carl S. [Solomon]). [. . .]

5. No word from my father on receipt of books. I'll let you know. However, I haven't received any copies, and haven't any, and there are none in Paris. Does Villiers still have that stock of them? I'd like to circulate some around here. I looked up George Whitman at the bookstore Mistral and I live around the corner from him. He has idea what's happening but hasn't seen any of the books and his bookstore is filled with old musty copies of *Epoch* and 1945 *Partisan Reviews*. Yet there are plenty of live interested cats here in Paris who would absolutely dig *Howl* and San Francisco scene. A few copies of *Evergreen* sold out here and all sorts people stop me in American Express recognizing picture; and I've talked to a few French types, etc. — and there is a large market here — unexplored so far partly because of full impact of San Francisco scene not hit here, where it would be gobbled up, and the texts not here either. Whitman said if he had material he'd make a window display, books, articles and pictures, whatnot. His bookstore is pretty central like yours is and would reach most of the hip-English speaking French poets, and all the U.S. and British local cats. So, please make arrangements — would definitely suggest you round up all the material you can, as inclusive as possible — get a few copies of *Arks*, *Needles*, Greig's Kerouac issue if out, all your series, ask perhaps Mc-Clure for his and [Robert] Duncan and make up a big care package to send to Whitman for his window and reading room. Honestly, it's a mad opportunity to make it an international scene, very rapidly. I don't know how much Whitman be able to sell, or what money terms you can make with him, but it be great advertising. In any case whatever you do with everything else, send him a number of copies of my book as soon as you can — either from Villiers or from you. I'm sure we can start disposing of them here. There's also, after Gregory's visit, a market for his book here, when it comes.

The impression, I mean, is that if our books were here they would stir and sell, just as in San Francisco. I'm thinking of looking around for a French translator, you know any? Whitman also ordering Kerouac's book. Did you see that great review he had in *New York Times* September 5? (Not the Sunday)

6. You sent me so much money, do I still have any copies due me at all?? If so please send them or cause them to be sent fast as you can.

7. Let me know, in a general way, without committing yourself, if you think they'll be any more money for me from 4th printing — I'm trying to figure out next six months.

8. That covers everything. Make sure you get in touch with Whitman to begin some exchange and sale here, whole series of City Lights, could certainly sell some, and it's important to sell them here, kind of a nerve center. Send any pictures of yourself, Rexroth, etc, he could display — that's what he said. He has *Measure*, from me, I'll get him *Combustion* too. [. . .]

Anyway, I'll leave for Amsterdam later this week. If there's immediate trial news, send me a fast note c/o Gregory in Amsterdam, where I'll be for two weeks. Otherwise for anything that can wait, American Express, Paris. I've located a room here near Seine, Rue Gît-le-Coeur, I can move in October 15, — it's dirty and small but it's got a gas stove to cook in. Costs I'm afraid it will be almost $35 a month for two of us (me and Peter O.) but it's all I can find so far and I have to have a place I can boil eggs, potatoes and tomatoes or I'll starve entirely. Great central location tho. Leaving Paris to save loot till the gas stove is ready. Later —

Yours from the banks of the Seine, Goon

P.S. Am writing Kerouac's agent to send you K's poems and complete Burroughs manuscript. Read latter through and have first choice. Jack and I both agree he is as good as either of us — you make big mistake to pass him up. DIG BURROUGHS HE'S A BIG GENIUS.

Thanks,
Allen

September 28, 1957: Lawrence Ferlinghetti in San Francisco to Allen
Ginsberg in Paris

Dear Allen,

[. . .] Will send you clips on final action on *Howl* trial next week,
when judge brings in his written decision and opinion. I am writing
it up for next issue of *Evergreen*, per request of Don Allen . . . Great
picture of you in *Life*. Where was it taken? Would like to get it for
cover of Fantasy record. Could you trace down negative of it and get it
and send it to us? . . . Re. Fantasy record, yes, why don't you go ahead
and get studio in Paris for recording, and I will foot bill for it, until
Fantasy forks over, that is, if you can rent a sound studio for an hour
or two for under $25. The idea is to make the sharpest clearest livest
recording, uninterrupted by remarks or extrapolations, etc. [. . .] Will
also send you *Ark* and *New Editions* and others for Paris display soon
. . . Will see to getting those manuscripts around as soon as they arrive
(Burroughs, Kerouac, etc) . . . At Art Festival here this week, there was
Grand Guignol puppet type show, with puppets of you and Corso and
Rexroth, with scene at The Place[37] for backdrop, lampooning all and
fingerlike penis flopping out and Kenneth intoning and Lawrence F.
[Ferlinghetti] and the Police Inspector and the Cellar jass scene with
Kenneth on the podium with Brooks Brothers suits and you get the
idea anyway — by [the way] you know Gerd Stern and Jack Gilbert;
and they are still reading Robespierre at Festival; and our Fantasy record (K [Kenneth Rexroth] and me) is really getting around — a real
sharp recording, no matter what you think of the poetry (I enclosed
printed record insert with books to you) . . .

---

37 The Place, at 1546 Grant Avenue in San Francisco, was a bar/cafe that often hosted
poetry readings during the 1950s.

I have also done the sound and words for a film on the City Dump[38] which went over big at Festival . . .

Yours trooly, write

LF

September 28, 1957: Allen Ginsberg in Amsterdam to Lawrence
Ferlinghetti in San Francisco

Dear Larry:

Am in Amsterdam sleeping on Gregory's floor, waiting for your list of poems so I can write introduction. If you haven't sent them send them immediately yes? [. . .]

What's with trial?

Finally have room in Paris October 15 with gas stove so will settle there then. Lots Dutch hipsters here, read Artaud. Windmills, cows, green fields, Van Gogh and Vermeer, art cafes, canals, museums, cheap Indonesian restaurants, no housing shortage much in Amsterdam. How strange to be in Holland with the ducks. And great Red Light district, girls are like wax dolls in bright windows.

I know everybody puts Gregory down there and am glad you don't, I am amazed by his genuine genius and originality. Gregory says right color for *Gasoline* cover is bright-solid red letters on white background. Have you used this already? (Red Border?, with label like mine, red letters on label). Is it possible to get a red explosive and solid like, like an <u>Esso</u> sign? [. . .]

Allen

---

38 This is a reference to the film *Have You Sold Your Dozen Roses?*, which was produced in 1957 by the California School of Fine Arts Film Workshop and featured a free-verse improvisation by Lawrence Ferlinghetti.

October 10, 1957: Allen Ginsberg in Amsterdam to Lawrence Ferlinghetti in New York City

Dear Larry:

Got your note with *Chronicle* decision page today, natch was glad and thankful and also surprised to see you've got 10,000 in print, that's fantastic. Well that's all great.

We sent you a big envelope a week ago containing my intro for *Gasoline*, plus list of *Gas* poems in order, plus some new poems and final word on what Gregory wanted in the book and what he wanted dropped — did you get it before you left San Francisco? By all means follow his advice and don't put in the few poems he puts down, and do publish those he sends to substitute. The book as now put together is great and about perfect he thinks, I agree. SEND PROOFS!!!

In New York City, get in touch with Kerouac — either thru his Agent Sterling Lord or else thru Lucien Carr (leave message with Lucien). He sent you last week his poems, you should talk about that, also he has copy of Burroughs manuscript (make arrangements to dig that with him). Also he should contribute some book jacket or prefatory note to Gregory's book, Gregory wants that. So by all means look him up even if he's drunk in Bowery and hard to reach.

Was decision news carried nationally anyway? Look up Harvey Breit on *Times*, he'll probably want to interview you. Also phone Rosalind Constable on *Time Life*, who's very sympathetic — inform her of importance of Corso book and arrange that she get copy so *Time* can review it — which they will if she passes it on to review department, I think. Also try arrange thru Breit, or see Brown the editor at *Times*, that they begin reviewing City Lights.

I hear from Jack that both Viking and Grove interested in hardcover *Howl*, however that be wrong, etc., so don't worry as I said I won't go whoring in New York. If you follow Corso with Kerouac and Burroughs you'll have the most sensational little company in U.S., I wish you would dig that, anyway — we could all together crash over America in a great wave of beauty. And cash. But do you think you can sell 5,000 more actually? How mad.

When I was in New York I saw [Philip] Rahv and [William] Phillips at *Partisan* [*Review*], [George Frederick] Morgan at *Hudson* [*Review*], [Louise] Bogan at *New Yorker*, spoke to somebody (Mrs. Abel) at *Commentary*; [Arabel] Porter at *New World Writing*. I yelled at all, about reviewing books. You might contact them (they all know about City Lights) and make sure they are getting books and insist on them reviewing — particularly Gregory's upcoming *Gasoline*. Breit too. With Porter above I yakked about San Francisco, Black Mountain and Boston poets; you might talk to her and see if she'll start printing us, or get someone to edit a mad poetry section in one of the *New World Writings*.

If possible, now that *Evergreen Review* issue is over, would like to get the single poem "Howl" reprinted more widely, perhaps in *Time*, *Life*, *Look*, *Congressional Record*, or more likely *New World Writing*. It would not hurt the book. Sterling Lord, Jack's agent, may be (maybe not) working on this. If you can get in touch with him and see if some deal to make us all some more money can be made, this way. [. . .] Gregory, Peter and I been writing long rocket chain poem about the moon ["Moon Prevention"]. Back in Paris October 14, so write there. [. . .] Is there chance of continuing the fight and freeing Miller, [D.H.] Lawrence, and maybe [Jean] Genet, etc.? That would be really historic and worth the trouble. [. . .]

Later,
Allen

◀ 1958 ▶

Ferlinghetti was fluent in French and had translated the poems of Jacques Prévert, which he hoped to publish. He asked Ginsberg in Paris to help him get permission from the Prévert heirs through their agent, Mrs. William Aspenwall Bradley.

ca. January 6–7, 1958: Allen Ginsberg in Paris to Lawrence Ferlinghetti in San Francisco

Dear Larry:

[. . .] Sterling Lord was here and took me and Peter and Gregory to supper and I asked him to try peddle my book to foreign countries, he's had a lot of success with Jack. I explained you'd said I was under contract to you in order to protect my interests, so there's no embarrassment for you in that untangling. He said to ask you to send him half a dozen copies of the book and he'll take the *Life* article and try selling it in France and Russia maybe. (Perhaps if you're interested you can make some same arrangement with him for your and Gregory's book or the series.) In any case please send him six or eight copies of the 4th printing. I haven't made any formal arrangement with him. He said he might be able to sell *Howl* abroad tho, but he'd try tho didn't know. He has nothing much to gain from it, there's likely not much money involved, in his terms of money anyway. [. . .]

Re Mme. Aspenwall Bradley: As soon as I got your letter with instructions I went to see her — I talked with her secretary, an old lady, at great length. The secretary said she didn't know why nothing had been done for you and was sure it could all be arranged. She said she'd tell Mrs. Bradley and call me. She didn't call, so I went back and saw her again. She, the secretary, said that it was all arranged OK and they would write you confirming your conditions and making it formal —

but they had no objections. I went back a week later and she said they were writing you that day, so I took it for granted that it was all done already and was surprised that you write you've heard nothing. I've been there four times already actually, there must be something wrong with them. Bradley has a huge office in an apartment building on the Île full of expensive foreign and French books, a respectable old secretary and a maid and poodle and telephone and her offices look like some publishing house directors meeting — I don't know what's the matter with them, they're not fly-by-night or anything, just perhaps too old and disorganized. I tried to get Prévert's address but they didn't have it. Well, as I say I will go back tomorrow and make appointment with Mrs. Bradley herself and find out the score. I'm sure it will be all right in the end. I thought I already had the situation straightened out — it's their goof again not mine — I saw them last about two weeks ago. I'll write you in a few days as soon as I see them again. I am taking care of it tho so don't worry I'm on ball.

I talked to Bernard Frechtman the other day — he translates Genet. He also did a lot of other French translations for *Transition*, etc., including the famous Artaud "Van Gogh" essay. As you may know Artaud is a pretty hot number, the trouble with U.S. publication has been in getting the rights — I think Grove is interested also but can't get rights. Frechtman said if you were interested he'd try to get rights for reprint of the Van Gogh and another sizeable mad piece of prose poetry — perhaps "The Judgment of God," or the Tarahumara-Peyote essay which was in *Transition*. Or better something as yet unprinted in English. In other words Frechtman would cooperate to get rights for a book of his and his wife's Artaud translations; possibly that could be extended to other people's translations. I think [Guy] Wernham has a translation of "Pour en finir avec le jugement de dieu" which is powerful and brilliant Artaud. If you are interested in the possibility of a pocket book of Artaud, send me a letter addressed to Frechtman saying you are interested in doing a book with Van Gogh, specify about how big or long the book should be and what kind of material you would be interested in — do you know Artaud's works??

I should think his madhouse "Letters from Rodez" would be the end — and there's another wild looking book about Mexicans and drugs and death — ("Vie et mort de satan le feu" or something). If you could come out with the first book of Artaud in U.S. you'd have a very fine item and probably sell it well. Are you interested? If so send me a formal type letter I can give to Frechtman to show Gallimard to get the rights; or I'll send you Frechtman's address (don't have it on me now) and you deal with him directly. Please write me what you think. Frechtman is a little weird by the way he talks in endless tangents and is, well not stupid, but very mental.

I'm glad you dug the new Gregory poems, "Coit Tower" is certainly approaching something really great like "Fern Hill" [by Dylan Thomas]. I was depressed when I finally saw his proofs because I really do think he's one of the greatest poets in U.S. but it wasn't in the book. I like his short poems, but I dig his genius most in the long wild incomprehensible blowing, the pure phrasing — His life is too unstable for him to sit down for long cool afterthoughts and assembling of book properly — it should have had more long wild poems — even "H.G. Wells,"[39] with "you Mexico, you know no Chicago, no white-blond moll." Well I guess that's somewhat remedied by the new poems — actually he has around in freakish half-finished form, like "Power" (which he's still trying to revise right) a great pack of singing poetry (not shouting). Nothing to do now but go thru as is, I guess — I hadn't realized in Amsterdam how much crap like the America fragment had crept in and short meaningless poems. But almost everything now is near perfect — strangely he's best when he's serious, I mean, not rip up and delay the book again to include "Coit Tower." Somewhere there is the makings of a brilliant *Gasoline* book, is it all in there yet, or is it just satisfactory still?

I bought a huge volume of Mayakovsky in French and a petite volume of Essenin and am reading in and out [of] them and translating a little, also reading the New Directions Pasternak book.

---

39 Gregory Corso's poem "H.G. Wells" is unpublished, but Ginsberg mentioned it and quoted the same line in his introduction to *Gasoline*.

Re the Burroughs manuscript. Don Allen has had it all this time, to take excerpts for *Evergreen*. There is enough, more than enough, to spread around, they won't wind up with the only choice printable parts. Since I'm here, Jack has taken over tasks of peddling the book in U.S., he's in New York now. I wrote him to send it to you next. Burroughs due here this month, we'll continue work, he has another new 100 pages.

What do you think of the Kerouac poetry? McClure wrote me he'd read it and apparently he dug it — at least his enthusiasm matched mine. What's up on that score?

Regards to [Peter] DuPeru and anyone else. Peter Orlovsky has written two pure and fantastic poems, I suspect he will be the next great wave to break out of San Francisco poetry — it'll upset Rexroth who may have thought I was in my queer dotage digging P.O.'s mind. But such is the justice of eternity, the meek shall inherit the earth.

Am writing (got four single space pages finished) long poem on "Fall of America"[40] — modeled on Blake's approach to politics in "The French Revolution" poem.

"and millions of tons of human wheat were burned in secret caverns under the White House

while India starved and screamed and ate mad dogs full of rain

. . . and the immortal Chaplin was driven from our shores with the rose in his teeth

. . .

thousands of fanatics agitated for the sake of the screaming soprano of industry

Money money money Mad celestial money of illusion leprous money made of machines

Money against Eternity! and eternity's strong mills coin out vast paper of illusion"

If poems can be made out of ashcans, you can write poems on political subjects without being temporary, also. No reason why not. I don't know why they couldn't in the 30's. Take a cross between Blake,

---

40 This was published as "Death to Van Gogh's Ear!"

Apollinaire and Whitman and you can sound prophetic about [John Foster] Dulles even.

OK, write, I'll
write after I see
Prévert people,
Allen

ca. late February 1958: Allen Ginsberg in Paris to Lawrence Ferlinghetti in San Francisco

Dear Larry:

My last letter undoubtedly confusing the issue [of the Fantasy recording]. Enclosing therefore the contract signed. Financial arrangements OK. Saw Delaunay and arranged to make the tape tonite, and will send it airmail to you or Weiss this week. Send me postcard with his address so I can mail it or give me instructions. Delaunay by the way is if you remember from 1936 author of jazz hot type discography and old jazz intellectual . . . now sitting behind layout cover desk of commercial record company . . . doesn't listen much anymore he says. I read his book in high school. Will try do good job recording. Would like to help advise on cover, I have a few ideas . . . let me know if that's impossible or not.

Mainly would like on cover a photo of Sir Francis Drake hotel monster visage at nite as photographable from corner of Pine and Powell — its picture of Moloch face could be capturable for teaheads interested. Discuss this later, let me know.

As I said in letter I have no intention of switching to Grove (haven't been asked anyway by the way) and present financial arrangements are fine. Best put book out in cheapest and simplest possible form as before, City Lights Pocket Series is both eccentric and distinguished, as is. (If, by the way, you change cover styles and use cover artists, I wish you'd try Robert LaVigne, Four Lakes, Washington, at least for mine.) But I don't have a book now. Actually I find it hard to write and don't like much what I've written and am getting too self-conscious and would prefer not to think about books for a long time. I keep trying to strain to sound off like a prophet in latest writing and it's not good. So will submit book when there is a real one, I'd rather not rush around and come up with bullshit. [. . .]

Jack [Kerouac] be in New York soon, arrange to send you the Burroughs manuscript. He's junk sick now and is recovering from slight paregoric habit and so inactive; later will assemble book of selections with him.

Will write later. Thanks for check, they always seem to come in when I'm broke. [. . .]

As ever,

Allen

Ginsberg had a lot of difficulty in making what he considered an acceptable recording of "Howl." As he mentions in the following letter, he had also been turned down for a Guggenheim fellowship grant.

ca. late March 1958: Allen Ginsberg in Paris to Lawrence Ferlinghetti in San Francisco

Dear Larry:

Been sort of low so not written. Well I've been to Vogue [recording studios] several times and tried reading but can't make it, don't know why. I'm not in control, either it comes or it doesn't. It may be the finality of the occasion and five year contracts and officialdom of it all and money for it chills the spirit. But the idea of facing the microphone again is too much. I mean I have tried but the feeling I have is awful — sort of like a young virgin boy who can't get it up in a whorehouse and freezes more and more. So I don't know what to do.

I may try again but I don't think it's going to come off, I don't know what's wrong, it would take psychoanalysis. I made a record for BBC which was great, weeping and wailing and sincere. Perhaps can use that. Also Locke McCorkle[41] at Mill Valley has good tape of the Berkeley reading we all gave. Gary Snyder can perhaps get a hold of it — he's back I hear. Perhaps it can be edited to get rid of interruptions and sound OK. It has a good reading of "Holy" [part of "Howl"] and "America," etc.

I'm broke, dumb, writeless and nowhere. Send on royalties as soon as you can. No Guggenheim so may have to come back to U.S. earlier than hoped — right now I'm living off Burroughs. You had better hold back $50 from the royalties in case refund is necessary for Fantasy temporarily. I seem to be changing personalities in midstream and can't Howl right now. Meanwhile I wrote to Warsaw and Moscow asked them to give me a hovel and daily kasha for a short visit if they can. I'd like to travel a little more before going home. [. . .]

Read and enjoyed, "I Am Waiting" — but I think you run into same trouble I have now on this politics poem — the specific poetry, the images, are not fine and permanent enough — too lax and coy. The music, or drive forward is there, but the concrete particulars are not wild enough languagely — but I am now riddled with self-criticism and shouldn't bring you down with the same drag.

Read a lot of Ron Loewinsohn he sent Gregory — they seem really good. Also reread all Whalen he sent Gregory and they seem, as Jack once said, "a pillar of strength." What's new in town?

Everything I've tried writing this year comes to a pile of spiritless miscellaneous junk so I give up for awhile. Don't know what next, broke, headed nowhere [. . .]

As ever,
Allen

41 Locke McCorkle was a writer and Buddhist friend of Gary Snyder and Jack Kerouac who lived in a cabin in Mill Valley, California.

April 15, 1958: Allen Ginsberg in Paris to Lawrence Ferlinghetti in San Francisco

Dear Larry:

Received your check, thank you, I was, as I said, broke and living off Bill Burroughs. And your postcard. Books not arrived yet, I'll let you know when they do. Re: recording, OK, will wait awhile and see what happens — hard to set up right scene, equipment, etc. Perhaps later in New York City if not here. I'd like to make record but don't know in advance exactly how — will wait till the spirit whistles.

Gregory back from Venice has room downstairs, also scrounging for money. He may write an article for USIS magazine here, on poetry. We'll both go to England for a fast trip, his first, in three weeks, a contemporary poetry society invited me for a paid ($15) reading. [Thomas] Parkinson[42] gave a BBC broadcast including a tape I made there last time and that stirred a lot of interest and was well reviewed. But there seems to be some opposition to playing the uncut complete tape — Parkinson just broadcast Part III [of] "Howl." Meanwhile [Stephen] Spender[43] turned down Burroughs manuscript complaining about having to wade thru yards of entrails. So anyway Gregory and I go try blitz England. Here we gave a small reading in George Whitman's store last week, Bill read prose too, Gregory took off his clothes this time, I read mostly new poems. Enclosed by the way a weird rhymed poem Kerouac and I once cooked up,[44] I was fiddling around with it the last few days. It reads better actually if you leave out the three beat lines (I threw them in now just to see). Rather like [Robert] Herrick. I have been seeing a very square toad anthologist Alan Bosquet who's compiling an anthology of U.S. poetry, young. I gave him my, your, Gregory, Levertov, Olson *Maximus*, two Creeley

---

42 Thomas Parkinson (1920–1992), a poet and professor of English at the University of California, Berkeley.
43 Stephen Spender (1909–1995), a British poet, writer, and editor of *Encounter* magazine.
44 "Pull My Daisy" was a collaboration written in 1949 by Ginsberg, Jack Kerouac, and Neal Cassady.

books, several volumes of *Black Mountain Review*, etc. etc. as well as a roll of poems by Kerouac. He says he'll include you, me, Gregory, and maybe Jack, but rejects everything else. He's a businessman and a bad one, I think he personally caused an enormous depression I've had for a month, like a French Oscar Williams[45] but worse since more staid. He'll probably get in touch with you for rights sooner or later. There will be more of a demand for City Lights series in England, is there any place there you stockpile your books? You ought to make some arrangement with Hand and Flower or whoever, to have a sizeable number on deposit, whence they can be ordered by English bookstores, some kind of English distributor for you. I don't know who. Received *Evergreen* #4, read Horn ["Horn on *Howl*"] article by you, thought [Mark] Schorer's[46] seemed faraway too, except for "god dying in America." No, I didn't change it, they printed it from that mimeo I made.

Re: Burroughs' manuscript. Enclosed find a letter from Bill, I asked him to indicate to you what would be his choice for a small selected prose book.

The manuscript of *Naked Lunch* that [Sterling] Lord is sending you consists of the sections we worked on and typed up in Tangiers. None is published anywhere except for the Yage City [section] in *Black Market Review*. The piece in *Chicago Review* is from a new book he's completing now (a junk picaresque pilgrimage New York to Lima). The manuscript you have consists of many parts that are not integrated, interwoven. However it contains his best writings so far. [. . .]

Well, as you can see, his method is to get going into a sort of routine, that's Burroughs's short form, the routine, usually starts verbally then he writes it . . . carries the material out where it verges on the psychotic often . . . some of them classic in my mind like the Talking Asshole or The President is a Junky. Maybe a book of selected routines. Or one long section like The Market. Or a long insane succession of

---

45 Oscar Williams (1900–1964), an academic poet and editor.
46 Mark Schorer (1908–1977), a writer and educator who testified at the *Howl* trial on behalf of City Lights.

images like Word. In any case I've specified above which are my favorite parts. There is a lot of other material but it is not in final form. Bill says to send you "Have You Seen Pantopon Rose?" which is a three page version of Word. He also has a thirty page version. You have the full sixty pages which I think is the best. It's the most extreme and pure piece of writing he's done and the logical extension of his method . . . which is to transcribe directly the succession of visual images passing thru his extraordinarily open inner eye . . . a faculty developed thru years by much meditation . . . and twelve years constant junk dream. Anyway, then, finally, please let us know when you've read it . . . take your time with it tho. Show anyone who's interested — Rexroth has read earlier books (not this) . . . and McClure might want to see the manuscript if it's around . . . or anyone else is welcome . . . Duncan, Loewinsohn, etc.

If you are interested and want us to work on a final selection for you let us know, we can do the editing and patching here . . . or make your own suggestions. Kerouac could do an introduction, perhaps a sort of portrait of Bill, maybe, I dunno. [. . .]

Love,
Allen

May 8, 1958: Lawrence Ferlinghetti in San Francisco to Allen Ginsberg in Paris

Dear Allen . . . .
Have been trying to find time to answer your letters for some time, and here's at least a try. I received Burroughs' manuscript from agent and am going thru it all; then I'll go over your notes on same. It will take time, and I am extremely doubtful, from what I've read so far, that any bookseller would dare to sell it in his store, becuz of the flow of junk and jizzom . . . . More on that later [. . .]

The few paragraphs of your poem about the Destruction of America which you sent me were astounding and great. Hope you don't throw that part away but build it into long work [. . .]

Guess that's all for now . . . . Am reading a prose tirade at Poets Follies this Sunday entitled "Tentative Description of a Dinner Given To Promote the Impeachment of President Eisenhower." My New Directions *Coney Island* [*of the Mind*] is out. Will send you a copy tomorrow . . . . Gregory too [. . .] so long yes.

larry
LF

Ferlinghetti continued to worry that Ginsberg might seek a larger New York publisher, but in this letter Allen again reassures him that he'll stick with City Lights.

ca. last week of May 1958: Allen Ginsberg in Paris to Lawrence Ferlinghetti in San Francisco

Dear Larry:
[. . .] Gregory's book [*Gasoline*] received, looks GREAT. Hurrah! You were so patient, wonderful — what would have happened if it went thru six months ago. Send me twenty-five copies, charge me. Or charge me for fifteen, I'll send the rest out for review here and England. [. . .]

Ah, it's not that Jack's book (of poems) is a good thing — it's that (I think) it's great unrecognized poesy. But no accounting for tastes. Jack published enough, prose, no worry bout that — it's the gist of his method in poetry that's interesting to me (and check with impressionable McClure the same reaction). But "Lucien Midnite" fine too — whatever, if you do anything with Jack, do something wild no one else will publish.

Burroughs: For God's sake, he's written so much, there's no fear anyone will skim the cream. However both *Partisan* and Grove have put him down. Tho *Chicago Review* took a great ten pages and wrote him congratulatory letters saying it was the best prose they ever saw lately. Grove hung on to the manuscript overlong, months, and returned it to Sterling Lord. Jack K. [Kerouac] will be in New York soon and send it to you.

The impression of chaos it apparently makes on everybody — Perhaps if we send you short trim selection sixty pages you'll be able to take it in easier. So Bill (who's here) and I will work on a selected Burroughs pamphlet for you and mail that in soon. Meanwhile you can have the whole manuscript as soon as they send it to you. I'm not there in New York to hurry things on so it's all fallen flat and is sitting around offices dusty for months. So read our selection and also look at the total bulk. Then decide what you want. [. . .]

The "new long poem" of *Evergreen* is the old duckbill platypus Mexican ramble "Xbalba" ["Siesta in Xbalba"]. As I said I am satisfied with you, more than satisfied, and will make no contrary arrangements otherwise, that's definite, don't worry. When I've written a book of new poems I'll send them to you — probably publish pieces in advance in magazines, but make no fuckup arrangements on rights, so will give you book. Yes I seem to be getting famous but I see now (alas too late) it is no blessing, but a mixed bag. I mean it's all illusory, the only thing really matters is wild writing. But fame or notoriety seems to invade my personality like a cancer, I develop an alternate self as author of *Howl*, and that's an absolute bring-down — you have no idea.

So anyway our arrangements and agreement you stay my publisher I your author stands stop or don't worry. [. . .] Maybe I'm paranoid, also broke, and see no future prosperity of any kind, in fact rather the bloody opposite and expect anyway in five years to be weeping after no gold and no god in some furnished room in Chicago. I am not exactly defenseless now, but if my poetry is to improve I will have to be, put myself, in a naked raw defenseless state somewhere someplace or other, outcast and I hope for that matter crucified, I mean it — at which time maybe I won't want that fifty percent. But then it may be a godsend. I would like to take out insurance while I'm still sane for I will break out in tears and not be in five years no matter how much publicity there is in *Mademoiselle*. And that's what I mean by the fifty percent, I don't expect to be a professional poet, I don't want that nor to make regular money on it (why I don't make contract) — but want what loose chance brings in, not steady return for steady production — for if I ever produce steady it will be bullshit not fright that is expressed. Well I'll think more. Yes, also, pocketsize cheap books better than largesize, I agree absolutely, I have no ambition about nice looking big book — the odder and truer the form of book the better. [. . .]

Love,
Allen

In 1958 Lawrence Ferlinghetti bought an old Victorian house on Wisconsin Street on Potrero Hill. He also purchased some land for a cabin in Bixby Canyon, north of Big Sur on the California coastline.

June 13, 1958: Lawrence Ferlinghetti in San Francisco to Allen Ginsberg in Paris

Dear Allen . . . .
As you see by the address, I've moved to Potrero Hill . . . . though at the moment I am in the Big Sur forest and have just finished reading the two black notebooks of Burroughs — *Naked Lunch* and *Interzone*. He wrote me a note suggesting a selection of it, as you did, and maybe this will do to answer both of you, since I see he's also laying where lies the Coeur [heart] (Ci-git)[47] . . . . Naturally, I agree, there is a lot here that ought to be published. But I have not been able to make any selection which could possibly be put on sale by any bookseller in this country, and anyone that published it as is would be indulging in pure and sure premeditated legal lunacy, as I am assured by the most liberal lawyers. The real place to publish it, in its present state, and all of it as is, is in Paris, like [Henry] Miller. If, however, you can make a selection, as you say on your latest card, which anyone here would dare

---

47 Burroughs was also staying in the Beat Hotel on Rue Git-le-Coeur.

to sell in a regular bookstore, I am interested. There are parts which could go as is, and I wish I edited a magazine like the *Chicago Review* just long enough to publish same. But enough for a book is another thing, unless something can be done along the following line. i.e. expand the actual description of the Visionary Yage City (pp. 64-67 in *Naked Lunch* and first part of "Market" at end of *Interzone* which is the same description). This vision of the Composite City (with the city of Annexia added) is at the heart of everything — certainly the end of the quest of the whole of *Naked Lunch* and also bound up in the junk climaxes in *Interzone*. At least that's the way it strikes the non-junked reader. As for specific parts of *Interzone*, this is how it goes with me, in a more or less yes-or-no evaluation: "The Word" first 5 or 6 pages filled with the best prose and visions and great sentences. This is the best section for my money. "Voices" — I don't dig except for "like I say junkies is ghosts and only certain people subject to see them." "Clerk" — Nix. "Interzone U" — Not much. "Islam Inc" — good last part. "Hassam's Rumpus Room" — you can have it. "Benway" — description of city of Annexia great. "AJ's Journal" — no. "Hospital" — parts I like. "Psych Conference" — good. "Market" — first part Yage City climax again . . . . I don't know what you can make of this, but, as I say, I'm hoping he will be able to make a new version based on Yage City, etc. [. . .]

so like
yrs trooly,
larry

By the time Ferlinghetti rejected Burroughs's manuscript, Allen had received word that the Chicago Review *would publish substantial selections from* Naked Lunch. *He had also heard about Neal Cassady's arrest in San Francisco for the possession of a small amount of marijuana.*

Dear Larry:

Passed on your note to Bill [Burroughs]. He's working on new novel, a lot of new material and patchwork of some old, for *Chicago Review* serialization, so he probably won't do anything on it for awhile. When there's time, I'll see if we can assemble sixty pages of publishable and legal selections.

Keep the notebooks at store, I wrote Gary Snyder and [Michael] McClure the manuscript was there if they wanted to borrow it to read — or anyone else interested — don't give it to no goofs who'll lose it tho. (Never forget Cassady's manuscript lost by Gerd Stern)[48] (Cassady I hear has been busted but I can't seem to reach him or anyone who knows what the score is.) [. . .]

I recently read early Tzara (and other Dada in Motherwell's book) and he seems the best of the writers of that group — livest. Here he's considered now a washout old Stalinist, but I really doubt that, the early writing was too good and the one French literary kid I met whose opinion I really admire says his later work is great, too. Guess he's undervalued. But seven dada manifestos are really vigorous and funny, I have been able to read the later work, it's not translated or too much known. Met Duchamp, Benjamin Péret and Man Ray at party the other night — and Tzara briefly at Deux Magots. [. . .]

Gregory writing a lot — he has more than enough for another book already I guess, but I guess he doesn't want to publish more so soon and's waiting to see what'll happen to his work in near future, how it changes, it seems to change every month. Best poems so far this year are final version "Power," "Army," "Food," "Park," "Withdrawal," "H-Bomb," — and some others — all long, 2-5 pages each.

McClure from letters sounds as if he's had a kind of internal explosion and's finished sixty-page collection, including new long Peyote

---

48 This is a reference to Neal Cassady's "Joan Anderson Letter," which had influenced Jack Kerouac's development as a writer a few years earlier.

poem — you seen that? Sounds from afar very good. . . . *Coney Island* arrived, I hardly had chance to glance at it and someone interested borrowed it, I'll get it back and comment next letter. New short poems seemed very good, where your images are discrete; the long political ones seem too loose, as poesy. Only sensible way to redeem long lines for use is to make each one as perfect as a line in a sonnet — "in this mode perfection is basic," said Williams when I asked him about some early rhymed poems I showed him. Well, later.

Love,
Allen

Ginsberg returned to New York in July and he and Peter Orlovsky found an inexpensive apartment on the Lower East Side.

August 20, 1958: Allen Ginsberg in New York to Lawrence Ferlinghetti in San Francisco

Dear Larry:

Been back for two weeks, found nice small apartment — new address is 170 East 2nd Street, Apt. 16, NY 9, NY, — so can always reach me there. Pretty crowded scene in New York, lots of poets — Edward Marshall here too, you know his long poem ["Leave the Word Alone"] in last *Black Mountain Review*? very good — he had lots of other manuscripts.

I gather that bad poets and commercialism have somewhat soured the scene here on poetry readings. But Gary [Snyder] and Phil Whalen and LaVigne say they're coming here this fall maybe so maybe, we put one on in New York with [Ed] Marshall and Levertov and O'Hara, who's here. Five Spot[49] asked me to read but I said no for the time

---

49 The Five Spot was a well-known jazz club at 5 Cooper Square in New York City.

being. I live near there and sneak in free every other nite and hear Thelonious Monk.

That fellow you asked me about, who said he knew me and Greg and Bill in Paris, yes, I knew him, his poetry is interesting tho in a way phony I feel, however he is sort of an untrustworthy con man, emotionally, I forget his name — told us he was dying of throat cancer, I doubt (now) that's true either. Said he was jazz musician, but can't blow, also told McClure he was big big poetry reading expert, etc., etc., which also sort of silly conning. I don't know what he's up to. Interesting cat tho, in that he's sort of a psychic conman. McClure thought he was fuzz — I suspect him to be the spiritual fuzz.

[Henri] Michaux said, no one had translated his *Miserable Miracle* and his following book after that, too — which was also further deathly experiences with peyote. Louise Varèse is his translator, and she has the manuscript complete — I mean, no one had published the translations — he was interested, and annoyed, in a nice way, that he was now having trouble in the U.S. on the mescaline books. You could probably get the last one easily. I sent you his address. I guess Gregory's still seeing him.

I'm going to sit around a few weeks and then get part-time job and work on manuscript for new book. I'll see also about Fantasy reading tape. What's new? [. . .] When Gary and McClure are finished with the Burroughs manuscript please ship it registered here, I'll refund stamps, or take it out of royalties. Let me know by the way when more royalties are due — is it soon or in several months you think?

Let me know anything you want done in New York City. Did you do anything about Céline — write him? If you're interested let me know, I'll write him, or — I think I sent you his address? [. . .]

As ever,
Allen

This is the first letter in which Ferlinghetti mentions the possibility of publishing Frank O'Hara's poetry. It took a long time, but eventually, in 1964, City Lights would publish his Lunch Poems *as part of the Pocket Poets Series.*

August 30, 1958: Lawrence Ferlinghetti in San Francisco to Allen
Ginsberg in New York

Dear Allen,
Just back from Big Sur, got yours. [. . .] I can get you much more long
green in the long run, if you refer all reprint requests to us; I think
you should have gotten much more for reprint in *Beat Generation and
Angry Young Men.* Maybe you don't care. But there's no reason you
can't live off "Howl" for a long time to come, especially if I continue to
uncover new reprints. We've got Canadian distributor now. And German one, for our own editions. Also have another German publisher
interested in German *Gasoline* [. . .]

Would like to get manuscript from poet you mentioned in letter
[Edward Marshall] . . . . Also from John O'Hara [*sic*: Frank O'Hara], if
you see him. I dig him a lot. I <u>think</u> I wrote him c/o Grove, but maybe
not. No answer. Could you call him in New York City for me?

Am expanding publishing a lot — going into prose books. Could
you ask Jack Kerouac for short novel or novella (10 to 20,000 words, or
even less)? Am publishing Gregory's *Bomb!* as broadside mushroom.
Boom boom. *Il est poids net, Andalous Raffine!*[50] [. . .]
                                                                                LF

September 4, 1958: Allen Ginsberg in New York to Lawrence Ferlinghetti
in San Francisco

Dear Larry:
Settled down here in New York City — got your last letter. All your
arrangements are fine, including splitting 50-50 on German contract.
I'll refer all future reprint requests to you, so everything will be OK.

---

50 *"Il est poids net, Andalous Raffine"* was an invention of Gregory Corso's that Lawrence
Ferlinghetti adapted to his own use. Andalous Raffine became the name of the main
character in his novel *Her.* When he asked Corso about what it meant, Gregory said that
"Andalous came from a can of fish soup, and Raffine from a box of salt. So there. The
entire mad meaning of your proposed hero. Salty Fish."

I'll contact Frank O'Hara, and I think it was Edward Marshall I mentioned, and have them send you manuscript to look at. Tho it's sad you don't put out Buddhist poems, [I'll] ask Jack to send you prose soon as I see him next. What's possibility of making a 10-20,000 word Burroughs?

Glad you're publishing "Bomb," it's great poem. I read it drunk one nite at the Five Spot (only six people there at 3AM and I climbed on platform and reeled it out). The vast audience liked it. Can peddle them in England too.

What is "poids net andalous raffine"?

I don't understand why you think Gregory has ambivalence toward "Bomb" and "Power." Because his straightforward "position" is really the whole <u>point</u> of those poems and what make them permanently valuable. He does love the bomb. Why not? Is his loving it, on the level which he loves it (the same level you love a lightning flash or volcano) going to do harm? Of course NOT. It can only do GOOD (from a sociological viewpoint even) — it is as if he is declaring the human spirit bigger than the bomb. To hate the bomb, says the poem, is to make yourself vulnerable to it. People who hate it will be destroyed by it literally or spiritually.

He says also, the bomb is coming to rid the universe of stupid man. If that does happen, he's quite right, and the poem can only serve as a prophetic warning — might save us from the bomb. Basically I think he has the only sane attitude toward the bomb. So lucid, sane, level-headed, and spiritually hip — that it's laughable that anyone should think he has destructive ideas or [should be] ambivalent. He's making a great scene. The first great poem on the bomb bigger than the bomb. It also ends prophesying an apocalypse and <u>more</u> apocalypses in future universes.

We will not get rid of the bomb by banning it. We created it to destroy our stupidity. We'll only get rid of our stupidity (unless it's blown away) by digging life, the bomb (the bomb is really life) — indifferently, digging — neither hating it nor banking on it politically. (The alternative common attitudes that brought it about). The bomb is really a symbol of Life. Power is really a symbol of Life. The poems are sort of Zen poems about life. They are not political tracts about democracy and politics and ideas, they are poems directly about life — digging it quite openly with all its fierce — tiger tiger burning bright. It's like somebody accusing Blake of having an unnatural immature worship of tigers, an ambivalent attitude to force.

Dig, that's all pretty clear. Greg sent me your letter, that's why this tirade. Things fine here, I'm writing and having mystical experiences.

Your lover,
Allen

The following letter reports Ginsberg's first experience sampling laughing gas at the dentist's office. The experience would result in a long Ginsberg poem called "Laughing Gas."

September 10, 1958: Allen Ginsberg in New York to Lawrence Ferlinghetti in San Francisco

Dear Larry:
[. . .] Had laughing gas and finally understood "swindleresque ink." Certainly is an accurate phrase for appearance of disappearance of the universe when consciousness goes. Very Buddhist actually. He [Corso] really does deliver a piece of Shelleyan dream. Wrote funny "Laughing Gas" poem, back to short lines, looks like Jack's crazy Blues.

Love,
Allen

September 12, 1958: Lawrence Ferlinghetti in San Francisco to Allen Ginsberg in New York

Dear Allen . . . .
[. . .] By the way, did you get any payment from new book-magazine called *Horizon*, published by American Heritage Press in New York,

which published a page of *Howl* without any permission from us? They list Grove Press as publisher? @*and_%$#" Fuck them. Also your picture in it. Glad to see it, however. It all helps . . . . I guess this is what [James] Laughlin meant when he told me about literary robbers taking your pants while you're walking down Madison . . . .

Re: Gregory. I guess you both must wonder why I publish a poem ["Bomb"] I so little understand. What I am saying is that his "position" is not exactly clear to the reader who only has the text to go by and doesn't know Gregory himself. In other words, there is an <u>unintentional</u> ambiguity in the texts of both "Power" and "Bomb." OK, so you and I and everybody who knows Gregory knows that there is no ambivalence in his attitude on these subjects, but it seems to me that the poems themselves have an ambiguity of meaning in them which the "outside reader" wouldn't be able to unravel. Now you're liable to say that any ambiguity there is, is actually <u>intended</u>. Like Rimbaud. Or Williams. Or Andalous Raffine. And that anybody who cannot comprehend just where the poet stands must be stupid and the whole question laughable. Still I think there is something to my point. The poem is going to be read by a <u>lot</u> of stupid people as well as by the hip and the informed and the swinging. That's all I meant. Pass this on to Gregory? . . . . I'll have poem from printer in about five days now, and I'll send you a few and send it to 8th Street Bookshop and other places. Paper Editions will distribute it on our regular list, which soon will have a lot more new books on it, I hope. Hayakawa, Ralph Gleason, Alan Watts, Donald Keene, Anatole Broyard, Norman Mailer are some of the ones I've written recently, to get books . . . . Haven't heard from Frank O'Hara yet. Hope you see him . . . . I really dig . . . . 10,000 words selected from Burroughs would be good, but as I said before I doubt you can find that many printable passages. It's all right to have the nerve to publish it, but if no bookseller can sell it, what's the use??? Could you or Jack Kerouac make a selection? I've tried to call McClure, without any answer. Did you get manuscript back from him? Hope so . . . .

lawrence

Dear Larry:

Received your nice letter, [. . .] O'Hara is in Europe, I'll ask him in a week or so when he returns, he's on a temporary trip — job for the Museum of Modern Art. I'll also ask Kenneth Koch to send a manuscript — you don't have to take it but he's of same school as O'Hara and you might be interested?? [. . .]

I went to dentist, had laughing gas and it changed my life. See William James *Varieties of Religious Experience* on the subject. Now I'm a Buddhist. Kerouac, Snyder and Whalen are all correct as far as I can see: the whole fabric of existence is illusion. If you can get the kind of explicit Nirvana thru meditation as you can thru nitrous oxide, contemplation here I come. I never saw anything like <u>that</u> before — whole friggen cosmos slipped into the void like lizard's tail into crack in blank wall. Sort of an immense obvious cosmic joke.

Yes, the poem ["Bomb" by Gregory Corso] is going to be read by the stupid and square — that's the experience he had in Oxford where they threw a shoe at him thinking he was hymning capitalist fascist American H-bomb policy. What I think is, his "Line" on the subject, his own personal party line, is so poetic and pure you can't alter it, you'd lose the perfect balance. So what to do? Not much you can do if people can't understand. I mean, how many people commenting on my poetry or Jack's have got the point? — look at an article like the *Horizon* — completely mistaken in everything — there's nothing you can do. It's like, you can only tell the truth — you can't make, force people to believe it — nor can you explain the truth (by changing it) to make it more palatable — then you lose out both ways. Nearest you can do is make a prefatory note or footnote saying "The author wants it clearly understood that this poem both has and has not to do with the actual bomb."

It's the old thing of the poem being the only possible way of saying what can't be said clearly otherwise. If you say, "He's really against the bomb," that distorts the delicate reality, if you say, "He's really for the bomb," that also distorts it. All you can do is write and print what you actually think — cast bread on waters . . . also, finally, I think it's gotten to a point in the U.S. or the world where the masses are wrong, the world is going to hell, there's no more hope for improvement, not even thru prophetic poetry, things will get worse not better, all the explanations in the world won't lead people to deeper understanding — there's nothing left to do but keep the light burning for whoever can understand now or later.

I don't dig prose, pure prose by Broyard and Gleason. Watts is just tedious on Zen, I think — though if you could get him to edit a great anthology of pure nuts of Zen poetry and haikus and riddles and koans — that would be a mad interesting book. [Norman] Mailer's essay on "White Negro" I thought was excellent and I hear he's on a new mad kick on death of God or something — that's wild. I know you didn't ask my opinion on Broyard and Gleason, but I'm offering it anyways. Though I don't know Gleason's prose — didn't he write long dullish article on San Francisco Jazz for *Evergreen?*

Have not received the Burroughs manuscript from McClure. I'll write him to send it. Please phone him again. I'll work on a selection, that's printable in the USA. *Chicago Review* said next issue would be Bill's "apotheosis" by them.

As ever,
Allen

September 18, 1958: Lawrence Ferlinghetti in San Francisco to Allen Ginsberg in New York

Dear Allen . . . .
[. . .] Other ones you mention: Am hoping to get prose series off the ground soon and would like to get short prose books or pamphlets from Olson, from Gary (he's not in town now but will see him when he gets back), and the others I told you about writing in my last letter. Anything good you can find? . . . . Burroughs non-fiction on addiction? . . . . etc . . . . How about Carl Solomon? . . . . he writing anything

now? . . . . I've gotten no answer from Broyard or Mailer . . . . Sent out over fifty review copies of *Gasoline* — but no reviews anywhere, except *Mexico City News* and a few very little mags like *Combustion* in Canada . . . . As for Paper Editions, New York, they've been ordering Pocket Poets regularly every couple of months, although they always wait until they are out before re-ordering. We sent them last order, including at least 200 *Howl*, about two weeks ago. Maybe three . . . . New Paperback Gallery in Village took over 1000 copies various books in series about six weeks ago . . . . including several hundred *Howl* and quite a few *Gas* . . . . Am spending about half my time on publishing now, and it's going like mad.

    Was down in Big Sur most of August writing or rather rewriting fiction book I wrote in Paris almost ten years ago. Hope to have it for New Directions by January . . . . *Coney Island* has been reprinted by them. I guess that must mean 10,000 so far . . . . Don't know . . . . Name of my prosebook is now *Hunger*.[51]

L.

Ferlinghetti was becoming swamped with ideas for publication and he decided to publish an anthology to handle a sampling of work from various writers. The project would eventually develop into City Lights Journal, Beatitude Anthology *and* Journal for the Protection of All Beings.

September 25, 1958: Lawrence Ferlinghetti in San Francisco to Allen Ginsberg in New York

Dear Allen . . . .
[. . .] Have called McClure and he promised to send you Burroughs manuscript right away, tho I'm still dubious about your finding even 5000 words that anybody would be able to sell over the counter, without chopping it up incomprehensibly . . . . Perhaps I've a better

---

51 Ferlinghetti's novel was published as *Her* in 1960 by New Directions.

idea now. How about making selections from Burroughs to go in an anthology to be published by us. Get everybody great that you dig, both famous and unpublished. You edit it. Get everybody like Mailer, Kerouac, Algren, Brossard, Broyard, Clellon Holmes, Carl Solomon, Whalen, Snyder, Corso, Rexroth, Trocchi, John Rechy, yourself, others from out here. I know Don Allen is working on anthology of new amurrican poets which will no doubt be largely along these lines, but our anthology would be both poets and prose writers (and both fiction and non-fiction prose) on the same general theme as *Beat Generation and the Angry Young Men*'s, but this latter is too wooden and limited and there is a real void existing for a real live anthology such as I have in mind and it would go like mad both here and in England. Anthology could be called something like *A Beat Anthology*, altho this term smells of Madison Avenue, and maybe you can think of a better title. The poetry section could be called something like Street Poets or maybe no head needed but intersperse it with prose throughout the book or use some much wilder phrase to characterize the poets. Get <u>all new work</u> from all above writers, since reprints cost too much and involve endless delays and correspondence and legal permissions and other hassles. You're in contact with everybody and could make a great haul, better than the one Cass is said to have gotten in New York City for next *Climax*[52] . . . . As for payment, Grove Press seems to get away with paying $3 per page, and we might be able to work up to near that — and also give you royalty payment advance for doing the selection and editing and even writing an intro if you felt like it, tho you might want to get somebody else to do an intro . . . . I've now got big outfit in New York that handles most U.S. publishers in Europe to distribute our books over there, and would be able to print 5000 of this anthology first printing, and it should be gotten out as fast as possible, by early Spring anyway. How about it? I think it would have to be limited to about 128 pages at the most, which would mean short, pithy selections from the prose writers but would allow an awful lot of poetry.

---

52 Robert Cass published *Climax: A Creative Review in the Jazz Spirit*, which featured poetry and fiction by a wide variety of writers.

One of the main things would be to get <u>everybody</u> represented by something strong, even though it's only a selection from a larger work-in-progress. Make the whole thing work-in-progress maybe . . . . Let me know what you think about this, and if possible do the whole thing right away, if you want to do it . . . . If you don't want your name on it as "editor" why then how about just being silent editor and do the collecting and selecting and we'll put it out simply as a City Lights selection, though you could still get paid for your work . . . . I figure you'd be ideal for getting this material for anthology, since you're in contact with all the people I can't seem to get any answer out of, etc. and it would seem almost impossible for me to do it all by correspondence without coming to New York, etc. . . . . The more I think about the great collection you could assemble the more heated up I get over it . . . . Hole-button everybody for new work. Tell them it'll get good publicity and distribution and that they'll get paid regular, etc. etc. [. . .]

Have, by the way, written Gary, who is out of town, about editing a *Zen Book of Koans* . . . .

yers trooly
L

September 30, 1958: Allen Ginsberg in New York to Lawrence Ferlinghetti in San Francisco

Dear Larry:
[. . .] Re: an anthology — it's a good idea and I'd like to do it actually, but there are problems.

First, all the information and material I've gathered over the last two years I've been pumping into Don Allen, who listens a little, and Irving Rosenthal in *Chicago Review* — so perhaps anything I would like to do will be done in one form or another by them — that is, Allen's anthology will probably include at least all the people I would dig.

Second, a lot of people I like (Levertov, Creeley, Olson, O'Hara, Koch) would probably object to being included in general title Beat.

Third, I am not well informed about prose: generally actually I only dig highly poetic prose for which reason I've followed Jack and Bill — but not read nor liked much Brossard, Broyard, even Holmes, Trocchi, etc. I mean for pure prose.

Fourth, the work: I'm bogged down with my own manuscript, and have been too much involved with literary maneuvering and ought to get out of the game. In any case I can't do it right away.

You know my own taste and interests and I've written you about various people so you could do it yourself, anyway, if you want.

What I will do, is look around and compile a mass of manuscripts of various people in the next few months, of exactly what I think is the classic writing of the period — most of it unpublished or if published, relatively unknown. Then I'll send it to you and you can decide — this doesn't make it necessary for you to print it or me to follow anybody's kicks but my own — see, actually, I would be interested in a book with Bill's best writing, Jack's best from unpublished late books (*Visions of Neal* and *Poems*), Gregory and my best, *Slop Barrel* and a few later poems by Whalen, fifteen pages Snyder, fifteen short poems by Creeley, maybe some prose of his though I don't know, five poems by Levertov, one long poem by Marshall, maybe some passionate surreal poems by O'Hara and Koch — I don't know beyond that. I know — yes, something by McClure — a few other things here and there — that's all too narrow a choice for you though I think — plus an introduction trying to explain the different movements that have converged into one scene in poetry the last ten years.

Well, this doesn't leave you anything definite. I seem to be indefinite all the time. I just have too much on my head — actually I get most now out of doing nothing but stare into space and go to dentist for more laughing gas which as I think I wrote you has turned me into a Buddhist.

In any case I'll begin compiling manuscript and you can decide later — or go ahead with plans of your own, alternatively.

LeRoi Jones bought a press for *Yugen* and wants to print books for everybody — Snyder, Whalen, Creeley, anybody — he can do it cheap and break even selling only 100 copies. If you have any ideas for him write him. Laughlin at New Directions said he'll look over Snyder, Whalen and Kerouac books of poetry, and also now Grove seems to be interested in doing their books. So at last it looks like the dharma bum boys will get printed up entire, by someone or other, maybe by the end of this year. I think that'll help clear up some of the illiterate confusion of Renaissance. They ought to strengthen the whole scene. But I will put together a book, of various people. [. . .]

Jack and I all nite drunk with Franz Kline[53] last nite.

I don't know how Gary will respond — don't know if he — why, yes, I think the Jap lady who sent him to Kyoto was working on a big semi-important collection of koans or poem-nuts of some kind, classical works translated — he might. Grove is bringing out his Han Shan translations, simultaneous with Jack's *Dharma Bums* — Gary's the hero of that and Jack quotes lots of his poems. [. . .]

You see all the involvement with the above literary logistics and publishings — I've been writing letters on and off recommending this and that — I'm afraid I'll get neck deep in it if I start off compiling your anthology on a real scale, I'd better not.

I'll look around for manuscripts of what I like as writing and send it to you in two months, with an introduction, you do what you like. [. . .]

As ever,
Allen

October 2, 1958: Lawrence Ferlinghetti in San Francisco to Allen Ginsberg in New York

Dear Allen . . . .

Got yours. You're so right. You should write instead of edit and con. But will be glad to have you gather manuscripts for me. Including your own. When do I get new book of yours? [. . .] Hope you don't mind reference to "Beat" on cover. Actually, it's the truth, as far as what most people think. (Weren't you surprised how famous-like you were when you hit New York this time? . . . . As for using Beat in title for anthol-

---

53 Franz Kline (1910–1962), the abstract expressionist painter.

ogy, I'd rather think of something else too. What would you suggest? *Protest Poets? Zen Lunacy?* Why don't you write that introduction <u>first</u>? It would help conceive and define the book? You might persuade me too, by doing this, of how Levertov, Olson, Creeley, fit into the picture. You might also persuade me on a lot of other things. I see Whalen and Snyder in anthology, but not separate books of poetry. Good for Grove and New Directions if they publish them . . . . Can you get Jack to send me *Visions Of Neal* now? Please like . . . . Try introduction soon, OK? (My Fantasy record of "Impeach" is out now.)

yes
LF

October 15, 1958: Lawrence Ferlinghetti in San Francisco to Allen Ginsberg in New York

Dear Allen . . . .

Am just going to Big Sur to get some writing done and will be gone for three weeks, but will have mail forwarded. So I hope you are really doing something about that Beat anthology. Have discussed it with Gary, and have asked him and Phil Whalen to contribute, either to you or me. Don Allen asked me, "What is this Beat anthology Allen and Kerouac are working on — when will it be out?" etc. . . . I told him this Spring, but that it would not conflict with his coming anthology of new American poets[54] — since I wanted to make it half prose, if possible. Keep this in mind anyway and get some short prose pieces, anyway, and a good sized piece from Jack Kerouac if you can. How about that *Visions of Neal*, which I have never read? Would it be publishable as a book in my new prose series? And a part of it in Beat Anthology? And have you thought of any better title for the anthology? Let me hear how you're coming with it, so that I can decide if and when I can announce it on our "Spring List." [. . .]

LF

---

54 *The New American Poetry 1945–1960* (New York: Grove, 1960).

[P.S.] Some of Kerouac's "Blues" too . . . Get the kind of poetic prose you like from others.

ca. October 23, 1958: Allen Ginsberg in New York to Lawrence Ferlinghetti in San Francisco

Dear Larry:

[. . .] I still admire your poetry in *Pictures* but I think you're going too goofy political. Street poetry OK but what street boy sings of Ike and Senators? Rather hear songs about combs and razors and shoelaces on the street. But later. It's none of my business.

I'm assembling manuscript for the beat-hip-high handbook, including an excellent thing by old jailbird [Herbert] Huncke[55] (vision at fourteen of cosmic sun in Chicago when he realized he was mad, as remembered dying in New York twenty years later). Jack says he'll work on it with me and we'll write an intro to it, probably sign both names, and make weird good book. [. . .]

Grove reading *Visions of Neal.* Jack's agent Sterling Lord has it, and I'm now too far away to wrestle with them for it. Please maybe write Lord and ask him for it next. There's plenty there for a small book [of] selections. New Directions bringing out private edition of porno parts when they can find a printer who'll handle it, says Laughlin. But lots of clean parts left. Also Jack has later books. Selections from *Some of the Dharma,* or *Springtime Mary* (100 pages, 1954) — and there are other books. They're all as good or better than *Dharma Bums.* I still think *Blues* should have been published, complete. But write Lord for it. Doesn't he answer you? Then write Jack. [. . .]

I have enough now for a huge sloppy book but it's all in messy manuscript and sooner or later will get around to assembling it all. I'm so overwhelmed with letters, people, and my own sort of

---

55 Herbert Huncke (1915–1996), one of Ginsberg's earliest friends and the author of *The Evening Sun Turned Crimson* (Cherry Valley, NY: Cherry Valley Editions, 1980).

gregariousness that I never seem to get much solitary work done. However, I guess there'll be time. [. . .]

Is it too early for another book by Gregory? He has all the poems. Somebody will steal him maybe if you don't tie him down. Or maybe next time, reprint *Gasoline* with three times as much material — "Army," "Power," "Bomb," "Marriage," "Food," "Park" (all new long poems). O'Hara writing a long appreciation for Grove, a review of *Gasoline* finally and unpublished poems. O'Hara thinks Gregory is the greatest U.S. poet so it should be mad review. [. . .]

Love,
Allen

October 26, 1958: Lawrence Ferlinghetti in Bixby Canyon, CA, to Allen Ginsberg in New York

Dear Allen . . . .
[. . .] Am down here working on prose book. Will send some of it to you eventually. You might think a few pages of it might fit in the anthology, though that's up to you, since I don't feel too good about publishing myself all the time . . . When do you think you can have manuscript for anthology all assembled? To get it out by April, it should be ready for printer by January at latest. December, if possible. Figure on 196 pages, 33 lines to the page, poetry or prose . . . . As for my poetry, you're so right. Pocketcombs and shoelaces, rather than senators. That Eisenhower tirade was just a blast I had to get off . . . . Fuck it. What about title for anthology? "No Name Anthology" would have to have a subtitle to explain it . . . . From Jack, *Springtime Mary* sounds like it would be just right for us. How about it? Can you make selections from it for anthology? . . . . I asked Fantasy to send you my record — let me know if you don't get it . . . . Wrote Gregory a month ago that I was ready to do next book of his or at least wanted to read the manuscript first . . . . I think separate book would be best for "Army," "Power" (re-written, he says), "Bomb," "Marriage," "Food,"

"Park" . . . . just long poems . . . . the greatest . . . . We could go to a lot more than 196 pages if the material warrants it, so send me all you can that you think any good . . . .

so long
lawrence

October 31, 1958: Allen Ginsberg in New York to Lawrence Ferlinghetti in San Francisco

Dear Larry·
So far, if things go as planned, Kerouac will go next month to Florida and type me up fifty pages, selections from all his works chronologically so it be self-selected anthology of his best. I have to get Burroughs' manuscript back in several weeks from *Chicago Review* who've got it to print what they can. That's all definite that I know. Gregory's headed to Greece and slept in Coliseum so it'll take time to get documents from him. I have to settle my own manuscript slowly, so don't know if it all be ready in January. I would like to get all this off my head, it being sort of final statement and henceforth after that retire from the literary world in which I've got too involved. I really don't know what to call it, could give you title now but that wouldn't be as interesting as one which I waited till I thought of a good one, so no point being pressed with time to take anything at hand — same with the material. I really want to make a testament. More I think of it may limit it to four to six people — leave me fuck around and see what I come up with. 196 pages be plenty. Good idea on Gregory book. Too bad last book not reviewed, but so what, it's probably paid for itself, maybe next book do better and *Gasoline* still be in print to sell, too. [. . .]

Anthology I guess will take time. I don't want to be sloppy.

I'm getting ten letters a day and have vast letters [to] answer, etc., so I'll have to settle all this and be done with literary type life and liaison interorganizations, it takes up too much time and my mind gets filled with it, bad medicine. Two years now of it, all my duties are discharged and I resign. [. . .]

As ever,
Allen

As the following letter states, the University of Chicago censored the next issue of the Chicago Review. *Fighting this became an all-consuming task for the editors, Paul Carroll and Irving Rosenthal. In the end they decided to create their own periodical, which Kerouac would name* Big Table. *Its first issue would include all the suppressed material.*

November 19, 1958: Allen Ginsberg in New York to Lawrence Ferlinghetti in San Francisco

Dear Larry:

Irving Rosenthal probably wrote you — the University of Chicago is suppressing his winter issue, which was to consist of thirty pages "Lucien Midnite" by Kerouac, thirty pages of Burroughs selected by Rosenthal and considered legal by him, and thirty pages of new prose by Edward Dahlberg. I told him to write you and see if you'd print, publish, the issue for him as a City Lites book (*The Banned Chicago Review*) — probably be good money in it and excellent art, and be able to outwit the University and be legal. They're not in trouble with cops or post office, they're being bugged by over-timid school bureaucracy afraid of local Chicago Herb Caens[56].

Happy
thanksgiving,
Allen

---

56 Herb Caen (1916–1997), an influential San Francisco newspaper columnist.

Dear Allen . . . .
Irving Rosenthal sent me the banned *Chicago Review*, but I returned
it to him, since I didn't see any reason why I should publish it the way
he wanted it published — as "The Banned Winter Issue of the *Chicago Review*" . . . . The Dahlberg writing had little to do with Kerouac
or Burroughs, and the Burroughs selections weren't the ones I'd have
chosen from him. Then too, I thought that if you were going to use any
Burroughs in the anthology, why go into it with the *Chicago Review*?
I'm not so sure I'll like what you choose from him either, since most
of the time I find his writing isn't worth the cruddy language and imagery he uses — that is, the content of the <u>writing</u>, what it is saying
in the end, isn't great enough to warrant the general puss of junk . . . .
The Kerouac selection from "Sebastian Midnight" was the only thing
in the *Chicago Review* which really interested me, and I think this is
the best Kerouac I've read yet, despite the Finnegan derivations or
depredations. How long is the whole of "Sebastian" and can you get
it? I wrote Rosenthal and said please to send you "Sebastian" for our
anthology. How's it coming? [. . .]

> Happy Geekyear
> Merry
> Goonsmass
> luv
> Larry

Dear Larry:
[. . .] I have so much work. Have been writing a lot, last week forty-
page poem autobiographical narrative, my mother in bughouses, ends
in big Kaddish funeral chant. But to assemble that, and politics and

three-part, six page "Au Tombeau Apollinaire," and four other long poems, and innumerable short, to a book is typewriter labor and nervous breakdown over revising etc. so take time. But base of book now ready. [. . .]

Allen

◀ 1959 ▶

January 10, 1959: Allen Ginsberg in New York to Lawrence Ferlinghetti in San Francisco

Dear Larry:

[. . .] Now, I have been working on my own poems and tho I was complaining last year it seems I have been writing like mad. It's just that I never typed anything up in final form, but went ahead. As it stands it's rather frightful. I have a couple short poems, then a lot of middle size poems — "At Apollinaire's Grave" (enclosed — Grove printing it in *Evergreen*).

Poem Rocket (3 pages) — in Gregory's German anthology[57].

Ignu (Goofy poem) — 3 pages in Gregory's German anthology and also accepted for local New York anthology ed. Daisy Aldan[58].

Sather Gate — 3 pages — will send to *San Francisco Review* and also Grove use it for their anthology.

World world World — 3 pages shortline London Vision (not sent out)

Lion for Real — 3 page unrhymed longline quatrains (a little like Corbière's "Rhapsodie du Sourd") unpublished

My Sad Self — 2 pages, a little like "Organ Music," unpublished

Laughing Gas — 6 pages broken style Xbalba verse, work on that to finish

To Aunt Rose — 2 pages about family Spanish War in Newark unpublished

American Change — 4 pages — pennies nickels and dimes first seen on the boat back — work on that to go.

Well that's all OK, but they never get higher off the ground than the Greyhound poem. Finally however, I am now typing a vast mad

---

57 *Junge Amerikanische Lyrik* was edited by Gregory Corso and Walter Höllerer and published in Germany by Carl Hanser Verlag in 1961.
58 *A New Folder* (New York: Folder Editions, 1959).

masterpiece "Kaddish" — so far in five different sections, the center one is a thirty-page single-space piece of strophic narrative interspersed with chants and hymns.

If we publish it all together it'll all amount — good poems, not just shit dribble notations — to 100 pages or more. So maybe a big mad full book. The "Kaddish" is for my money better and wilder than "Howl" — I mean huge sections of Bach-like construction, as well as lots of Newark detail, politics, etc.

I still haven't started working on all the material (about thirty pages) I assembled on Fall of America, either, and mean to do that this month, too.

I don't know what to do. I'll bring everything I have done, when I come in May to read for Berkeley and San Francisco State. We'll worry then. I work on them all at once, at the same time. I am busy and overworked and still mostly broke, tho this month things fine since Peter, Gregory and I are getting $18 a day for a week working on an experimental movie (script by Kerouac)[59] — so exhausted from everyday under camera. Flying to Chicago to give readings on January 29 for *Chicago Review* to raise money for them. Trying to prepare cut Burroughs manuscript for Viking and unexpurgated possibly for 8th St. Bookstore–Jonathan Williams undercounter edition. *New York Post* reporter and *Tribune* people following me around (*Post* be out to see you next week — Al Uranowitz [*sic:* Aronowitz]). Therefore — therefore — I can't work faster than I am on the manuscript of poetry for the moment, and as I said I'd rather take time and finish it right, slowly. I guess by summer. The *Goofbook* will have to wait till I'm done with my poetry. Meanwhile *Howl* is still selling fine so no loot's lost and it'll only build up vaster audiences for next book. *Howl* will probably continue spreading in sales because I've been reading at universities — scheduled for Princeton, Columbia, Yale (done already) and Chicago, etc. and the *Post* series will probably sell a lot here in New York, still.

While we're on subject — it seems to me, I mean, is it possible now — that after 20,000 copies you start upgrading my royalties?

---

59 This was to become *Pull My Daisy*, filmed by Robert Frank and Alfred Leslie.

%-wise? All other sales are pure gravy and I'm paying for a lot of the publicity with my blood (the readings and interviews, etc.) — and I begin to think final sales before it's all over may reach 40 or 50,000. So if it is now pure gravy for you, beyond the 20,000 already sold, what about increasing my share in it? Same for next book *Kaddish*, which ought to do well — after a certain number of thousand when you've got return on your investment, etc. Let me know. [. . .]

Later,
Allen

January 17, 1959: Telegram from Lawrence Ferlinghetti in San Francisco to Allen Ginsberg in New York

I READ "APOLLINAIRE'S TOMB" THUNDERSTRUCK AND POOR YOU ARE HUGEST DARK GENIUS VOICE ALIVE STILL UNRECOGNIZED DESPITE ALL. HOWEVER ABOUT BOOK NOW OF NINE POEMS YOU LIST IN LETTER TO BE IN PRINT FOR YOUR VISIT HERE IN MAY. "KADDISH" AND "FALL OF AMERICA" SEPARATE BOOKS LATER. PLEASE MAKE SURE GROVE PRESS DOES NOT RESTRICT OUR RIGHTS TO REPRINT POEMS THEY USE. YES BIGGER ROYALTY SEND YOU ALL PROFIT LATER LOVE

LAWRENCE FERLINGHETTI CITY LIGHTS BOOKS

January 23, 1959: Allen Ginsberg in New York to Lawrence Ferlinghetti in San Francisco

Dear Larry:
Thanks for your encouraging telegram, it made me feel fine for two days and Gregory's upset you haven't responded to his poems, help him too.

Enclosed find "Ignu." A book of these poems in May would be

a good idea, if they are all finished by then, but let us plan on a book when I'm done with them, I'd rather not work by deadline, it doesn't help composition, and I'm trying them out for defects at readings. But there's no rush, actually, from commerce angle.

Grove said they'd print Snyder and Whalen but only if in a book with some poems of mine or Jack as third part, and neither Gary or I or Phil dug that, each for his own reasons. Don Allen wanted to print separate books, but [Barney] Rosset nixed it. So Allen gave them to [James] Laughlin who said he dug the books but was too busy, too full up, and wanted to give Denise Levertov's upcoming books special promotional attention, and not confuse his salesmen with too many poetry books at once. So they are left out again. I don't think it's good, all this, everybody getting books and books and nobody willing to print the two central Classicists. LeRoi Jones proposes to and that's a good idea, but he has hands full and no apparatus as yet. Won't you please put their books out? They are good poets, they write and deserve audience after all this time, they are important in the U.S. poesy renaissance and their poems still get nowhere as far as publishing. I be willing to finance the costs for both of them if you are too overloaded with other manuscripts in preparations you can use my future royalties on the new 10,000 *Howls* for that — should cover Villiers costs for two books. I mean, they are so historically important for San Francisco Muse and you are the historically important San Francisco pioneer so it would work out madly great if you'd relent. Besides they'd sell enough to pay in long run and be well received prestigetidinous items, etc. I remember originally you said you just weren't that moved by their poetry, I'm writing this now in hope that acquaintance and recent readings of last two years in their visits have made them more dear to you. Otherwise it means me running around spending more time, LeRoi overburdening his shop, etc. and sadness a little for them, too. I mean, the romance of us all having the same publisher and United Front. Well put this under your pillow dear Larry.

Leaving for Chicago next week to read several times to raise money for Rosenthal's independent magazine, he has almost enough now and the manuscripts are at the printers already. Magazine to be called *Big Table* and that issue lovely, the Burroughs selection is very good. Also read this Monday night for the Living Theatre with Paul Goodman, another benefit to raise money for them, they're putting on Williams' (W.C.) *Many Loves* play. Then February 5 with Gregory big free attack on Columbia at McMillan Hall there, maybe Jack join us. Then with LeRoi, Raymond Bremser and Ed Marshall to read to the Shades[60] at Howard University in Washington DC. Gregory to Chicago and Washington, too. Then April 25 be in San Francisco for a few weeks, read for Poetry Center and University of California. I tried to get both to try arrange for Corso and O'Hara and said I'd share costs out of my loot but they are too bureaucratic and or slow or unwilling to put themselves out so I'll come alone, I guess. OK. Write about the Zenmasters' poetry [Snyder and Whalen].

As ever,

Allen

Ferlinghetti decided not to publish Corso's next book of poetry. James Laughlin at New Directions was more enthusiastic and became Corso's primary publisher. In this letter Lawrence makes his strongest statement about why he won't publish all of Ginsberg's friends as Allen would like.

February 5, 1959: Lawrence Ferlinghetti in San Francisco to Allen Ginsberg in New York

Dear Allen . . .

Returning Gregory's manuscript to him makes me a first class peanut cacoethes[61] I know. Also Gary's. I read and reread both Gregory's *Starmeat* and Gary's *Myths and Texts*. Yes, I still feel the same as to Gary's — I'm just not sent far enuf by it. I'll wait for later works by

---

60 Although not politically correct today, this is a slang term for African Americans that Ginsberg used on more than one occasion..

61 Cacoethes is used here to mean a person who enjoys doing evil.

both of them, for there's going to be much better things coming, great ones, and I hope to have a chance at them. (And I don't mean first-class highclass straightforward protest poems, which are for square consumption.) I'm getting literally stacks of manuscripts every month now, and I just can't publish all that's good that comes my way. I dig all you say about the United Front (!); but I don't wanna. You're a move-ment in yerself, but you carry this little band of cohorts around with you in portfolio like a prospectus for the Revolution as if their writing had very much in common with yours. Gregory's certainly does, and I'm not out to run a press of Poets That Write Like Allen Ginsberg, [in the margin of the letter Corso has written: "Dat's a lie, a big dirty lie, I don't write like Allen Ginsberg — Gregory"] but Gary and Whalen couldn't be further from you, given a certain great type dharmabums base, and I certainly see nothing classical about either Gary or Phil ex-cept classic Northwest American sawmill buddhism . . . . (even though I feel Gary is going to do great Zen work in the future . . . . and I love Whalen's Berkeley poem[62] which is on Lipton's recording . . . .) These New Yawk publishers hem and haw and say like well we'd LOVE to publish yer great friends but would it sell and I'm overloaded and this and that — everything but that they really don't want to publish the writing; well, I'll say I see the romance of publishing the classical poets, but I'm too stuck on my own poisonal [personal] tastes to do it. Enuf.

Read in a United Press story of your action in Chicago and wisht I was there.[63] *Big Table* will be wonderful. Am going to advertise in it, natch. Re, your reading here, in May, I told Paul Naden at Coffee Gallery[64] about it and told him to write you about a reading at the Gallery. As for [Thomas] Parkinson's panorama of the beat,[65] I told him I wouldn't show up for any panel discussions, but just wanted to

---

62 "A Dim View of Berkeley in the Spring."
63 While Ginsberg, Orlovsky, and Corso were in Chicago to help raise funds for *Big Table*, the media reported on what they considered to be the juvenile antics of the poets.
64 The Coffee Gallery was a bohemian cafe at 1353 Grant Avenue in San Francisco's North Beach.
65 Thomas Parkinson was editing an anthology that became *A Casebook on the Beat* (New York: Thomas Y. Crowell, 1961).

read poetry and have everybody just read great poetry and no goosy footnotes and seminar mumblings and droolings. In fact, I think he should just have you and Jack and Gregory and no others. Or just one at a time on different nights . . . . And why won't they take O'Hara? Can't you get him to come? And get him to send me manuscript? You asked him for me once, but he never sent anything, though you said he was pleased, etc. I have a lot of his Grove Press books at store — probably the last copies available . . . . I bought them when Grove wrote to say they were clearing them out . . . .

Your poetry, OK, whenever you get ready. You're right to take your time. I'd sure like to see "Kaddish," too, Please send. "Ignu" I'll save for first book, it's strong [. . .]

luv . . . .

larry

While Ginsberg became ever more sought-after for readings, the mainstream press tended to report on the bad behavior of the "Beatnik" instead of on the poetry of the Beat Generation writers. Time *magazine was no exception, as Allen indicates here.*

February 17, 1959: Allen Ginsberg in New York to Lawrence Ferlinghetti in San Francisco

Dear Larry:

Your letter 5 February received, sorry so slow answer, too much mail, too many poems to type, too much Chicago, Columbia readings, etc. I'm quitting readings after I go thru with three more I promised, at least for a long while, too nerve-wracking, had to say no to Yale and Princeton but will make a Harvard shot with Gregory March 25, Brooklyn College March 4, and Howard Spade University in DC with LeRoi Jones late February sometime. Chicago was great beyond *Time*'s version and we read at Columbia last week, 1400 came and another 500 couldn't get past the police at the door, too crowded, and the reading started a small revolution at Columbia, at last. [Lionel] Trilling boycotted but his wife came and dug it, ran off and told [W.H.] Auden it was a "great success" which he reported back to us over coffee yesterday. It's my old school I was kicked out of so I suppose I'm hung up on making it there and breaking its reactionary back in fact I almost went mad on the stage weeping over a poem ("Kaddish," and my pop in audience) and denouncing the English faculty as a pack of ignorant amateurs, gave long lecture on prosody, etc., and we answered questions, even Peter [Orlovsky] read two poems, strange nite. All ok.

I sent a poem ("Sather Gate Illumination") to *San Francisco Review* and they rejected it. I thought it was a good poem, in fact *Evergreen* will print it in their anthology, so I don't know what *San Francisco Review* wants. They also rejected an excellent (I thought) little poem of Jack's I typed up for them, and apparently couldn't find anything they liked in Gregory's collection. I don't trust their judgment, considering the insipid poems they printed already. Bodes no good. Are they for real?

As I said, I thought Gregory's new book[66] better and wilder and deeper (even socially conscious deeper) than *Gasoline*, but it is hard to get into all at once, is that what you found wrong I wonder? Anyway, follow your own insights; but I will bet you ten dollars that in two years (by February 17, 1961) you will like them, I mean really be crazy about them. I bet. (Deposit loot with Harpo Marx.)

Our writing is similar, tho his line is shorter; but he has influenced me in the last two years — "Ignu" for instance; the Vachel Lindsay poem ["To Lindsay"] imitates his shorts in *Gasoline* (elliptical jump) — and other things in the mad phrasing I try to learn from him — so that it is a two-way process, as it should be. I see him as having a rich Shakespearean line. As the end of "Food," "when this table goes / I'll music my eternal meal to the dew." Like, I think he's a more imaginative poet than I am, in his phrasing, more free, and that's why I study him, and that's loosened my own phrasing. It's the weird quality of

---

66 This became Corso's book *The Happy Birthday of Death*, but it was published in 1960 by New Directions instead of City Lights.

phrasing and those long poems are great examples of it even when he has comedy enuf to parody it as in "Marriage" with shots like "Pie-glue, telephone-snow."

Oh, well, I've said all this before. Yes, I agree, Gary and Phil are miles away from me stylistically, which goes to prove that I've not been urging you to "run a press of Poets That Write Like Allen Ginsberg." I thought of them as classical because they work on old Williams-Pound shortline measures, Snyder more than Whalen, and their content is more (like Pound) literarily learned and allusive, than freestyle à la French poetry.

[. . .]

God, reporters all over, all asking the same questions and no end in sight, it's getting stranger and stranger, life. Beginning to get invites from TV programs but have been holding out for scene where I can read poetry rather than discuss Beatnikism. The world is really mad. That *Time* account of Chicago was so wrongly done I wonder what they do to politics. No wonder there are wars. I sent "Apollinaire" to the Germans. And *Playboy* asked me and Gregory for poems — Spectorsky, the editor, was the moderator at our Chicago readings and dug the audience digging the poems. Maybe come up with some solid loot — I'll send him "Ignu."

Well, that's all I can think on.

As ever,
Allen

March 12, 1959: Lawrence Ferlinghetti in San Francisco to Allen Ginsberg in New York

Dear Allen . . .

Thanx for Lion ["The Lion for Real"]. Good. When do I get to read "Kaddish"? Columbia reading must have been the living end [. . .]

San Francisco Review turns out to be pretty sad affair, from point of view of what they like in poetry. Sorry to waste your and Gregory's efforts on it. I gave them a long poem which I wrote first years ago —

and they took it . . . . *Yugen's* latest is the liveliest on the whole scene at the moment, I think . . . . Hope *Big Table* can keep going issue after issue. Sent them long poem just written on "The Great Chinese Dragon" . . . . But I wouldn't be surprised if first issue were seized by police here or somewhere . . . . if they are printing exactly the manuscript I read . . . . As I said then, in this case I don't think the Burroughs writing (in the selections they made) is worth the obscenity, and I'd hate to have to defend <u>it</u> in court, on these grounds . . . . the best in it is Kerouac's "Midnight" . . . . Yes, saw Totem [Press] list, and have ordered all for store . . . . Please could you goose [Frank] O'Hara again for me? He never sent a line . . . . Am going to LA to read probably in middle of April but will be back in San Francisco by about the 20 or 21st . . . . Have made arrangement with Poetry Center to sell all your Fugazi Hall tickets at City Lights. Hall only holds 400 at most but it's a great place to read. None of that poetry central-heating, etc. . . . . Whalen back, living in town. You probably stay with him? . . . . Gary gone to Japan, after helping fix up City Lights cellar — you should see it — we have whole basement under building cleared out now and have underground press section under sidewalk, etc., open to public . . . . was holyroller meeting hall forty years ago; you remember signs, biblical quotations . . . . just opened it . . . . You're right, don't go for those TV programs discussing Beatniks . . . . Me, I'm bashfaceful and won't show up for Parkinson's symposium and will only read poetry for that University of California scene . . . . Could you maybe record for Fantasy when you're here, and get that done at last? . . . . Read your letter in *Time*, very astutely cool, exactly what *Time* does with every story just about . . . . you master propagandist too . . . .

see you soon . . . .

larry

Ginsberg was back in San Francisco from May to August 1959, hence no letters were exchanged until August, when Allen reached home in New York City following a cross-country drive. After Allen left San Francisco, the poet Bob Kaufman was beaten by the police.

August 13, 1959: Allen Ginsberg in New York to Lawrence Ferlinghetti in San Francisco

Dear Larry: Fast note:
I got on phone (having talked to Bill Margolis[67] this morning and gotten sleepy story from him, a little unsure what the situation exactly is with [Bob] Kaufman) — and sent you a telegram today — here's the text in case it never gets thru . . .

"Cops arresting poets they don't like and stepping on their toes ridiculous soon they'll be beating up people near bookstores and coffee shops and demanding kickbacks at poetry readings. Call out the spiritual fuzz and put cops back where they belong on level of streetcar conductors and public servants. Who wants to pay dues to a nasty illiterate gestapo? Stop and down with police state laws against the holy weed marijuana."

The Western Union phone operator gave me trouble and it caused a slight nervous breakdown at the local office, they finally refused to take it, saying — "I'm sorry sir we can't accept this telegram by phone it's defamation of the police." So I sez, "what was that, can you repeat that, I work on a newspaper and would like to have an official quote from you on why you won't accept this telegram, Madam." They asked me what newspaper and I said I wrote articles for *San Francisco Chronicle* and they went into conference and came back on phone and said they'd accept the message and deliver it. But god knows what they'll do on the other end of the wire so I thought to send this to you immediately. Use this telegram as you see fit and cut out the marijuana war cry if it only obscures the issue. Tho leave it in if you can. [. . .]

Love
Allen

---

67 William Margolis was a San Francisco friend of Ginsberg's and one of the founding editors of *Beatitude* magazine.

After years of trying, Ginsberg finally succeeded in making an acceptable recording of "Howl" for Fantasy. Dealing with Fantasy wasn't as easy for Allen as Ferlinghetti had hoped, though. Allen never made any money and he was continually trying to get royalties and tax statements from them.

October 24, 1959: Lawrence Ferlinghetti in San Francisco to Allen Ginsberg in New York

Dear Allen . . .

Just read your writing on back of *Howl* record which we're now selling at store. Wild picture — how'd you get it? And writing is the true end. Some blast! . . . . We now have new printing of *Howl* book in quantity — copies not rough like copy I gave you . . . . Take your time on new book manuscript — doesn't matter if we're late getting it out — the sooner the better, of course, but don't rush it . . . . Had 700 at *Big Table* reading in Chicago. Barbara Siegel[68] publicity, wow what scenes with newsreel cameras and tvs. Gave best reading, much better than New York . . . . I gave Paul Carroll idea to blast *Poetry* magazine in 4th issue — get wild statements from all *Yugen*, City Lights, *Big Table*, etc, authors, all of your best cohorts. You think this cornball idea? Is it worth it? Please don't give up on Paul [Carroll] and *Big Table* yet. Please remind Frank O'Hara please to send me that manuscript of *Lunch Poems* soon . . . ! Wish I were still in New York. Everything quiet here — tho Rexroth still doing poetry-jazz at Blackhawk[69] this week. Not me baby.

Hello —
larry

Ginsberg continued to promote the writers he liked. In this letter he tries to interest Ferlinghetti in Michael McClure's poetry.

---

68 Barbara Siegel was a literary agent and owned a bookstore in Chicago, which she modeled after City Lights.
69 The Blackhawk was a jazz club at 200 Hyde Street in San Francisco.

Dear Larry:

[. . .] McClure has written some sex poems which are so fantastic and truthful and full of huge heroic cunts and cocks I think he is a Genius. He read one at Muhlenberg [College] and, it was like the audience ran into a Brick Wall of the Real — gasps. Yet tho the poem is totally sexy and full of porno words, the whole thing is so gigantic and true no one can dare put it down — like *Lady Chatterley* sort of but concentrated. I was amazed. He's really broken the sound barrier. Look them up when he gets home, they made me ashamed of not telling the all-out sex truth before — I'm all mental — his new poems are physical orgasms — never seen the like. What a gas. [. . .]

Love
Allen

◀ 1960 ▶

In January 1960, Ginsberg and Ferlinghetti attended a writers conference together in Concepción, Chile. Allen decided to stay on in Chile for an extended visit while Ferlinghetti and his wife Kirby visited Peru. Lawrence and Kirby headed back to San Francisco in February, but Ginsberg would stay in South America for the next six months.

February 7, 1960: Lawrence Ferlinghetti in Lima, Peru, to Allen Ginsberg in Chile

Dear Allen —
Am leaving for Mexico tomorrow. Had good reading here, got paid 300 *soles* by Salazar Bondy. He wants to do same with you . . . . Raquel Jodorowsky (she has American boyfriend Stewart Monroe who has big apartment and offered to put me up free. He might do same for you.) Almirante Guisse is beautiful chick poet you ought to look up — I told her you might. She says she is *vagabunda, titiritera y poeta* . . . . José Miguel Oviedo did good translations of my poems for reading . . . . friend of Bondy's. They are both professional journalists (on *La Prensa* and *El Comercial*) . . . . They really knocked themselves out for us . . . . I found yage in Cuzco Indian mercado. [. . .]
                                        Love —
                                        L

[P.S.] Writers, painters hang out at Cafe Zella on Plaza San Martín.

February 20, 1960: Allen Ginsberg in Santiago, Chile, to Lawrence and
Kirby Ferlinghetti in San Francisco

Dear Larry and Kirby:
Well I'm still here in Southern Chile and never even yet started to
travel. I stopped in various towns on the way down (Temuco, Valdivia,
Puerto Moutt) — and stayed on farms and right now in a fishing village fish-canning factory — been here two weeks, great panorama of
snowcapped volcanoes and channels and islands and fisherman's sail-
boats — looks like a Breughel canvas. Still have $90 left. This should
reach you this coming week in San Francisco?? I never got to Tierra
del Fuego, spent so much time here. Heading north in a few days. Will
go via lake region here, pass a few more days in Concepción and then
Santiago. I have no idea what mail has reached me in either place. If
you can please find out if the $200 from Fantasy has been sent to me
in Concepción Hotel Pan-American. If not, have it sent to me c/o
U.S. Embassy in Santiago. I'll wait for it there. But if I get to Santiago
and find that mail has been screwed up due to my long delay, etc. I'll
telegraph you what the circumstances are. Write me in Santiago also,
saying where to go in La Paz and Lima and let me know what you did,
where you went, etc. I'm ok — had a touch of the Chilean National
Disease a few weeks ago and it passed — Monstrous variety of strange
shellfish here I never heard of — eat sea-urchins and vast mussels a
foot long (well six inches anyway).

                                                        Love,
                                                        Allen

March 25, 1960: Allen Ginsberg in Santiago, Chile, to Lawrence
Ferlinghetti in San Francisco

Dear Larry:
[. . .] Well, despite all your warnings, I think I will proceed to La Paz
— just for goofs, to see the city for a day or so. I know it is a crappy
place — have been reading various books of South America and Bo-

livian history — there is an old Bolivian dictator who sounds like a Burroughs creation: "Once in power the new president (Melgarejo) showed a complete contempt for legal restraints and private rights, cruelly suppressing every evidence of discontent and using the public funds for gratification of his vices and the enrichment of friends. During his frequent periods of drunkenness he was capable of atrocities that terrified even his unprincipled associates." He flourished sometime last century but presumably the tradition still carries on. Been reading *Life of Bolívar* by J.B. Trend, Isherwood's *Condor and Cow*, a book on Machu Picchu by Hiram Bingham, another on Cuzco (guidebook of 200 pages), and various accounts of travels of Humboldt, Darwin and Spruce (who first named yage) in the Amazon region — in any case I expect to spend a week around Cuzco, move on to Lima, and then go up the Ucyali river to Pucallpa, where (according to Burroughs) there is a Brujo named Saroya who knows the right way to prepare yage. Then I hope to continue up to Iquitos on the Amazon, which is the jump off place for ships that go down the Amazon. So I may spend a few weeks going a little way down into Brazil — see the Jivaros maybe. They use yage for headhunting inspiration. [. . .]

Vicente Huidobro probably is a great French-style Chilean poet (dead) *ami de* Apollinaire and the free-est around South America. I've bought books by him, Vallejo, Pablo De Rokha, and Nicolás Guillén (alive in Cuba) and Neruda — who are the great poets of South America this century, so everybody advises me. [Luis] Oyarzún left for China. I saw Volodia Teitelbaum and arranged to receive Chink and Russian books and mags. Everything fine except I have a non-malignant infection tumor in my asshole from bad toilets and enteritis. I'll probably have to stay here to have it fixed for another week. [. . .]

Love,
Allen

April 6-10, 1960: Allen Ginsberg in La Paz, Bolivia, to Lawrence Ferlinghetti in San Francisco

Dear Larry:

Arrived here the 1st and was immediately struck down with the Wrath of the Air Gods — in bed twenty hours eating some spare morphine tablets to kill headache and fatigue — finally recovered after a day and except for constant slight fatigue am in good shape — I go every day to the huge markets around Calle Sagarnigas and Buenos Aires — living in a place called Hotel Torino for $1 a day and eating great juicy red pork stews in the market — the prices here are cheaper than Mexico or Tangiers — my hotel is just off Plaza Murillo where all the local buses start from. I have been having a ball — mainly the last five days doing nothing but wandering and eating in the markets — it must be a web of streets twenty or thirty blocks long, crisscrossed, and I've been thru practically all of them. I've bought a lot of tourist junk — little pins of silver (flies, spiders, butterflies) and five cheap mantas (the colored shawls the women carry their babies in) as well as a few hats (and especially one big black hat to wear with my beard). All told I dig Bolivia — I like the Indians and chew a lot of coca — I like the color and the landscape and avoid the Spanish downtown. Tomorrow I take a bus to Sorata, a town off over the mountains some-where north. There are a number of small trips I want to make so will be here maybe two weeks more. However above and beyond all this Bolivia shit, next door to my hotel is an antique store where I found a few Chinese scrolls which are of great value — I suppose, I don't know — in any case several of them are really extraordinary, so they must be valuable.

I bought one for $30 and there are several others for same price and one for $60 and another huge magnificent magical one of the seven or eleven immortals for $100 — it's huge. Anyway I bought the nicest and cheapest — having it wrapped and will ship it to New York from Peru — mail is safer there.

I also came down (in Chile) with some kind of rare disease of the ass — not from incontinence as I've been sexless as a creep since I got to S.A. — So it cost me $40 to fix that — a non-malignant tumor type shot. So I have enough money to continue traveling with all the checks I got — but after doctor bills and scroll buying and tourist buying I have no great excess. [. . .]

The scroll I got has some clouds disappearing into strange green cubist mountains. It's a late decadent interesting style. I don't know what century. The $60 scroll is quite old, real old.

Otherwise the mountain scenery's great. I took a bus up to Los Altos and a town 20 km beyond on the altiplano yesterday — very dull, tho the plain itself is like the sea, endless. I've looked for poets here but found none.

I spent the last month with [Nicanor] Parra in his house at the foot of Andes on outskirts of Santiago. It got to be depressing — he is a sort of rational Marxist and with his trip to China is obsessed with Marxist-poetry-politics as the only way, sort of Catholic-Reichian style fundamentalism that got on my nerves after awhile — and I got on his with my obsession with drugs. We would cover up after arguments but the abyss was there. I got so desperate after awhile I told him I didn't give a shit for the sufferings of the proletariat. Which was heresy, and he was justifiably shocked. I also spent lots of time in a cafe (São Paulo) on Calle Huérfanos and met several dozen famous old decadent Chilean poets — including Pablo De Rokha who is-was one of the great geniuses.

So far as I gather from talking a lot and reading a little, the really great poets relatively unknown in the U.S. are César Vallejo, Huidobro (friend of Apollinaire) and maybe a live Cuban negro communist, Nicolás Guillén. I've read a little of each and they are very striking writers — much more up San Francisco "renaissance" lines than academic European or American — and relatively easy to translate, since they write open free poetry. Also of course Rokha and Neruda. If you could get someone to translate a book each of theirs I think it would be a great series and very striking in America. Vallejo particularly covers in great tragic way the prewar Spanish Revolution with a kind of political action poetry of a finesse and passion not seen in English during the U.S. thirties. Huidobro is more like Corso — "Creationism" was his creation, i.e. pure cubist mad verbal poetry. He is the most influential among the young, since the least fucked up politically. [. . .]

As ever,

Allen

April 13, 1960: Lawrence Ferlinghetti in San Francisco to Allen Ginsberg in Bolivia

Dear Allen . . . .

Was in New York last week and saw Peter [Orlovsky] at Gold Medal Beat Anthology party at Living Theatre and ate with him at El Faro, but then lost track of him. I also had a great weekend with Jack, starting in Northport and ending with De Kooning some days later. Among other activities en route we, but mostly he, broke up bad poetry reading at Gaslight,[70] and I stumbled out to Burlington, VT, where a drought was in process (liquor laws) and I was introduced by a minister and read in a chapel with hymnbooks in seats to 1500 students and then got in big public argument with Dr. CHRISTofilos, atomic scientist who also addressed Vermont Conference . . . . etc. . . . . etc. . . . . All in all, I am glad to get back to the Potrero Meadows . . . . I got your last letter yesterday, the one you wrote March 25 just before leaving Santiago for La Paz etc. and am relieved to see you finally got those checks. Fantastic — three months to get them. Hope you made it thru La Paz by now without dying of Gory Asshole. And Machu Picchu. My "Hidden Door" poem was published in Lima and also in Mexico D.F. University of Mexico *Revista* (by Jaime García Terres who was at conference), and there have been reports on conference with a lot about you in same magazine (by Moreno) and in others (by Sabado, Alegría, etc) . . . . Can you do some translations of Huidobro for City Lights? and maybe Rokha? I read some of each in English but never found the right poems, I guess . . . . I also know Guillén in English

---

70 The Gas Light Cafe was a basement coffee house at 116 MacDougal Street in New York City.

only . . . . In meantime, I'll be owing you more money for payment June 1st — or can send some to you when you get back to New York City. We have just printed another 10,000 *Howl!* That makes 50,000. Also have received payments for you for reprints in Germany, Sweden, etc. plus $100 from Thomas Y. Crowell for Shapiro's *American Poetry* in which you're the last poet in the book, latched on to 200 years of American poetry and you the only new poet in it. It's chronological and I think you follow [Richard] Wilbur who is at end of line, and so you represent Modern Poetry all by yourself in the book. I sent a copy to you c/o 170 E 2nd, since it was too big for lugging around South America and you'd probably never get it anyway . . . Also, Bosquet's anthology came out with you in it, although he never wrote me for permission or sent any money. Let me know if he didn't send you any loot, in which case I'll write to put the bite on. All in all, I think you will get enough to live on during the next year via our various scrapings and threeball pawnshop activities in the field of poetic usury . . . . Now everybody is hollering for *Kaddish* — since I did put it down for July six months ago, thinking that would give you plenty of time extra, and we already have back orders for over 2000 copies and will print 10,000 first printing, etc. and so when like can I get my cornball hands on it? If you could let me have it by June 1st, we might have it out by the middle of July. Let me know what to expect as to time. Why don't you figure on 72 to 94 pages, 33 lines to a page and let me know about how much you've got already . . . . Am doing new [Bob] Kaufman broadside, first section of novel, this part called *Die Now Pay Later.* Also have been working on Djuna Barnes anthology, Kerouac's *Book of Dreams* (he gave me original manuscript of it — I got it here), O'Hara's *Lunch Poems* — which I haven't got yet — he in Europe; also have been thinking about doing an anthology from *Beatitude*, choosing from all the issues to-date. What do you think of that? [. . .]

yoohoo
larry

102

Dearest Larry:

Back this week (half year gone) and found 300 letters and your exquisite signature. Was clearing my desk of mail so can't write much and got manuscript to do. Wrote a whole book (poems) in South America also — it's just I write so much; I hate to look back and clean up. I'll do *Kaddish* before August 15 (one month after return). Had ayahuasca (yage) eight times in Peru, also brought back gallon. Once I thought I was death, it was horrible. After all my bleating. [. . .]

Love

Allen

By mid-September Ginsberg had put together the collection that would become his second City Lights book, Kaddish and Other Poems.

Sept. 16, 1960: Allen Ginsberg in New York to Lawrence Ferlinghetti in San Francisco

Dear Larry:

Enclosed find manuscript of *Kaddish*, I finished reading and re-correcting items tonight, so send it special delivery onionskin carbon — to get it in mail, in fact it's midnite — I don't know what it'll look like to you, poetry or not — huge white elephant maybe — you figure out what to do with it.

If it's ok to print I guess start setting in type — I still have to show my father this week, anything he objects to I'll have to cut — things that pertain only to him — he's never seen it before.

I have good poem "Magic Psalm" from Peru, still to type and send as well as a raft of others — Maybe "Mescaline," maybe "Lysergic Acid," maybe use "Laughing Gas," [. . .]

Too much for one book? Or just select the strongest things to go with "Kaddish"? We'll figure when I send you the rest. Meanwhile can set up "Kaddish" in type?

"Laughgas" not spectacular enough for *Broadside*? "Fall of America" might be, don't know yet. Thanks for lovely card. I'll go mail this now. Let me know what it looks like to you — I have lots of doubts.

As ever,

Allen

September 20, 1960: Lawrence Ferlinghetti in San Francisco to Allen Ginsberg in New York

Dear Allen:

Thanks for *Kaddish* manuscript which arrived couple days ago and which I have now copyread for printer. [. . .]

In any case, I am ready to send whole manuscript as-is to Villiers printer in England, and the following questions are only copy-printer questions, etc. [. . .]

Got your "Moon Prevention" which I think is too long for *Beatitude* magazine, but I'll keep it awhile just to see — the next issue is already done — so it would be for a later issue anyway . . . . it's gassy all right . . . . I also dug notey from Peter [Orlovsky], especially "I took walk over Brooklin Bridge and saw sun orange between Wall Street cockey buildings".

As for other poems for *Kaddish* book, I would want to be sure to include all those great poems — "Aunt Rose," "Apollinaire," "Poem Rocket," "Laughing Gas," "Mescaline," "Ignu," "The Lion for Real," "Europe! Europe!" (And "Politics"? "Sad Self"? "Fall of America"?) (never saw "Lysergic Acid") and "Magic Psalm" from Peru which must be beautiful . . . . I got to hear about the rest of your South American trip, after we left, I suppose it's too much to write — when you coming out this way? I'm going to Caribbean in November [. . .] and hope to get your book sewed up at printer well before that, and get finished copies by sometime in January at the latest . . . . Am going to Big Sur for five or six days tomorrow, so you have time to finish *Kaddish* and other poem manuscript — I could send them off to England when I get back from Big Sur about September 29th . . . .

Generally speaking, there seems to be some slight <u>repetition</u> in Narrative section — you might prune it a tiny bit more? . . . . repetition of events mostly . . . .? Narrative doubling back on itself, repeating details?

Love —
L.

ca. late September 1960: Allen Ginsberg in New York to Lawrence Ferlinghetti in San Francisco

Dear Larry:
I will go over "Kaddish" and reduce its length, it's too long and repetitious as you say. This may take a week or less or more, but it's got to be done. The fuckup inside it is what's kept me paralyzed on it so long. I'll send you original new manuscript.

OK — Later
Allen

October 10, 1960: Lawrence Ferlinghetti in San Francisco to Allen Ginsberg in New York

Dear Allen:
Have been swamped with work, Shig on vacation, etc. . . . . and have not finished copy-reading all of your manuscript. Will send you complete run-down of copy-questions separately when I've done whole manuscript. In meantime, here is Section II (Narrative) of *Kaddish* which I feel you've had the most trouble with; and this version is more concentrated (slightly) and more <u>found</u> (more melted and fused together, more forged into one piece) than the former version you sent me, which is good; and the reason I'm sending it now is that I feel/ sense/that you have not quite reached the final point of compression

and clarity in this section — due to the fact that I am pressing you for the finished works and you don't have any time to get a perspective on it and see it from the outside. You are so submerged in it that you can't get an objective outside view of this section as a whole. By the time the proofs came, I think you would be doing some more weeding out — and it's better to take the time right now, for a few last touches. I think this narrows down to, roughly, pages 18 to 23 (last paragraph on 18 to line near bottom 26, "Your last night in the darkness of the Bronx"). In other words, the whole period of her life in the Bronx. Here I find still some repetition or what seems like repetition to the outside reader, tho not to you — to you, every detail counts whether repeated or not, etc. And I think you can improve the dramatic effect of the whole by some slight cutting especially in these pages, clarifying some spots mostly by cutting (I know there are dear phrases which are like pulling teeth to take out) but since <u>this section has to sustain itself</u> in the midst of other sections of pure poetry, if it were just a very little shorter, the effect of the whole would be more potent. As it is, I feel that the "narrative" drags a little thru the above pages, there's a slight lessening of dramatic tension due only to the tortuousness and reiteration of parts of the story . . . .

But if you want it just as-is: OK. Airmail it back. The rest of the book — Great as-is!!!

Love —
[unsigned]

October 11, 1960: Allen Ginsberg in New York to Lawrence Ferlinghetti in San Francisco

Dear Larry:
Eureka! Here is the entire book complete, retyped, ready to roll.

I went over "Kaddish," read it aloud to Jack new slightly cut (five pages cut) version (enclosed) and it sounded foursquare and right what I want. I take back earlier doubt as to whether it should be published.

Only two poems are missing I want in, which you have copies of

— "Mescaline," and "Laughing Gas." Put them in in place indicated on contents page. This makes quite a long book — but I have also left out a lot — "Sather Gate," various psalms and short minor poems, things I've already published all over — nothing important: "Cottage in Berkeley," etc. If I can finish the "Fall of America" in a week I'll send that too — to put in preferably if time, or make a broadside of it convenient. [. . .]

I guess make one big monster book and charge a lot, I just wrote too much. Note it's only poems 1958-1960. I left intermediary stuff out — another little book. My father's seen and approved, I'll get legal letters from family for you this week. Will read *Her* this week too when finished "Fall [of] America". OK

OK, OK — write
Allen Ginsberg

ca. November 1960: Allen Ginsberg in New York to Lawrence Ferlinghetti in San Francisco

Dear Larry:
Assuming this book comes out alright, I was thinking, later, in a year or so, would you be interested in a book of miscellaneous poems 1954–1958 —*i.o.*

Epithamion (*Beat Coast East* anthology)
Sakyamuni, Seattle, Over Kansas, etc. (from *Beatitude*)
Green Auto (from *Mattachine*)
Siesta in Xbalba
Strange Cottage in Berkeley
Sather Gate Illumination
Dream Record (about Burroughs' wife)

And a whole bunch other — Psalm III from *New Directions 16*.
I could leave it behind with you, large book actually, to publish when and if convenient. I wanted to keep *Kaddish* book just recent

sharp [as] axe poems, but these are also good poems I guess. Rather than wait till *Collected Works*.

OK

Allen

In early December 1960, Ferlinghetti visited Cuba to witness first-hand the effects of Castro's revolution. Ginsberg was also planning to go to Cuba around this time but his trip was cancelled and he wouldn't be able to re-schedule it until 1965.

December 23, 1960: Lawrence Ferlinghetti in San Francisco to Allen Ginsberg in New York

Dear Allen

Have been back a week but snowed under with piled up manuscript and letters and trying to get "Cuban Notebook" off to Grove for next *Evergreen* . . . . just sent it, so you'll read about it I hope and I won't put it all down here again: it was GREAT and not really very weird but certainly not evil . . . . You got to go there: I met Neruda and he asked about you (said he followed our/your "antics" in Chile), he said give him names of poets to invite to Cuba, I did give him your address, which he gave to Casa de la Amistad there, and they were going to invite you right away. (This is new Friendship House founded by Fidel this Fall and Neruda was first one they invited.) I went to big scene at Capitol with Neruda in limousine, that was weird-like, I'll tell you more about it next time I see you, I didn't come by New York because wanted to come back thru New Orleans and see Kay Johnson[71] (if you go there, be sure look her up — she in love with Gregory, by correspondence, she great undiscovered Djuna Barnes-type writer and poet I think, am going to publish her. Maybe you know her already?) [. . .]

[unsigned]

---

71 Kay Johnson's book *Human Songs* was published by City Lights in 1964.

108

‹ 1961 ›

Around this time, Ginsberg became involved with the psychologist Timothy Leary and the experiments he was conducting with various drugs. He wrote the following note under the influence of Leary's mushrooms.

February 10, 1961: Allen Ginsberg in New York to Lawrence Ferlinghetti in San Francisco

Thursday nite (weird syrups in my veins). O what a great working ser- aph you are to be there in the faraway, holding your faith 3000 miles for years waiting for me to send message, book, I wanted to send you something sublime — naked mama or trumpet of divinity — anything real beyond materialist illusions — and wish I could thank you for when I envision you like that so kind a messenger, making secure the communication gets sent across cold Atlantics and vast empty voids so men can know someone is guarding the signal and the great impulses of being are really sent back and forth by the specters of this dimen- sion who are gathering to decide what to do with the cosmos, whether to recognize the vast image of being and publish it to all gathered con- sciousness — that you are so there on side of angels, it's so beautiful. Life is waving, Larry.

Hello
Allen

I wrote big hymn to electronic-telepathy-mutations of human con- sciousness tonight.[72]

---

72 This was the poem "Television Was a Baby Crawling Toward That Deathchamber."

February 13, 1961: Lawrence Ferlinghetti in San Francisco to Allen
Ginsberg in New York

Dere Allen

I read your poem "To an Old Poet in Peru" (Cesar Vallejo?)[73] in *Rhi-
nozeros* in Germany and think it Trumpet of Divinity which you were
looking to send me from New York with syrups in your veins but here
it comes from Peru . . . . (It must go in next book) . . . . No *Kaddish*
book yet, but I told them to send you airmail copy direct, so let me
know. I wrote Villiers goosing them four days ago [. . .]

    Later and Later

    [unsigned]

February 17, 1961: Allen Ginsberg in New York to Lawrence Ferlinghetti
in San Francisco

Dear Larry:

"Old Poet in Peru" is for that next book of miscellaneous poems I
wrote you about — that, "Aether," "Sather Gate," etc. — I thought
there wouldn't be enuf room in *Kaddish* volume — just be too much
at once. [. . .]

    Received a copy of a letter Knopf wrote you. I got a telegram
from them offering me book and spoke to them by phone. What I said
was that I didn't think it was necessarily a good idea as I probably can
make as much money and keep things simple publishing with City
Lights. They said, they can put out hardcover book for libraries and
carriage trade that City Lights haven't reached, and there would be no
conflict financially with you they don't think. Also this editor's angle
that it would open up Madison Avenue a little to some public fucks
and cock sucks on poetry pages. I told them to write you and I would
leave it up to you, also warned them against writing in such terms that

---

73 Although César Vallejo and Martín Adán were both Peruvian poets, Ginsberg was
probably addressing this poem to Adán, since Vallejo had died in 1938.

it would cause you guilt conflicts. I am more or less indifferent. Stay with City Lights I keep my preferred amateur standing as far as the Industry goes. Money I have enough right now. Also it keeps a kind of purity, one thin book issuing from City Lights every few years. My career might get muddy and ambiguous if Knopf put out a book. On the other hand there would be some money and maybe it be a best seller and be read in White House by Mrs. Kennedy's social secretary. So I dunno. You figure it out as now you got the rights to the two books. If you think it a possible idea, you get sizeable chunk of reprint rights I assume. It's tempting but not enough to make me feel strongly one way or other. Also remember it's not the only chance for a book in New York as I've had offers from Grove, New Directions would do one, and Dutton and other would do it too — even Macmillan once asked. So there's no emergency. Let me know what you think. Only charming aspect is that Knopf is so ultra respectable it's funny to think having them as publisher. I suppose somebody might as well put out a hardcover selected-collected poems of mine sooner or later or it might happen inevitably anyway and they are as good as any, tho now might be premature. IF you think it's OK you can have them delay it a year till *Kaddish* starts selling. Or two years. Anyway, whatever you decide.

I'm leaving for Greece in a few weeks now for sure. I just wrote another huge ten-page single space weird poem, next step after magic psalm — same night as I wrote you that postcard — I took methedrine, junk and some mushroom pills and sat at desk from 8PM to 12AM next day typing steadily — roughly the same combo as I had for "Kaddish" — this more political maybe a better poem, gotta look again. Actually I have enough between that and all the other huge politics poems for another book with "Aether" etc.

Went on John Crosby TV show and gave eight-minute lucid advertisement for pot, outright — this the first time it ever got broadcast, and in detail — the FCC is now investigating, but there's nothing they can do. We win. Also got the *New York Times* to work — they're going to do exposé of Anslinger.[74] Also *Playboy*, *Harper's*, etc. etc. — and I

---

74 Harry J. Anslinger was the first commissioner of the Federal Bureau of Narcotics, a

brought LaGuardia Report to Grove to be printed so there is now a big conspiracy which will explode in April.

Love,
Allen

February 26, 1961: Lawrence Ferlinghetti in San Francisco to Allen Ginsberg in New York

Cher Allen . . . .
Am going to Big Sur for a few days (on Tuesday) and want to get this off, even though I've not heard from you in answer to wire I sent on Tuesday last, asking for "gassier jacketblurb" for American printing of *Kaddish*. The one I wrote is all right for the British, but . . . . We received repro proofs from Villiers last weekend and I put it to press the next day — I hope you received airmail copy of British printing, as I instructed them to send same direct airmail to you — I've not gotten finished British copy of book yet but repros look beautiful, and I think you'll be happy . . . . If I don't get any new jacketwords from you by tomorrow night I will have to make out the best I can with my own — Jest like you, I can't write this sort of crap. I would rather print nothing but "It Is" on the back . . . . but . . . .? [. . .]

Re. Knopf offer: J. Simon wrote me nice letter about it, after talking to you, I haven't answered him yet, having been unable to make up my mind. I asked one big editor (who is in New York and doesn't want me to bring his name into it) what he thought, since I'd no experience in these bigleagues, and I was greatly surprised to find he thought I was out of my mind even to consider it, etc., and said among other things: that "Knopf couldn't do anything for you which I already hadn't done, and done better." Then there was a lot more about "the big elephants rushing in after all the discoveries were made and trampling down the

---

post he held for more than thirty years. In 1944, Anslinger disputed the findings of the La Guardia Report, which stated that marijuana use did not lead to insanity or addiction as his department had claimed.

wheat" etc . . . . (This not from a <u>small</u> publisher) . . . . He also said that
if Knopf had published you originally in a hardcover edition, everyone
knows the book would have disappeared without a ripple . . . . etc . . . .
In any case, I was for letting them go ahead, until the above dissuaded
me . . . . plus <u>your</u> letter, which also doesn't seem too hot for the idea,
all in all. The way I look at it now is that, eventually, this is going to
happen — eventually you will have a big hardcover *Selected* or *Collected*
Poems from the biggest New York publishers — The question now is
(since <u>all</u> the doors now seem to be creeking open —) just <u>when</u> you
want to <u>let</u> it happen. If Knopf takes you in now, it's like being accepted (in contrast to being attacked by) Time Inc. etc. etc. And when they
and the rest of the Square World accept you, then all the excitement
is over and you're "one of them" NO???? This is why I say for the time
being, let them go ferk themselves for awhile. In the end, if they want
you bad enuf, they'll offer you fortunes — and when you are ready
finally to be canonized like T.S. Eliot, you can do it. (I think Knopf is
about the only one I'd consider at all now, if I were you — even though
Grove or New Directions would certainly do book of yours at the drop
of a copyright . . . . ((Laughlin has said as much, tho he also said he
would never <u>ask</u> for another publisher's author unsolicited.))) I would
say that after your third book gets out next year, or a couple of years
after that, you might like to get some hardcover edition going. And my
latest thought is that City Lights can also do a hardcover edition. (We
have just done a beautiful $3.00 edition of Patchen's *Love Poems*.) Vil-
liers could produce a beautiful larger size hardbound of *Howl* and/or
Kaddish, in black cloth, like those British T.S. Eliot books. And what
would you think of that? . . . .

Love
Lawrence

P.S. Thanks for more or less leaving it up to me. I sure appreciate your
sticking with lil ole City of Light, for the time being at least. I'm going
to write Knopf and tell them No for right now but leave the door open
for another year . . . . OK?

March 3, 1961: Allen Ginsberg in New York to Lawrence Ferlinghetti in San Francisco

Larry:
Fine anything you arrange with Knopf for far future OK by me. I usually do good on blurbs but — I dunno — blocked, could come up with nothing [. . .] Peter been sick and myriad things to do before leaving — file and forget masses of letters and mass of notebooks pack books give away possessions, etc. I dunno if good idea to send [Kerouac's *Book of*] *Dreams* and *Kaddish* out at once, might distract space-attention from each. But I dunno. I think newspapers give more space to *Kaddish* if they receive it as single event. On other hand mebbe not? I dunno. I'll write when can soon. Dutton Company wants Jack or me to make an anthology, I guess I'm just too busy (anthology of beat) — I gotta get out of here.
    Love
    Allen

Ginsberg asked Ferlinghetti to return his original manuscript of "Kaddish" to him. He had promised to give it to Julian Beck and Judith Malina to auction as a benefit for the cash-strapped Living Theatre. This was to be the only manuscript of Allen's that escaped his enormous archive.

March 16, 1961: Lawrence Ferlinghetti in San Francisco to Allen Ginsberg in New York

Dear Allen Alvah Irwin Garden Goldbooker . . . .
You crazy to give away original *Kaddish* manuscript right now! Am sending it to you surface mail today, along with former manuscript you sent me. This latter includes four or five of the principal poems in *Kaddish* as well as earlier version of "Kaddish" itself, and I beg you to lay this manuscreed on Living Theatre and save the final manuscript

(which is in black folder) for yourself. What do you figure anarchists will have to eat in 1975? If you will please save this manuscript until at least ten years from now, you will eat off of it from 1975 to 2000. Even right now you should (and I could) get at least muchos $ gringos $ for it from a big library. Please do not throw away your shoes in order to walk barefoot thru India, because when you get back to U.S. you will need them shoes again. (By way, what did you do with original "Howl" manuscript? I hope you still have it?) . . . . You crazy goofball . . . . Sending out review copies to all new names you gave me. Books ready in gross here tomorrer! Trublu. [. . .]

[unsigned]

Ginsberg had long realized that if he stayed in America he would be caught up in the business side of poetry, so he and Peter Orlovsky decided to leave the country for a while. They would not return for more than two years.

March 20, 1961: Allen Ginsberg in New York to Lawrence Ferlinghetti in San Francisco

Larry:
[. . .] The book [*Kaddish and Other Poems*] looks great. The jacket blurb is so rhapsodic the poems'll come as an anticlimax maybe. Wow. When I get to Europe I'll try write one for next edition.

I did give the original manuscript to Living Theatre — of the poem "Kaddish" not the whole book. I'll keep the whole set you sent me. I gave them all the earlier versions. I have too many things to keep track of anyway including all old "Howl" manuscripts, which are in basement in Paterson with original manuscript of *Naked Lunch* and fifteen years of letters from Bill, Jack, Gregory plus five years correspondence with you, Snyder, Whalen, McClure, Wieners, Lamantia, Dorn, Creeley, etc. etc. several boxfuls plus fifteen tapes of everybody reading poems including old 1955 Berkeley stuff, etc. etc. I got all that off my back and packed away last week. Arrangement with Living Theater is if they ever get rich on Broadway they support me anyhoo. It'll all be alright. [. . .]

Peter and I have tix on SS *America* for this Thursday March 23 and'll be in Paris on April Fools Day, join Burroughs and Gregory who's now tired of waiting for us in Greece and going to meet us in Paris. After that a complete blank, I dunno but will keep you informed. Can reach me next at American Express, Paris France — I'll write you when I get settled there.

The book looks excellent — just right size and neat.

I sent you the subsidiary manuscript.[75] There is no need to publish it for awhile until it's convenient. Also I am taking along with me to work on the manuscript of about forty pages of "Fall of America" which I should finish sooner or later. If I do get that done soon, maybe best give *The Bunch of Poems* to Auerhahn and I'll supply you with the new poem. I already agreed some time ago to give them a small volume of journals. I'll type that up in Paris. Also Totem Press will bring out *Empty Mirror* early poems this year; further subsidiary. They haven't started rolling on that yet, I had them wait on that till *Kaddish* was out. I told [LeRoi] Jones to go ahead now when he wants — probably be a half year.

I saw *Book of Dreams* on sale here, can you send me a copy by regular mail to Paris?

Spent an afternoon with W.C. Williams — he's more decrepit physically but finished another book of poems which New Directions has — short poems. He asked after you. [. . .]

OK — I'm cleaning up generally here and removing all evidence of my being from 170 E 2nd Street — signing off forever from here, maybe phone you before I leave.

Love
Allen

---

75 Eventually this manuscript would be published by City Lights as *Reality Sandwiches*, although for the moment Ginsberg was calling it simply *Bunch of Poems*.

Dear Larry:

Peter and I are in Paris, 9 Rue Gît-Le-Coeur for the next month. Gregory arrived from Greece the same day and we all wind up broke a week later now, so please send the German money now if you haven't already sent it.[76] I think I wrote in on the contract that you get 25% of foreign rights? So take that out and send me rest, yes? Don't send advances of *Kaddish* (unless I get in trouble) — just keep money coming for past sales in my direction, every few months, if business is good enough. I already have a hundred advance on that, don't I? How is reaction to the book? Particularly curious what Rexroth thinks, tell him if you see him, and give regards from all.

Are you really coming to Paris? [George] Whitman is still here and in good humor. Has a little apartment for voyaging poets above his store, but we haven't used it.

I saw Italian translator-critic Nanda Pivano — I gave her note to send to you — she responsible for interest in our writing at Mondadori and Feltrinelli[77] and very well informed, etc. She's editing the Feltrinelli anthology and also had suggested the Mondadori book; supposed to write introduction to my poems on Mondadori. So best she be the informant-liaison-decider on how to apportion poems between each. She suggests you tell Mondadori to make her the editor of my book there, and I think that be a good idea because she knows the problems of translation and can do best job of supervising it, she's interested in scholarly way. She translated *On the Road* and Hemingway, etc.

Also saw [Maurice] Girodias[78] who is very friendly — we gave him some mescaline yesterday. He says he'll help arrange for a book for me in France; so please check with him before anything is fixed

---

76 Allen was asking for the money City Lights had received for the publication of his work in Germany.

77 Mondadori and Feltrinelli were two important Italian publishing houses.

78 Maurice Girodias (1919–1990), the founder and publisher of the Olympia Press in Paris, who found profit in publishing great literature as well as dirty books for the tourists.

finally with L'Arche. Or let me know what you do. He also owns a big great new restaurant-cave. Weird Gregory Candide-like novel[79] coming out in a week or two with Gregory's drawings in it. Did you get the bunch of poems manuscript I sent you? Paris is lovely all old grey stains familiar.

Allen

ca. April 17, 1961: Allen Ginsberg in Paris to Lawrence Ferlinghetti in San Francisco

Dear Larry:
Thanks for German check which I did receive; also enclosed find the forms, no need I guess henceforth to check them with me. Maybe let me know roundup every few months. I would like to see reviews of *Kaddish* if you get spare copies, if not, not. Bunch of poems, I sent that off to you rather than bury them in Paterson basement. I don't know what to do, probably in a year have other material; also bunch of poems could be cut down to exclude minor fragmentary things. I don't have a list of the poems, someday if you can send me table of contents page. It needn't be published, the whole thing, except there are a few good poems "Sather Gate," "Aether," etc.

Gregory, Peter and I all at 9 Gît-Le-Coeur, probably go down to Cannes for two weeks stay at someone's house film festival, *The Connection* cats are around. I see Jouffroy[80] often, saw Michaux with him the other day. Then in another few weeks join Burroughs back in Tangier or Southern Spain. [. . .]

So no special plans. Gregory has a novel coming out with Olympia a sort of great Candide-type children-adult book with dozens of his own mad illustrations — next Monday, Olympia throwing him a huge party for 500 people at La Grande Séverine restaurant which Girodias owns — biggest restaurant and chicest in Left Bank. They

---

79 Gregory Corso's novel *American Express*, published by Olympia Press in 1961.
80 Alain Jouffroy (b. 1928), a French poet and writer.

never do this in Paris anymore so it'll be an international literary event of the season or something. That's what Girodias wants. Gregory's book called *American Express* and Olympia hopes American Express will sue. Peter going to gym to workout and Alliance Française to learn French finally. We sit at Deux Magots daily and goof around St. Chapelle.

OK, Love
Allen

May 4, 1961: Lawrence Ferlinghetti in San Francisco to Allen Ginsberg in Paris

Cher Allen . . . .
[. . .] I still have not read all the way thru your *Bunch of Poems* manuscript, but you wouldn't want to put it out before late Fall, anyway, would you? — too much at one time — saturate the scene — This is what happened to Jack (Kerouacker) — He pooped out so many books all at once during last three years that suddenly people in general had enough and now his books just sit on the shelf in bookstores (even City Lights — we ain't sold but a handful of his books during the past couple of months — except of course for back orders of *Book of Dreams*, which amounted to 1000 or so) — But whenever you want to go ahead with it, we'll shoot — I certainly want to publish that "Fall of America" — maybe do that all by itself first — before the *Bunch*? How long is it now — good for a broadside? Probably too long . . . . Yes — I see you said it's already forty pages. Make separate booklet! . . . . OK?
 . . . . McClure wrote you bout our new great revolutionary *Journal for the Protection of All Beings* — Hope you can really catch some of those big dogs over there like Sartre and Beckett (especially Beckett) and Genet and Céline and get page or two from each — prose blasts or capsule essays on whatever subject they're heated up about at the moment — revelations — McClure covered all this to you — It will be large size newsprint journal, format like [Alfred Leslie's journal] *Hasty Papers* only not that large — We'll print a lot and get it all over

country. So send something in prose yourself. It's going to be terrific, if all the writers we wrote come thru . . . .

LeRoi [Jones] is now bugged with me since, after big exchange of telegrams, I refused to sign his declaration by poets and artists, sponsored by Casa de las Américas in Havana and also signed by many South American writers. I wouldn't sign because no one in U.S. government is going to be persuaded to change U.S. policy toward Cuba (or to change its plans for future invasions) by our declaring our solidarity with foreign writers sponsored by Cuban organization. Who does he think such a declaration would influence in this country? It would only give bait to witchhunters wanting to hang any of us who oppose U.S. government policy in Cuba and would compromise independent position of dissent. I wonder if [Norman] Mailer signed this? Did you and Gregory? No one here (in San Francisco) did, far as I know . . . . I bet Jack didn't (He got his own Revolution out there) . . . . I figure we're not playing games anymore, daddy . . . .

Let me hear
(Love to Corse)
Cookoo
Lorenzo

ca. end of May 1961: Allen Ginsberg in Cannes, France, to Lawrence Ferlinghetti in San Francisco

Dear Larry:

There is no rush to publish *A Bunch of Poems.* I'll send "Fall of America" when and if ever done. I have no idea what or how to end it. I have not yet worked on typing up journals and have nothing to send McClure, etc. yet, except our spontaneous manifesto on Cuba which was published in Art Buchwald column with corrupt text — real text is being mimeographed by Olympia and will reach you soon — Can you print that? Am not now in touch with anyone of big dogs so can't collect material. I haven't signed any Cuban manifestos except those I wrote myself — did you see the Buchwald column about two weeks ago?

Grove Press (Dick Seaver) has copy of the La Guardia Report in microfilm which I got indirectly from Dr. Karl Bowman, ex-head of Langley-Porter, who is in Frisco retired now. He has a copy and probably lots of other material. Can reach him thru Langley-Porter probably. Bowman can give you details on rights. Lawrence Lipton published excerpts in *Holy Barbarians*. Olympia Press, Girodias, can get you excerpts from Burroughs and new Corso novel. I'll send material from us when we have some. We're all working on silent projects in the sun Riviera, isolated. All well — Jack is on phono and I'm in a rose arbor writing.

I think you will in long run be covered in your Cuban activity since U.S. will have to change cold-war policy or get blown off the map. From here the U.S. fix looks absolutely weird and hopeless, which is just fine. U.S. will have to come around.

Spending time at film festival and St. Tropez with a rich junky friend. Will try to make a meet with Burroughs here or Tangier — after that, no known plans. [. . .]

Love,
Allen

June 13, 1961: Allen Ginsberg in Tangiers, Morocco, to Lawrence Ferlinghetti in San Francisco

Dear Larry:
[. . .] I made a copy of a tape of Artaud and [Roger] Blin doing "Judgment"[81] parts, and sent it for safekeeping and use to LeRoi Jones. If you want a copy ask LeRoi to make one and send you. Since the one I sent him is one of only three or four in existence, best not mail the original around, might be lost. I had had a copy of Wernham's translation which I laid on LeRoi a long time ago and he wanted to put it out. Is this for *Journal* or a book? One of you should [publish it], it's really

---

81 *To Have Done with the Judgment of God* (1947), a play written by Antonin Artaud.

wild. Especially after you hear Artaud's bloody superhuman screams on the tape.

However — Paule Thévenin[82] told me that the text that was published was very corrupt — I loaned her my copy and she corrected it in detail, and I sent this copy with the tape also for safekeep to LeRoi. If Wernham is willing, why not get the right text and correct his translation. It's worth doing, since some of the mistakes make the poem more incomprehensible and goofy than it really is, seriously. The corrections do also jive with Artaud's taped recitation. So you can get that corrected text from LeRoi. I hope Wernham is around and willing.

Also I asked Thévenin were there any other comparable Artaud late poems-texts and she suggested the following uncollected untranslated material. Letters, poems and articles published in the magazine *Tel Quel* [and others]. So these are weird texts recently published in Paris, and rights are available from the magazines and OK'd by Gallimard, all one has to do is write to get the magazines and have them translated. Actually, "The Judgment," plus the Van Gogh letter, plus Letters from Rodez, (that were in *Evergreen*), plus the letters to Pope and Dalai Lama, plus the above would be more than enuf for a real stunning paper book — and rights for such a book are available from Monique Lange, etc. Why not? By the time it was all assembled and readied you'd have enuf back from *Dreams* and *Kaddish* maybe to afford it? I hope. [. . .]

Love,
Allen

---

82 Paule Thévenin (1918–1993), a translator of Antonin Artaud's work.

August 19, 1961: Lawrence Ferlinghetti in San Francisco to Allen
Ginsberg in Tangier, Morocco

Dear Allen . . . .

Enclosed are clips you may not have seen. Been meaning to roundup all kinds of little bits of news and info concerning you which have piled up . . . . here's a few items I can think of at the moment:

Tapes you recorded at WBAI in December 1960, I've just paid for and gotten copies of same (two reels, about an hour in all) and have just played same, having missed them when broadcast on KPFA here. Anyway, I wanted to get them for the record. Vincent McHugh[83] thought there might be a little book in them called *Ginsberg on the Cosmos* . . . . but there isn't enough, aren't enuf remarks about "the cosmos" to make more than a few pages . . . Maybe add to them, later? However, I think mebbe the whole interview might look good in print — for a future issue of some journal City Lights will put out — if you like the idea, I could get the tapes transcribed and send them to you for editing . . . . sometime . . . . Swami, there're some great fantastic beautiful lovely remarks therein . . . .

After we get first issue of *Journal* out (it'll be ready in another two weeks or so) and after I go on small junket around Southwest this October, I'll get to your next book and send you all you left me in some suggested order, etc. — or send you manuscript prepared for printer — so we could get it out early in 1962 . . . . First issue of *Journal* will be good and true . . . . I translated Artaud for it. [. . .]

I may be going to Italy a year from this Fall — I'd sort of like to live there for a half year at least — have been doing a lot of intensive drawing (from models at School of Fine Arts here) this summer and am all steamed up about it, it's marvelous, much more <u>fun</u> than writing, and just as powerful, terrific terrible incisiveness and tragedy and punch and Goya vision in it — so may apply for one of those big studios at American Academy in Rome . . . . That's my latest idea . . . . Would probably do some publishing from there — a small book

---

83 Vincent McHugh (1904–1963), an American poet and writer.

or two — maybe Italian poets, if any — or drawings — or an issue of a *City Lights Journal* — been reading the old *Little Review* — Exiles' Number,[84] gives me lots of ideas on *Journals,* etc. . . . . Met translator from Italy — editor of *El Contemporaneo* — who published my "Castro 1000 Words" in it in Italian — name of Romano Giachetti — and he wants to do translating of you in Italy, as well as Gregory and others — I told him get in touch with Mondadori and Feltrinelli to see if they had translators enough — he's young, with American Brooklyn Jewish wife who helped a lot on Castro poem, and I think they'd produce good translations . . . . I'll send his name to Mondadori and Feltrinelli too, next time I have reason to write them [. . .]

Mike [McClure] gone to live in New York City . . . . Jack [Kerouac] back from Mexico — had his bag stolen in MexCity — and returned to Florida instead of coming out here as expected . . . . Will write you more about *Journal* soon — Will send you copy airmail, if possible . . . . to London . . . .

love
Lorenzo

During the summer the group in Morocco split up, all going their separate ways. Ginsberg wasn't certain of his plans but hoped that he'd find a way to reunite with Peter Orlovsky before moving on to India. Back in San Francisco, after wanting children for years but having no luck, Lawrence and Kirby had just adopted a baby girl named Julie.

<hr />

84 The *Little Review, Exiles' Number* was edited by Margaret Anderson and Ezra Pound in 1923 and contained work by H.D., Gertrude Stein, e.e. cummings, and Mina Loy.

August 22, 1961: Allen Ginsberg in Tangier, Morocco, to Lawrence
Ferlinghetti in San Francisco

Dear Larry:

I'll sail to see the Parthenon day after tomorrow; thence on to Egypt to inspect the Sphinx. Send the *Journals* to Athens. Burroughs and Corso are in London now. Bill B. to go work on consciousness alteration at Harvard in two weeks — mushrooms and electronics. Delighted to hear you added babe to your house — lovely idea, you be happy? Love to Kirby, and hello to McClure — how's Philip Whalen now? Send regards. I wrote $750 article on Cannes for *Show Business* in twenty-four hours — so we all had loot for planes and boats to make a Diaspora. Peter is in Istanbul in the Blue Mosque. Burroughs new book *Soft Machine* is beyond words beautiful and rare. I'm amazed.

Love
Allen

August 27, 1961: Lawrence Ferlinghetti in San Francisco to Allen
Ginsberg in Athens, Greece

Dear Allen . . . .

Just got your card with group photo on front. It's one of those immortal pictures, naturally I wish I wuz in it (Laughlin had copy I saw before). But listen, I thought you had already cut for London and so about a week ago I wrote fairly long letter to you c/o American Express, London. I also wrote half of card to you on card to Gregory and in with this card were four or five clippings of reviews you got. (Scorpion Press in England has really been getting you reviews there — they sent out large number of review copies there.) So anyway please write to American Express, London, for first letter — which had a lot of semi-important publishing type news in it. And Gregory has card with your reviews . . . .

How come Peter go off by himself? Mad and sad? . . . . I hope you go to India from Egypt . . . . Is Olympia publishing *Soft Machine*?

I hope so. If not, I would like to see manuscript. But I suppose Grove has fancy dibs. [. . .]

Today Vincent McHugh's review of *Kaddish* came out in *Chronicle*. Next to Paul Carroll's in *Evergreen*, this is about the only review you've gotten here that was at all fair to the book, even tho he goofs in a couple places . . . . Real nice of him . . . . Enclosed

frick-frak —L.

ca. October 1, 1961: Allen Ginsberg in Greece to Lawrence Ferlinghetti in San Francisco

Dear Larry:

Been out of Athens for a week, now answering letters. [. . .] The book of poems you have, that's so far arranged in chronological order. If there's anything should be left out, suggest it.

Well, I've been in Greece a month — a week in Athens screwing Greek street boys and hanging round Ammonia Square Times Square area, then to country to Delphi, walking over Mt. Parnassus to shepherd valleys, pure idyllic sheep bells and country paths, then around Peloponnesus to ruins at Olympia, back to Athens, then to Isle of Hydra, then a town Methana where old Greeks take sulfur baths for bones, then the Plains of Argos where the chiefs gathered for *Iliad* wars, and wandering in valleys on foot around Mycenae, and tomorrow leave Athens again and stay two weeks in Crete, I'm almost broke again, go there wait two weeks for man to send me 100 dollars for *Empty Mirror* manuscript (Yale collector) — then after that two weeks at Mt. Athos with ugly monks. Then Israel and then dunno till India January 1 meet Gary [Snyder]. This week sat in cafes and met Greek poets, it's just like Chile, also today got drunk with Miller's Katsimbalis[85] who actually is a fantastic storyteller, looks like combo Sidney Greenstreet and Raimu with popeyes acting out feeling like a butterfly in observation car going over the rockies jacking off un-

---

85 Henry Miller's book *The Colossus of Maroussi* is a portrait of George Katsimbalis.

der full moon to howl of American jackals. Found Spiro the Berkeley kid and met his gang, and also Vassilikos[86] and Leslie Fiedler[87] too and tomorrow Crete. Greece is really Greece, everybody's sexy and the light's immense. Peter disappeared into Istanbul, angry at Burroughs for cutting up Love. I don't know what I'm doing, just wandering and having strange dreams about losing mind in amnesia. Some kind of lonely changes.

OK Love
Allen

P.S.: Yes, *Soft Machine* is already in print at Olympia, I wrote dust jacket. I think astounding idea, the book. His point is, to mutate consciousness, get it outside of language. To do that, cut up verbal consciousness, like Zen koan. I can hardly write poesy anymore, it's so great as a technique for kicking language habit.

Peter's home address is care of Kate Orlovsky, post office, Northport, L.I. [. . .] We've lost mail contact, I don't know where he is, last address was Istanbul American Express (Turk Express) — but no word from him all month though I've sent various packages and letters. I'm writing him care of Northport tonight. We had big arguments about future of universe in Tangiers, he wanted it to be sex-love mutation out of bodies, I was undecided, confused. I still am, except Burroughs seemed to have killed "Hope" in any known form. *The Exterminator* is serious. Peter wanted innocence and sex apocalypse, it got very serious, I was vomiting, then [Timothy] Leary from Harvard came with further mushrooms and took Bill back to Cambridge for research in consciousness alteration, and I'm fleeing to India to think. Peter said he'd meet me there. Meanwhile I'm trying to dissolve in solitary, it's hard since I built up such heavy poet karma, hard to be nothing again. I took some opium tonight to get thru these letters then I go walk in Crete wilderness mañana. All's getting amazing.

---

86 Vassilis Vassilikos (b. 1934), a Greek writer.
87 Leslie Fiedler (1917–2003), writer and literary critic.

October 7, 1961: Lawrence Ferlinghetti in San Francisco to Allen
Ginsberg in Greece

Dear Allen . . . .
Got your great letter from Greece and I sure wish I was there to go
to Mt. Athos and Crete and Delphi, but I'm going to make it next
year, leaving here about September and staying in France and Italy til
Spring and then going to Greece and I hope to Alexandria and then
India and then back here, by myself, Kirby and baby Julie returning
to San Francisco from Italy/Greece by themselves — that's me plan.
[. . .] So next year, maybe about time you get back to San Francisco,
I'll be taking off — or maybe, better still, you'll be still in India and I'll
see you in Benares trotting along the river toward yellow love, me with
my ankh [the City Lights logo], my alpenstock . . . .

So anyway, I think all this correspondence as literary agent for you
and others will have to be laid on some real literary agent like Sterling
Lord next year. You said in one letter you knew of another in New York
who would be better than Lord for you, and we could arrange it before
I cut out, so that he would handle all the pre-lim arrangements and
words with various publishers leading up to City Lights signing contract for reprints for you as we do now. [. . .] I have just signed a contract for you with Mondadori (the son was here this week — Fabrizio)
— Alberto Mondadori signed it, and they are to send $150 advance
upon signing, which should come thru soon, so I'll send you a couple
of hundred in this letter, advance against next annual report from us.
(Enclosed is the Mondadori contract for said book, both *Howl* and
Kaddish together, and Nanda Pivano is to be translator . . . . But please
return it to me before you take off. You will have to send them the two
prose statements (in contract) since I do not have them [. . .] Sure
yes I met Amaral in New York City — took him to party at Living
Theatre for Beats Gold Medal book — and lost him there when I got
drunk and fumed at some other address or should say some other joint
. . . . Sent you *Journal* to Greece by surface mail over a month ago, so it
should show very soon. If not, send me your next Far East address, and
I'll airmail one there — it's heavy, that's why I didn't send it air before

. . . . Enclosed are also all kinds of clips, some of which you might have seen already. If you don't know what to do with em, send them back here and I'll put in your voluminous file . . . . I just lent Don Allen your next book of poems manuscript since he wanted to go over it to see if there was something he like for his new Grove Press anthology which is to be a follow-up and continuation of his *New American Poets*. . . . . By the way, you will see in your interview in *Journal* that word Fuck came out "f . . ." since printer absolutely refused to set or print the word in full and rest of *Journal* was mostly set so that we owed him enormous amount of fresh bread and he said that's the way it has to be or pay or else, etc. etc, (and see also same dictation in deletion of word in |David| Meltzer "Birth" article — printer couldn't even say cunt, didn't know what cunt was, couldn't spell cunt, never knew cunt existed before we showed it to him). Wouldn't even use ferk . . . . So we have to find printer for next issue, if we ever put out another — McClure has moved to New York and may produce print issue there this coming Spring . . . . When you see *Journal* I think you'll agree it should be kept going but give us your advice baby, you can be editor on it if you want to, natch . . . . Swami . . . . guru . . . . hoisted up in a basket to them high Athoses, are you? Me here down below like . . . . but I got me own strange mystic scene going, this summer I had interior revolution at School of Fine Arts drawing the models like crazy and produced (and still producing) enormous drawings charcoal and black ink wash and it's greater than words any day, I'm going up there every day, Victor Wong[88] and me. He and Jack became great buddies when Jack here last year and other night we try to call Jack in New York and Florida and get him to meet us in Taos next month, etc., but Jack very sad these days . . . . Victor and I take big sketchbooks and pads and charcoal and paints and sleeping bags and take off in a few weeks . . . .

Now, to get back to your next book: will send it to printer in January at latest, in chronological order you set up, just as you sent it in, although when I get around to "copy-reading" it I'll probably have

---

88 Victor Wong (1927–2001), a San Francisco friend of Ferlinghetti and Kerouac, who later became a well-known actor.

lots of copy-questions to ask you, so let me know where to send same about December . . . . Your manuscript now is titled *Some Poems* (with dates) but you previously said maybe call it *Hiccup*. I prefer *Hiccup*. But it's yours to decide . . . . Will make it same format as your other two books, so all yours will be uniform . . . . But then after that I think I will start a "Second Series" in the Pocket Poets and use photo cover but exact same size as present series. (Of course every paperbook now has photocover instead of just typography — so that our plain typographical covers stand out now more than the others — *n'est-ce pas?*) Which do you prefer? (You got so many questions to answer people in letters, don't bother to answer any of this if you don't feel like it) . . . . For new Second Series I have in mind a long railroad poem about his father by Robert Nichols (you think him interesting?); a literary hoax fake translation by myself from some non-existent French; (also Artaud book, maybe). Maybe something of Stan Persky's[89]; and can you get me anything from Paul Bowles or Burroughs? . . . . I am definitely going to write Peter's Kate [Orlovsky] to ask for his manuscript since as you know I wrote Peter long ago (when you still in Peru) to ask if he would let me print book of his, but he never answered and I remember in New York once how he looked at books on shelves in horror, saying something about "Is that what you (Allen) want to end up as, a book on a shelf a thousand years later?" . . . . but I still want to publish him . . . . I am sorry he took off without you, and you without him . . . . I opened Poetry Center season at San Francisco Museum last week, boy was it a dull scene, like a morgue, but my white snake and small nuts came out looking fine on museum walls, I bounced them off it . . . . my next letter may catch you in extermination itself; I hope not. [. . .]

let freedom wring

. . . .

[signed with drawing]

---

89 Stan Persky (b. 1941), a Canadian writer and teacher.

October 14, 1961: Allen Ginsberg in Athens, Greece, to Lawrence
Ferlinghetti in San Francisco

Dear Larry:
[. . .] Got *Journal*, it looks fine, am passing it round to Greeks. Got
check, I just arrived from Crete back with 30 cents and the picture
enclosed expressed my feelings perfect. You look lovely. Yes *Journal*
should be kept going if it pays. I can't edit anything, I already got
too many letters to answer, swamped with appeals from LeRoi Jones,
Marc Schleifer[90] in Cuba, etc. I just can't make up my mind what to
do about all them sympathetic politics, I really don't believe in it. But
I got nothing else to offer. So I guess I got to refuse being Swami and
do nothing but go to India escape and run out. I do little drawings too,
Orlovsky style.

I still can't think of title for book. *Hiccups* is funny, but has nothing
to do with the case. *Some Poems* is dreary. This time there will probably
be endless typos, so be sure send me proofs, and now there's no rush
and plenty of time to do it leisurely, why not. Don't publish it unless
Kaddish sales justify as business investment. There's no rush by me to
print any more writings. I left it with you just to clean house in case
anything happened like I got et by dinosaurs in Upper Pakistan. Is
selling at all? Don't bother answer all this till real letter is due for some
state occasion. Photo covers are fine if photos are good and titles don't
bug the eye.

Burroughs' *Yage Letters* are now complete between *Big Table, Kul-*
chur 2 and the Roosevelt skit in *Floating Bear*, that's a small book. He
has lots of material. I'll write and mention it but you might send note.
I not read Nichols, don't know anything new. Bowles is always ap-
proachable and probably has something; or could prepare a volume of
stories by Ahmed Yacoubi, see sample in *Evergreen*. Ask him? I owe
him note and will mention it too. I still got endless mail. I think the
Artaud be the best. In back letters I think I outlined material available.
Regards to all girls in bathrooms everywhere.

---

90 Marc Schleifer was the first editor of *Kulchur* magazine.

Title of book — *A Lot of Words*. OK? I'll have to write some note explaining placement and chronology for errata page. Or *Further Yakkings* by Allen Ginsberg. Yes! Just *Yakkings* — then we have *Howl*, *Kaddish* and *Yakkings*. Everybody satisfied! Is *Yakkings* okay? I'm off to answer more letters.

Love to Kirby and Babe.

I thought your death poem lovely, I don't know if it was the pictures but it did seem back to poesy.[91] Also thought Meltzer's actual description of babe birth, couch scene — well read it amazed. Duncan also makes sense, especially when he confesses.

Crete, I walked a lot all around, valley of Lassithi, enclosed by mountains, where Zeus was born in Dicte Cave, explored with flashlight, read *Odyssey*. Now reading *Iliad*. Dreamt plenty. I still have to type up *South American Journals* for Auerhahn. When that's started I'll send some for *Journals*.

> How do we ever
> keep going? OK
> Allen

October 20, 1961: Lawrence Ferlinghetti in San Francisco to Allen Ginsberg in Athens, Greece

Cher Allen . . . .
No need to answer this letter, else you'll never get caught up with your mail . . . . Just got yours and am happy you got check so fast and *Journal*. By the way, that's my translation of Artaud in it — you may not remember the Wernham translation of same, but I found it pretty inaccurate in some crucial places. I'd like to translate some more of him, and will, if I ever find time, hoping to do that little book of his, following your suggestions as to contents as given in your former letter which I have — I'll be writing Mme. Thévenin about it — but I

---

91 This is a reference to text accompanying the photographs of James Mitchell in the first issue of the *Journal for the Protection of All Beings*.

may very well be in France by next year this time, which would be an excellent time to do the whole thing . . . . I also did the lettering on the cover of *Journal*, which I guess you must have recognized as mine [. . .] I'm not too enthusiastic about your title *Yakkings* (since critics will say "Yah Yakkings is exactly what they are"), but I'll go along with you on it — unless you think of something better — I think your manuscript (which Don Allen has at the moment) is entitled *A Bunch of Poems* (not *Some Poems*, as I said before). Ok, so we'll probably not get your book out until September next Fall, and we'll take time and get everything straight, no typos, send you proofs of course. *Kaddish* going slowly, but still much much better than most poetry: we printed 10,000 here and 2500 in England, and have 1500 left in England and 4000 here, not bad for half a year. Will catch those remaining few typos in *Kaddish* when we reprint, which might be this summer . . . . or before. [. . .]

Love
Lorenzo

Ginsberg and Orlovsky reunited in Tel Aviv in November after their separate voyages, and began to plot their trip to India. Unfortunately they found themselves stranded in Israel, because they could not travel directly from there to any of the surrounding Islamic countries. Meanwhile, not long after the adoption of Julie, Lawrence's wife Kirby unexpectedly became pregnant after all, with a son who would be named Lorenzo.

December 18, 1961: Lawrence Ferlinghetti in San Francisco to Allen Ginsberg in Tel Aviv, Israel

Dear Allen —
Saw your picture with Peter in *Jerusalem Post* — Glad to see Peter back with you — card from Nanda [Pivano] came a while ago — but didn't know where to send it — Will hope all this is forwarded to you from Tel Aviv — Paul Bowles wrote to me, thanks — offering hashish

stories — that's great — Will do — I wrote Peter's sister about doing his poetry — no answer — (Peter, how about it, now???) — Am also working on Artaud translating from Vol. I — Gallimard. (The greatest stuff hasn't even been touched!)

Kirby just got pregnant — so it looks like that's the end of our trip to Europe next year! May go to India by myself, West from here — Have written cave play, *The Soldiers of No Country* —

Love —
Lorenzo

December 20, 1961: Allen Ginsberg in Acre, Israel, to Lawrence Ferlinghetti in San Francisco

Dear Larry:

All same here, living with Peter in Acre, old Crusaders' city near Haifa, stuck like in flypaper trying to get out to India in time to meet Bowles and Snyder [in] Ceylon New Years. Looks hopeless, no boats, Arab borders blocked for travel, etc. May have to double back to Istanbul, change passport and get boat thru Suez. Don't know yet. Meanwhile mail here forwarded if I leave and also will send you forwarding address before I take off.

[. . .] Long dreary days waiting for boats and bureaucrats to get me on one. Outside window old medieval forts, Mediterranean and Arab medina and Turkish battlements and Israeli apartment houses.

Merry Xmas. How's your family? Babes on your nerves or is that fun? I guess you got Xmas tree with presents this year. Nothing special new here. A few poems and lots of bus rides and potato pancakes. Israel not interesting.

OK, later
Allen

Allen Ginsberg, 1959. PHOTO BY CHESTER KESSLER

Bob Donlin, Neal Cassady, Allen Ginsberg, Robert LaVigne, and Lawrence Ferlinghetti in front of City Lights, 1955. PHOTO BY ALLEN GINSBERG

Left to right: Philip Whalen, Robert Branaman, Ann Buchanan (aka Ann Plymell), Allen Ginsberg, Bob Kaufman, Lawrence Ferlinghetti, Alan Russo, and Charles Plymell, in front of City Lights, 1963. PHOTO BY ALLEN GINSBERG

Lawrence Ferlinghetti and Allen Ginsberg, London, 1965. © ESTATE OF JOHN VICTOR LINDSAY HOPKINS

Allen Ginsberg and Lawrence Ferlinghetti, early 1970s. PHOTO COURTESY OF THE CITY LIGHTS
ARCHIVES

Allen Ginsberg, Yevgeny Yevtushenko, and Lawrence Ferlinghetti, 1972. PHOTO BY MICHAEL ZAGARIS

Lorenzo Ferlinghetti, Lawrence Ferlinghetti, and Allen Ginsberg, Suva, Fiji, 1972. PHOTO COURTESY OF THE ALLEN GINSBERG COLLECTION

Standing left to right: Gregory Corso, Miriam Patchen, Kenneth Rexroth, Allen Ginsberg, and Lawrence Ferlinghetti; sitting left to right: Joanna McClure, Laurel Reuter, Shig Murao, Janie McClure, Gary Snyder, at a Beat Conference in North Dakota, 1974. PHOTO BY D. SORENSEN

Left to right: Lawrence Ferlinghetti, Minette LeBlanc, Peter LeBlanc, unknown, Allen Ginsberg, Harold Norse, Jack Hirschman, and Bob Kaufman at the Caffe Trieste, San Francisco, 1975. PHOTO BY DIANA CHURCH

Allen Ginsberg, Lawrence Ferlinghetti, and Nancy J. Peters, 1981, in the City Lights doorway. PHOTO BY CHRIS FELVER

Lawrence Ferlinghetti in his office with Pooch, Whitman photo, files,
coat racks, book bags, posters, at City Lights up on balcony, B'way
and Columbus Avenues, San Francisco, October 1984. Allen Ginsberg

left to right: Lawrence Ferlinghetti, Lucien Carr, Sheila Carr, Allen Ginsberg, and Harry Smith. PHOTO BY
SIMON PETTET

Lawrence Ferlinghetti in his office at City Lights, 1984.
PHOTO BY ALLEN GINSBERG

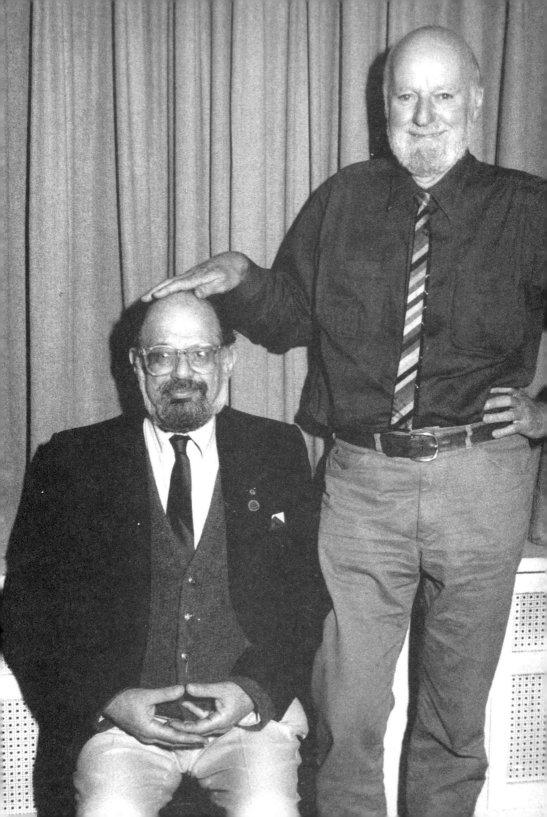

Allen Ginsberg and Lawrence Ferlinghetti, 1988. PHOTO BY ELIOT GREENSPAN

Lawrence Ferlinghetti and Allen Ginsberg, 1996. PHOTO BY CHRIS FELVER

◄ **Dear Allen** ►

CITY LIGHTS BOOKS

261 COLUMBUS AVENUE, SAN FRANCISCO 11

15 Nov 67

Cher Allen:
Sorry to hear you were sick. Shall
we continue to forward your mail to
Milan or hold it for a new address?
Let us hear. Stuff is accumulating.

Peter is here, having arrived last week
in VWbus from NY with Irving (Rosenthal
andhe is verySpeedy; and has had trouble
with VWbus. There is a $450 estimate
for repairson it, new transmission etc,
and we will payit so that he can get
the car out tomorrow. I hope this
won't upset you, but I imagine it's
still your car, and we'll charge it
against your royalties....

Just a quick note....Thanks for
laying my SEGOVIA poem on Nanda.

Love to her andEttore & you....

larry

(Kind of worried about Peter. Any
words of advice?)

16 Jan 69

Dear Allen: Dreamt last night you handed me a copy
of the VILLAGE VOICE with complete POEM ON THESE
STATES in it, about fifty pages of Voice pages.
Not a bad idea for a first complete printing of
it, I'm even dreaming genius publishing ideas,
and it reminds me to tell you I am ready to do it
in Pocket Poets Series whenever you are.....
I am also wondering, what with your new singing
career, wouldn't you like to do a little Blake
edition with your music for the poems you have
done? It would be lovely; but maybe you want to
give the idea to some bigger publisher......
We are, infact, really beginning to get out of
the Little Press category, with several "real"
books coming along for the Fall.....
I just saw Gary (at a party for him in Muir Beach,)
and he has two ideas for new Jap books, one with
Alan Watts, and I hope to do at least one of them,
soon.....
Just sent you the last ad for PLANET NEWS to come
in, CORNO EMPLUMADO. There's one more coming in
RAMPARTS, amd I think that's about it. We spent
between $750 and $1000 on it, I'm not sure exactly
how much, but the book sure is flying along under
its own power. You'd better proofread that British
edition for us soon as you can, so that we don't
get caught short on the reprint....
Talked to Daniel (Moore) on phone yesterday, and
he hopes to see you when you come in Feb; maybe you
will have time to go to Bixby Canyon for a few
days, with Gary, Phil, Daniel, or whoever.&Your
room here at the publishing pad will be available
if you want it (Got a more comfortable mattress).
Let me know when you're coming exactly, if you
can....

Love to all there,

LF   Larry

CITY LIGHTS

BOOKSTORE
261 Columbus Ave.
San Francisco 94133
362-8193

PUBLISHING HOUSE
1562 Grant Ave.
San Francisco 94133
362-3112

Jan 26? 71

cher allen.   the two thousand was sent you this morn by Bob McBride....

still no word from Australia. will call you one morning soon as
                    word arrives....
got yr stuff about the Italian Mondadori censorship. I don't see
anything to be done except let them suppress the words they feel
    they have to suppress,if you want the book published there.
    However, I would rather personally tell them to shove it: tell
       them to take it or leave it in its entirety, with not a single
       cut, put up or shut up, all or nothing,take it or leave it.
       That's what I prefer. But it's your decision. (There's no
          way I can see that City Lights could strengthen Linder's
              "hand" in the matter, if the Italian publishers won't
              go along with him against the fuckinstate.)

Re. German publication: enclosed is a letter from the headman at
                    Hanser, Fritz Arnold. I asked him to
       discuss with our agent, Dagmar Henne, the possibilities of
       breaking the Limes contract for Howl on the grounds that words
       were suppressed in your text in the German edition. Please return
          the letter. (We've added the artist credit to the Winged Biblio
              Gins.)

              will be talkin to you soon i hope....I just heard from Michael Horowit
McNellie's ▆▆▆▆▆▆▆▆▆▆▆ contact in the Holding Together, that Tim is"under house
       arrest"▆▆▆▆(This is CONFIDENTIAL at this point.) And it is the Pant
who are doing it, not the ▆▆gov. or police. Confirms theory ▆▆▆ he is"hostage"of Thir
World,like i sed a month ago.....
       I have just produced a goofy book: FUCK YOU WILFRED FUNK
          (wrot at 5 AM)

       love

              LF

REMINDER: if you haven't sent photo of Neal which you thinkwd make gud
              cover, please airmail.....
          Also any one or two page of words you'd like to see at beginni
          of FIRST THIRD, comme Intro.... Going to press with this in
          two weeks or three. I hope.

20 Oct 75

V1011

Querido, Allen —
Took off from Mexico City yesterday for here
on the Gulf of Mexico without any baggage —
just what I could carry in my pockets — —
Back to Mexico City later this week for poetry
reading at ▮ Palacio Nacional de Bellas Artes —
Hope your health has mended — (Go swimming
every day!) I enclose a Fotomat photo in bus
station, remembering ours in
Panama — Love — Larry

mystic volcano)

El Pico de Orizaba, 5500 mts. de altura, visto
desde La Posada Loma, Fortín de las Flores.
18,200 foot "Pico de Orizaba"
Veracruz, México.
Foto: Mark Turok

CITY LIGHTS
BOOKSELLERS & PUBLISHERS
261 COLUMBUS AVENUE
SAN FRANCISCO, CALIF. 94133
(415) 362-8193

13 Jun 86

Allen · Thanks for clipping from
<u>Philly Enquirer</u> + comments
on <u>Howl</u>.

About your family photo album,
I knew where it was all the
time, but didn't know you'd
been searching for it! I kept it
in an old fireproof safe we used
to have up in the old Grant Avenue
office. We also have in the same
safe an (incomplete) copy of
your filmscript for KADDISH.
(It is probably incomplete because art →

one time (when it was in an ordinary
file cabinet) Mark Green broke
into our editorial office and stole
it and distributed pages of it to
everyone in the Trieste Caffe.
(Someone gathered up most of the
pages + returned them to us. I
think you know the story – Mark
claimed his tranquilizers had run
out + that's when he always gets in
trouble.)
Re-your annual royalty check, see
enclosed –
I'm off to Italy in a couple of weeks
for a month or so....
                    Ever yours – lawrence

CITY LIGHTS
BOOKSELLERS & PUBLISHERS
261 COLUMBUS AVENUE
SAN FRANCISCO, CALIF. 94133
(415) 362-8193

31 July 81

Dear Allen —

Back from Nica +
10th Anniversario of
Sandinist Rev....

→ * You should have
been there. Great
stuff going on.

Love. Lawrence

9/1/90

Dear Allen – I sent the original of the enclosed
to you at Naropa c/o Anne, to hold
for you there.....Curious what happened
on stage that day of the sumi-brush
event.....After I asked you how to
spell <u>bodhi</u>, "elephants fucking" flashed
upon my brainpan-- then you said it!

love – L.

24 Aug 76

Dear Larry:
Returned home tonite & found your Aug 8 note in pile of letters — I'll stay here till go to Berlin with W.S. Burroughs sept 20 - oct 5 — Then w/ Peter oct - Dec 4 retreat N.W. Wisconsin sitting on breath all day + technical Void studies — Then open space till Next Summer at Naropa (will Teach one Course "Literary History of Beat Excursion) — Aspreatures retyped most of Mind Breaths — ready soon I hope — wrote to you — Louis died peaceful + philosophic little pain — Love

in haste
Allen

Larry Ferlinghetti
48 5 Filbert
S.F. 94133

Naropa 1111 Pearl St Boulder Colo. 80302

2RM 61   Photo: Don Harmon ©

Dear Larry: Up here vacation
re June + Trungpa + fellow sitters
+ Seminary — writing lots of postcards.
Anne Waldman 3 months. Request, & I wish
Braunstein marrying his girl Lizabeth & Larry
Fagin in N.Y. marrying Susan Noel May 21.
Peter upstate N.Y. tending my nephews +
nut trees. I have to finish some kind of
reply to Clark / nation etc. and finish editing
+ preface to P E N ~~Scal~~ Club F B I harrassment
of Underground Papers report, then have? any
A day retyped + edit last revision, I don't
think I can get all that done till Summer's
end. For Spring Maybe. Also completing editing
of Meyers / Cope / Clausen book. I finally tackled
Clark's book head on + finished Manuscript of
Errata "Big Mistakes" in his book.
Also transcribing long sections of my
interview with him which he didn't
*** *** *** *** *** ***
*** *** *** *** *** ***
*** *** *** *** *** ***
It's getting interesting!
was by Shy before, not wanting to Challenge or disprove etc. Love Allen   77/89c box 25

Disturbutor: Byron Harmon Photos, Banff, Alberta, Canada.

FROM THE ROOF OF THE
CANADIAN ROCKIES

LAKE LOUISE affords a magnificent view of Mount
Lefroy, Mount Victoria and the Victoria Glacier. The
view is from the lakeshore path that skirts the north
shore of the lake. This trail eventually leads to the
Plain-of-the-Six Glaciers

Printed and Published by John Hinde Limited, Cabinteely, Co. Dublin, Republic of Ireland.

May 21, 1980

CANADA 17

Larry Ferlinghetti
261 Columbus Ave.
S.F. Calif
94133
c/o City Lights.

Åbningstider alle dage
kl. 11.30-02.00

SØPAVILLONEN · GYLDENLØVESGADE 24 · DK-1369 KØBENHAVN
TLF.: 01-151224

Dansk Foto-Tryk A/S

PAR AVION

AIR MAIL

Larry Ferlinghetti
℅ City Lights
261 Columbus Ave
San Francisco
California
94113
U·S·A·

77189c box 2

[handwritten message, largely illegible]
Nov 18, 1985: Dear Larry —

ALLEN GINSBERG
P.O. BOX 582
STUYVESANT STATION
NEW YORK, N.Y. 10009

6/7/86 NY

Dear Larry:

Still struggling with Annotated HOWL.

Enclose an interview, Philadelphia Inquirer 2 months ago,

As you see I hadn't forgotten you, in fact had just done preliminary editing of Publishing/Legal history section.

What wonderful news for me that my family picture album turned up at last in the City Lights safe. What kind of vast cavern is it, what other treasures besides Powell seizes you got in there !?! I'd despaired of finding it and my brother Gene (now 65) and stepmother were upset ~~to~~ with me for taking it out of their house back in 1972 or so. I must have brought it back from L.A. and left it at City Lights in 75 when I visited with my father — probably with some idea in mind of K adding Film Script book, or Collected pieces. Who found it and how?

How are you? I'm back from weeks of travel — Naropa, New Orleans, Mississippi, Maine — have as ever Allen

P.S. I spent time with Kenny
Paul & Philip Lamantia at U.O.
Book Fair. Philip was in fine mood!

◄ 1962 ►

Here Ferlinghetti mentions an anthology that Penguin Books wants to publish in England. Deciding on the selection of poets would end up consuming a great deal of energy for months. In the end Penguin would publish Ginsberg, Ferlinghetti, and Corso together in one paperback volume, a grouping that appears to have made none of them happy.

January 5, 1962: Lawrence Ferlinghetti in San Francisco to Allen Ginsberg in transit to India.

Dear Allen:
I wonder when you'll catch up with this. [. . .] Looks like my trip to France and the world in the Fall is OFF: Kirby just got pregnant! . . . . Me, I'm just a normal American Boy . . . . Keep sending me bookstore addresses and we'll follow thru . . . .

A Mr. Richard Newnham at Penguin Books, Harmondsworth, Middlesex, England, is wanting to make selection from you to go in *Penguin Modern Poets III* — an anthology with a first printing of 25,000 — They want thirty pages of you. I told them YES, on principle, and that they should submit their exact selection for your approval. In the meantime you could write him and give your preferences . . . . There are to be three poets in the volume, including you: he didn't name the other two. [. . .] So that's the last word on the home frontier . . . .

Things sure are dead here, as far as poetry readings, etc. go . . . . Wish I could find a great new poet to publish! Know any? Everyone here seems to be writing plays. I just finished one myself. I'm the Bert Brecht of the 1960s, in case you didna know.

> Salud in six
> languages
> Lorenzo

Dear Allen and Peter . . . .

You'll get there [to India] yet — hope Gary is still there by then. (Your
meeting seems to be known all over the U.S., in the bookstore circuit,
that is. Everybody saying Allen got to India to meet Gary yet? Like
some kind of international sorcerer swamis' conjunction on February
4th maybe? . . .). I sent you airmail letter to Ceylon address almost a
month ago — no money in it, but some enclosures of interest. So now
here's annual royalty report and checks: you sure sold a lot of copies.
Dig them totals . . . . Let me know if and when you get this check . . . .

Yep, we have Bowles' book almost to the printer, with title *A Hundred Camels in the Courtyard*, which is a quote from proverb in story.
Four stories altogether, one new. Thank you, he wouldn't have sent it if
you hadn't writ him three letters. For this Spring I also hope to have:
Selected Poems (Mexican Cantinas, etc.) of Malcolm Lowry. (I am going to Vancouver BC by freighter tomorrow to see ancient professor
up there [Earle Birney] who has all Lowry manuscript cornered; also
to give potry [*sic*] reading at University of British Columbia) . . . . Also
hope to have *Poems of the Thaw* by Yevtushenko and Kirsanov (translated by Anselm Hollo); also Robert Nichols, *Slow Newsreel of Man
Riding Train* (one long poem); then your next book, which I am just
about to get ready for the printer. Don Allen has had your manuscript
and gone thru it for his new antho, but I don't know what he has chosen from it. As far as you're concerned, are all these poems now exactly
as you want them, and can I go ahead and shoot them to Villiers? Also
tell me where you'll be about May 1st, so that I'll know where to send
the proofs . . . . Am also working toward that little Artaud volume
but haven't had time to do any of the translation myself as yet. (I been
writing plays) (More important to me) . . . .

Well I guess that covers the world for the momento.

> See you in some
> temple
> Lawrence

Dear Larry:

India is MORE, yes, we met Gary a few days ago here in New Delhi and we leave day after tomorrow for Himalayas, go stay in Yoga forest school, talk to the Dalai Lama maybe, climb in snows, everything is fine. India has everything Mexico has, poverty and dead dogs, I saw a body scattered on RR tracks like toe cover of *Kulchur* only it was in six pieces, also it's got hoods like Morocco and Moslems and shrouds and Indians like worse Bolivias and garbages like Peru and bazaars like Hong Kong's and billion of people like nowhere I seen. So that's all fine. I also have this backlog of two months mail, I'm woozy what with 16 cent morphine you can get here easy here, and sitting in a Jain temple dormitory to answer. Gary's down street in the Hindu YMCA.

I got the check, fine. Actually cash is the best thing here since you get best black market rate for that exchange, but it's too risky I suppose to send hundred dollar bills in mail so send on the other money in same type check. American Express cashes them, no trouble, and gives me travelers checks ok. I'll be back in Bombay the end of March with Gary and Peter and Gary's wife [Joanne Kyger], so will pick up next mail there, I guess send the money on there by then.

Gary looks older and a little more domestic-acting now that he's married; his face is more seamed and wrinkled and the baby look is gone, and he comes on very straight and simple — I haven't seen him for six years and change is noticeable. He's staying here till end of March, we'll travel till then all together; and then he to Japan and Peter and I stay here till seen enough maybe a year, then go to Japan-Kyoto. Music here is great — night before last we went to hear farewell speech of a holyman who's going to stop talking for the rest of his life — he's thirty-two now — and a couple of the greatest musicians in a drummer (tabla finger drums) and lady sarod (guitar drone sound) serenaded him improvised for an hour straight, ending in trance-celestial speed — such classical music as I never heard.

So far spent two days in Bombay and sped here to meet Gary and we've hung around met a few writers, walked thru alleys and streets and saw Nehru give election speech and shopped for a little Tibet statue for Whalen and ate cheap 25 cent curry dinners, I haven't settled into any routine here yet and am disorganized and got too much unanswered mail. Anyway India got more than anywhere else, especially great cheap horse carriages to take you around cities for 15 cents a hop, lovely to lean back and clop clop thru fantastically crowded streets full of barbers and street shoe-repairmen and bicycle rickshaws and Sikhs in turbans and big happy cows everywhere stealing cabbages from pushcarts.

Your Spring list Lowry and Russians is great. *Poems of Thaw* is, comparatively, drear title. If the poems are really lively why not something lively like *Thaw Heads* or *Moscow Gold* or *Beat Moscow* or *Hip Moscow* or or *Red Cats* — yes RED Cats! — (subtitle *Poems of the Thaw*) *Red Cats* sell better.[92] But are the poems good? I hope. [. . .]

That's astounding about your being a poppa after all. The rich get richer, good thing you adopted that babe, he [*sic*: she] brought you blessings. Peter write you soon. Doubled congratulations to Kirby from the Indic depths of bacheloral morphia. Send interesting books and pamphlets slow boat to Bombay, they'll eventually reach me. [. . .]

Love,
Allen

[P.S.] If anyone wants to sell Tibetan cheap statuary rajput nice miniature paintings and Indian dancing statues, you can get crazy copies and originals here real cheap for export. Be a good business. I'll send you some souvenirs when I get settled long enuf to pack and ship gifties.

---

92 Ferlinghetti did indeed use *Red Cats* as the title for the collection.

March 10, 1962: Lawrence Ferlinghetti in San Francisco to Allen
Ginsberg in Bombay, India

Dear Gins . . .

[. . .] OK, so I'll put your new book to press next month. What is final
idea for title: *Hiccup*? I think I like it best. That message from *Time* you
got no doubt was for story which just appeared this week on "*Modern
Poetry: 1945-62*" which is the usual Shit Fuck You Eatshit Shit which
they always emit, full of the usual lies and hypocrisy. They contacted
me for permission to use twelve or so lines from *Howl*, weeks ago
when you were incommunicado, and I wasn't sure you'd let them have
anything anymore, after their past crap, but I finally succumbed since
they said all the other publishers of all the other poets in article had
given permission. Since it was under twenty lines, there was no payment for use. So then the usual shit shows up. However, maybe you
won't be so unhappy since you came out of it better than everybody
else on what they call the uncouth side. They can go shit on their hats
the next time around, I'll hang up on them the brownnose finks . . . .
Yes we are changing title of Russian poems to *Red Cats* or *Red Heads*,
thank ye, good idea . . . .

Am gathering translations by any and all for *Selected Artaud* which
I will probably get out a year from now, and have gotten stuff so far
from Michael Benedikt, David Ball (friend of Hollo's). Have written
Frechtman, but so far he hasn't produced anything but the old gob-
bleygook [*sic*]. So if you run into or know anyone doing any Artaud,
prose or poetry, please tell them about our project and ask them to
send stuff. I've just translated A's *Jet du Sang*, play. LeRoi [Jones] has
Artaud tape — I never had it . . . .

This week received mysterious sarcastic card from Jack (K) in San
Diego saying Castro is going to start wax museum of figures like me
and Gleason and Rexroth (Guess he doesn't know Rex's now 100%
Hearst). I just came back from Lenny Bruce obscenity trial, for saying
cocksucker in Jazz Workshop, and he was acquitted. The schmuck. I
got Al Bendich, sharp lawyer from *Howl* trial, to defend him, and now
Bruce won't pay him — thinks he should've done it for love and glory.

I told *Examiner* reporter "Go Fuck Yourself" for one phony scene he was trying to get me into there, drumming up a story, and so am getting paranoid like a good poet.

Hello to Peter. Hello to Gary. Hello to JoAnne. Kirby says hello too. So does Julie Ferlinghetti. [. . .] Would love to have crazy little Indian dancing statue. Or send Indian maid. I have written two plays this winter, working on two others. Really turned on to it. Got poetry all beat. I am Artaud's Aunt and Brecht's American Noseswiper of the 1960s. One I just finish is called *Three Thousand Red Ants*.

Lorenzo

March 17, 1962: Allen Ginsberg in Delhi, India, to Lawrence Ferlinghetti in San Francisco

Dear Larry:
Just got back with Gary and others from two weeks up in foot-hill stations of the Himalayas — climbed hills and saw 200 mile spread of vast snowy inner Himalaya peaks, Nanda Devi and all down into Nepal, huge white walls of Tibet. We stayed cheap at Ashram and eat 20 cent vegetarian meals sleep all night on trains and saw swami Shwanander and cave holymen and Lama Govinda a Tibetan scholar and lots of naked sadhus (yoga-Shiva worshiper ascetics) who are all congregatory — all the holymen of India — once every twelve years going on this month, we saw the opening day — at Hardwar, where the Ganges comes onto the plains from the mountains. I didn't see *Time*, even.

[. . .] *Red Cats* is best I think. *Hiccups* is not so good, I'm still stuck. OK fine about permish to *Time*, I let them take my pix here too, anyhow. I hear *Lunes de Revolucion* is closed down. Paranoia always justified but now I'm too tired and try to stay patient with one and all, after all now I'm vegetarian. I take vitamins to make up. Gary is fine, I'm learning lots about Zen from him. Love to Kirby and Julie and all babies, everywhere. I'll mail you a statue in next month. *3000 Red Ants* is great title. I want to re-write jacket blurb for *Kaddish* second edition if any. I'll write soon.

Love,
Allen

Negotiations with Penguin over the three-poet anthology continued. Allen didn't think that Penguin's idea to pair him with two British poets, Martin Bell and Charles Causley, made much sense, and he wrote with other suggestions.

March 25, 1962: Lawrence Ferlinghetti in San Francisco to Allen Ginsberg in Bombay, India

Dear Allen:

I'm wondering if Bombay really is a Bomb-bay these days . . . . Have just sent on your letter to [Richard] Newnham and told him you were completely RIGHT, and that I was holding contract here (just sent to me by Penguin) until he wrote his decision in answer to your letter. We can still back-out. Nothing signed. I also told him he should definitely use your letter as Intro to your poems, if he would not change selection of poets . . . . (I see you mention Creeley as a possible selection. I like Creeley but I wish you would explain to me sometime why you consider his poetry particularly "wild" or "exciting" (words you used in Newnham letter). He fitteth the image personally, in the flesh, but where, specifically is it in his poetry (which isn't even Beat!) ???????? Would you point out to me a major poem by Creeley? I always wanted to do a book of his but never could find the poetry (that is, since the *Black Mountain Review*, published ten years ago) which lived up to the man . . . .)

cuckoo —
Lawrence

[P.S.] Have just read *Soft Machine* and think I have been wrong about Burroughs all these years. This is great book!

Dear Larry:

I don't feel like arguing with Penguin any more, I said what I had to say. He says he'll include "Sunflower" and "Magic Psalm" and I think that sufficiently solid mess. And it seems too mean to insist on blackmailing him against other poets, there must be some other way, that's too negative. So let's leave it at that. I'll write him card saying I wrote you giving ok to accept and sign contracts, or make any other arrangements you think wise.

Yes, "wild" is misused with Creeley. Just that in comparison with [Martin] Bell and [Charles] Causley, Creeley is <u>there</u>, a live human talking laconic, and makes sense. I had lots experience reading Creeley's poems to audiences, about twenty of them ("I Know A Man", "If You", "The Hat", etc. etc.) were so simple and straightforward and intrinsically funny humane little statements that they charmed and woke listeners to the fact (like in Williams) that a little lyric poem could talk straight — so they then listened to whatever was read them, having come to trust poetry to be something other than highfalutin' bavardie, listened to what the man was saying. No single major poem, but I think a group of twenty (<u>not</u> the highfalutin' abstracter selection in Don Allen[93]) all together make one major poem, I don't mean that, I mean one real piece of writing you can depend on to be awake. Which? Lots in "The Whip". The one "so he gave up loving, and lived with her."[94] Also one about "my enemies sent a spy in form of woman"

---

93 This is a reference to Don Allen's anthology, *The New American Poetry 1945–1960*.
94 This line is from Robert Creeley's poem "A Marriage."

(I'm misquoting)[95] — there's a whole bunch of clear ones. I'm less at-
tracted to later aesthetic ones like "The Door", and don't understand
them. Too much [Robert] Duncan.

Soft Machine amazed me in Paris. I wrote the dust jacket blurb.
But I thought all his earlier writing, step by step as it gets further out,
builds up to *Soft Machine* like logical steps. He's now one step further, new book *Nova Express* almost done — I think a cut-up imagery
science fiction with cut-up mosaic plot, subject I think being cosmic
explosion (like Nova stars that flare up) as result of science gone mad
or mind control gone mad.

Gary sailed back to Japan the other day, Peter and I settled down
in Bombay for a few weeks in huge room with rush mats in house of
spiritual Indian family who are friends of Krishnamurti. Last four days
answering all accumulated mail at once. [. . .]

Not written anything for exactly a year, almost, and not kept journals. Clean slate. I wrote *Root and Branch* so.[96] Peter, Gary and I gave
a few small readings, the first in all this time, and I'm slowly coming
back to, I hope, poetry. Burroughs cut-up was a Chinese wall in my
path, it makes so much sense as method of creating imagery and as
method of self examination of contents of one's consciousness.

I haven't been able to send poems to anyone because I've not
written much at all and not typed any of that. I still have to stay in
one place long enough to type *South American Journals* for Auerhahn,
which for some reason I dread doing, same unwashed dishes like completing *Kaddish* manuscript. Immediate life too distracting to want to
go back and work on yesteryear's hang-ups. [. . .]

Peter and I found opium den in Delhi and have been trying local "charas" like pot. Apparently there's also a liquid-milk-pot drink
[called] bhang used by pious old Hindoos for devotional occasions.
We're being taken to a temple to try. I sent you two statues, one a dancing god and another one, give one to [Michael] McClure and keep

---

95 The line is actually "My enemies came to get me, | among them a beautiful woman,"
from Creeley's poem "A Form of Adaptation."
96 *Root and Branch* was a little magazine that had requested material.

whichever you like. When'd I last write you? We all climbed to 9,000 feet in Himalayas, to snow, and same day visited Dalai Lama and had long conversation about breathing exercises and pot and mushrooms, and U.S.A. Lots of Tibetan tankas on sale here (refugees selling them) first and last time in history they be on market so cheap. I'll buy one for 100 when I have enough loot, some are like great super-Disney cosmic cartoons, mad colors, and delicatest drawing like Persian miniatures.

India is the best place to visit, and great for easy living, and I'm even getting sort of happy since being here. I'd felt hopeless all last year. [. . .]

We all went thru Sanchi, Ajanta, Elora, Karli and Aurangabad cave-temples. Huge fantastic sculptures makes renaissance look pale — six-handed Kali goddesses with strings of skulls murdering buffalo demons, dancing on dead gods, Vishnu in dwarf incarnation doing the cosmic can can, elephant head Ganesha my favorite — Indian businessmen reverence him the most, with his four arms and fat belly and snake belt and trunk in a bowl full of sweets, his body in this realm, his head an elephant's because it's beyond being and non-being, he's the only god that can destroy demons because he doesn't exist, the demons take one look at him and realize the game's up, they don't exist either. His vehicle he rides on is a rat, to show how slyly he slips in and out of existence and non-existence and being and not being and all them places like that. They even make movies about him — Indian mythological movies the most, outclass *Wizard of Oz*, all sorts of magic with gods kalpa science fiction. Also met Jains and Zoroastrians here. The Jains have weirdest cosmography of anyone — the universe is a big dream machine that repeats itself exactly and no one can get out — Hindus, Jains, etc. all agree we are now in the Kali Yuga, the lowest and beatest part of the cosmic cycle, where things get thicker and eviler and finally everybody will be four feet tall living in caves forgot about fire even — then the whole cycle slowly start up again. Actually a few "Thirthankaras" got free but the last died long ago and the nature of things is hardly anyone gets out — still a living tradition for Jain super-saints to starve themselves to death on fixed date, so as to get out of the universe and float above it like a pure free bubble of nothing bliss. But they have to have permission from their guru to take this step. Most of the other Jains are jewelers.

The Parsi sect are old Zoroastrian fireworshippers I'm not sure about their universe, but when they die they take the bodies to Tower of Silence and vultures eat the corpse in five minutes. This is their big serious funeral custom. Actually everybody here is on big science fiction cosmos spiritual kicks. A really great stockbroker I spent all day with yesterday — his kick is Bachti, Bakti — a yoga of devotion. He worships Krishna as his own child. His wife and he spend hours with statue of baby Krishna every day, bathing it, giving it food, taking it to bathroom, covering it at night, playing tops with it, pushing it on swing — they have whole centuries old little swings and tops and all them plaything jazz — by means of which meditation and play and attention he says he gets his mental rocks off and finally merges himself in love with Krishna thru this ritual and gets cosmic vibrations — a very funny fat fellow — carries flowers around all day — flower petals, and hands out handfuls to everybody for kicks — and he's just a normal middle class businessman who follows just one of many traditional cults — everybody follows one or another or a couple — Peter and I are hooked on Ganesha — it's a big happy game, like a Walt Disney religion, Hinduism, almost funnier than Buddhism which is real seriously atheistic, and solemn. The people we stay with follow Krishnamurti who preaches <u>no</u> sadhana (no discipline path) — (no tops no goya no thoughts no attempt to get enlightened) — There's a big classical School of Droop for almost any kick you intuit, with huge histories and saints and legends. Finally they all say you can't trust anyone but your own heart, 's what it all boils down to.

OK — Later

Allen

May 22, 1962: Lawrence Ferlinghetti in San Francisco to Allen Ginsberg in Bombay, India

Cher Allen . . .

So I am just back from staying with Creeley in Albuquerque (where he arranged big reading for me at University of New Mexico), Taos, Las Cruces, and then Mexico. I got the usual touristas in Chihuahua and Topolobampo and was considering sending you some of my bones from there but then I recovered and made it back. Reason I took off was mainly to write big play, *Meat Unlimited*, which was coming along fine until the diarrhea laid me low-down. So things have piled up on the home front. (Actually I've been back over a week and sent your and Peter's notes on to [Richard] Newnham at Penguin in England by air, after they'd lain here only a day or two). You're right and Peter's right — why be in a book with those two versificators? I've still got Penguin's contract here and will hold it till I hear further from you, despite his urgings in the enclosed, which crossed yours . . . . Creeley moving to University of British Columbia for next year. As you probably know, his beautiful wife Bobbie[97] had a girl who was killed in a cave-in in the desert near Albuquerque this last Fall, a terrible tragedy, and I guess that's main reason they're moving . . . . It happens that Creeley's collected poems (*For Love*, Scribner's, 1962) just came out right after I wrote you about his poetry, so I now can see what you mean, and I do dig a lot of those short poems, altho I think maybe I am right, too. Anyway, Creeley is great person, so is Bobbie, beautiful Cherokee, and we had lovely time in Albuquerque and I hope to see more of him, sometime . . . .

Yup, I been Vancouver and stole [Malcolm] Lowry manuscript, plus some rare photos also coming out in *Selected Poems* (I had to go along with some selection by professor up there who sits on all Lowry manuscript, so selection is not exactly what I wanted but still very good (and about 100 pages). After I get this and the Bowles book out

97 Poet and musician Bobbie Louise Hawkins (b. 1930), was at one time married to Robert Creeley.

of the way, I'll get to your next one: during the summer . . . . Will also be getting to work more on the *Selected Artaud*; have been corresponding with Mme. Thévenin about it; so if you run into anyone who has other Artaud translations or interests, put them in touch, will you? (Nothing has come from LeRoi [Jones] by the way.) . . . . Max Weiss called while I was away and wants to do another record of my poetry, but will get him to do something about yours before I do anything more with him . . . . That's wonderful re. sending us statues. I've told McClure one's coming for him . . . .

Well, that sounds like a strange fascinating existence there and maybe you'll stay forever. There's no reason, except for Family, to ever come back. Very curious things are happening to this country. Flying from Tucson over LA to here, I saw it lying there like a big white rhinoceros whose horn is said to induce potency in males but doesn't . . . .

I'll see you one of these big days, maybe in India or France.

xxx

L.

June 26, 1962: Allen Ginsberg in Calcutta, India, to Lawrence Ferlinghetti in San Francisco

Larry Dearie: Typewriter being fixed.
I got back from a side trip several weeks to Darjeeling and Kalimpong and into Sikkim. I met refugee lamas of far out red hat [Buddhist] sect and made arrangement to live in Tibetan monastery later and take some instruction in magic practices from them and in return give them some mushrooms and mescaline for experiment. Really great opportunity to contact teachers of esoteric Tibetan tradition (for the first time in history outside of Tibet). [. . .]

There is no rush on my book, do that strictly at leisure. Do you really want to do it? I don't think it'll sell so great. *Kaddish* is not doing so great, I guess. I know you are not supposed to pay me mid-year royalties anymore. But if there is any practical way of sending a mid-year check please do so as I am going broke. I haven't figured next money move. I can write an article for *Playboy* — but not sure what I'll do for loot, yet. [. . .]

I'll be here for a year more, traveling — and then a year in Japan — and then back to states for a year — and then (finally) I wonder if I'll go to Russia and China. The Red countries is the one place I've really missed — part of a twentieth-century education I'm lacking.

I've started writing a lot but mostly bad loose poetry — a long diatribe on Laos, and a hymn to Kali — and have accumulated lots more on long politics poem — but nothing is finished — and I haven't settled long enuf to type out *South American Journals* for Auerhahn — so I won't have anything to publish till I get back or settle in Japan in one place for at least half a year — Now I don't write very well, that is, I feel need for some kind of basic change in composition as violent as cut-ups — but haven't found the way.

Have you thought again of printing Burroughs' collected South American letters? — They're all available in *Big Table*, *Kulchur* and *Floating Bear* — it would make a nice small prose book and it's all there in print now. [. . .]

Well, as I say I will come back to the U.S. as soon as finish my postgraduate course in the world scene — I'm just traveling to improve my education not to escape U.S.A. life which I enjoy, I'm not an expatriate.

There is lots of poetry here in India, classic and modern, all great — but very poor translations. I haven't located anyone who can assemble anything that would interest you yet. Bengal and Marathi poetry both are very live, also Tamil.

Love,
Allen

PS: The Lawrence poem[98] is very fine particularly the old portable and the six-line cycle at the end gets near naked, (expression great) (except last mistral bones is maybe too poetic).

---

98 A reference to Ferlinghetti's poem "The Man Who Rode Away," about D.H. Lawrence.

Ferlinghetti ended up sending the text of Ginsberg's next book to his typesetter while still trying to come up with a suitable title for it. Meanwhile, he was more than a bit irritated by Peter Orlovsky's criticism of his surrealist novel Her, *which had recently been published by New Directions. Peter had also told Lawrence that he wanted to publish his own book in India and sell it for a few pennies. Nothing ever came of that idea.*

July 1, 1962: Lawrence Ferlinghetti in San Francisco to Allen Ginsberg in Calcutta, India

Dear Allen . . .

Finally got around to sending your *Poems 1956-60—Bunch of Poems—Hiccup* off to Villiers, and it looks like it'll make a 100-page book, almost. It's being set in same type and style as *Howl* and *Kaddish*, natch, and we should have proofs by mid-August or September first. "Aether" enclosed since there were quite a few little questions of spelling (mostly) which I wasn't sure about. Generally the manuscript of this poem is in rougher shape than any of the others, and I figure you might as well be the one to straighten it for printer. So let me have it back as soon as you can . . . . (Word "aether" spelled two ways, etc.) Title I thought of for the whole book: *Alba*. How about it? Or give me better one. That *Bunch of Perms* is a little flat. How about:

ALBA
1956-1960
*Allen Ginsberg

PETER, I receive your epistle of June 10 and have sent [Richard] Newnham back his empty contraceptive, unsigned, unfilled . . . . Thanks for the insults to my book *Her*, but I am as used to same as any Edward Dahlberg always professes to be, having recently received worse put-downs from Corso, among others, not to mention earlier ones from most of the mob who consider me a business man with a loose pen and very drooly. I am also put down very subtly in Jack's new

Big Sur but am not mad at him just shaking my head a little and who cares I've gotten such draggy reviews and remarks of miscomprehension about my last book of poetry, *Starting From San Francisco*, that I aim to shut up for some years and not publish anything in the way of poetry, and in fact have written nothing but plays since last October, and may never publish anything but plays anyway being completely bugged with the whole petty "poetry scene" in the U.S. . . . . Peter, yes please send me all the copies of your India book of poems that you can spare me, and I will gladly sell them and send them all over for you at whatever price you want: 8 ¢ each, fine . . . . If you want to put the City Lights sign and symbol on book, OK, since you know that for longtime I have been turned onto your poetry and wanted to publish it. If you need cash to pay printer let me know, and I'll send same. I don't want and never have wanted to make any $ pimping poetry around the country, and have tried to give Allen everything not used for paying expenses, but if you insist on still thinking of me that way, oh well . . . . ferk it . . . .

ALLEN . . . . Hey! Your two statues from India just arrived and are now sitting on my mantel and I will give McClure one, like you said. They are both beautiful and I am having a hard-on trying to decide which one to give Mc . . . . Holy Smokes, as me brudder used to say, they're on fire, and I thank you, that was a beautiful thing to do
. . . .

> Well let me hear,
> I hope you send
> Peter's book
> love and flowers
> Lawrence

Dear Larry:

Our letters must have crossed in the mails. I got your July 1 sad letter today, and had written you one on June 27 or something, so you can see even without your saying anything I did hold your hands and look in your eyes soulfully and said I liked D.H. Lawrence poem and told you about Jyoti Datta Bengali poet who also said how nice he liked your poetry and said you should send him your books. I don't consider you a business man honey (I'm full of chandul — opium — we just got back from the Chinese den here). Larry, I do "consider" you a poet and I do and always have I admit complained about your loose pen but I wouldn't complain to you about it if I didn't think you were fine enough to complain to and your poetry solid enough to complain about non-solid frills in it. Don't feel so bad! Remember, Gregory is a narcissistic put-down artist and he doth exaggerate his put-downs — i.e. for instance he was putting down Peter and telling him he was no poet and should stop writing poetry forever and accept position as my prat-boy and weak sister friend. And that sure bugged Peter because Gregory was drunk and absolutely serious. At the time. Actually however Gregory changed his mind as usual a few weeks later. He (Gregory) just claims the right to put people down occasionally to preserve his own independence and let off some steamy insight in usually exasperating and momentarily unfair manner. He do it to Jack too, and Burroughs and (rarely) me (because I got him by the balls in some other way, like hold his head and dry his tears when he gets hysterical like when we all arrived on Tangier dock last year and his passport had expired and they wouldn't let him off the boat for forty-eight hours.) So that's Gregory, neither take him seriously nor don't take him seriously.

Not seen Jack's *Big Sur* — is it out??? But remember he puts almost everyone down in kind of crude subtle way, including me and Peter. I mean, the pictures he paints of me in *Town and City*, *Subter-*

raneans, Dharma Bums, etc. is actually sort of a creepy image and sometimes I got quite bugged, except I figure (by insight and hindsight, too) that there's a basic sympathetic intention underneath and some real insight ("Ginsberg, you're nothing but a hairy loss," he said to me three years ago looking up from my kitchen floor drunk) — so God knows what kind of good time Charlie lost Denny Dimwit[99] he saw you as — but it isn't, like, a sophisticated coterie type exclusion hatchet — it's strictly Jack's own genius — grotesquerie, home made in his mama's attic. Probably it's actually funny.

Jack seems to save his full range of understanding sympathy for the few heroic hero-worship loves he has — That is, the only people he pictures in full 3-D as human round heroes are I think Neal, Burroughs occasionally, his father and mother, (himself less directly) — Gary almost — one or two Huncke others — the subsidiary characters he generally treats with rough impressionist sketches, almost caricatures — including myself and others close to him. You too, I guess. It bugged me at first but after all it's only a novel and, alright, his main energy and reality goes to his obsessive hero, he hardly has one now? I am always so amazed and gratified he has the power and energy to be recording angel of so much detail of the last two decades' seasons — more work and drive and inspiration than I have summed up in my couple books of poems — that I don't feel right to be mad at him he hasn't seen me thru my eyes, or you thru yours, or make completer pictures of everybody — he done what he could do — with all his own needs and inner crazy — and that, when I read his books (the sum of them) seems so much, that the faults seem inevitable. I mean at times I was bugged, he didn't treat me right. Tho some characters do catch him eternally, like Huncke. Anyway I just mean, don't be bugged, there is no lasting ill here. *Starting from San Francisco* either you never mentioned or I never noticed. I didn't know you have a new book poems, please send us and we'll send you big letters of criticisms. I don't want you should stop writing or shut up poesy and neither does Peter. I think maybe it's the too closed in local literary atmosphere that's putting you

---

99 A cartoon character.

down so low in soul — it bugged me in San Francisco last time, it's a local malady and not too serious tho, it's like a cold, persistent and unobtrusive. Whether Rexroth is being sympathetic or obtuse, whether Duncan, etc., or letters from afar are being understanding or shitty. So don't feel bad — well anyway, you know all that. I should have written you more seriously line by line about your poems (as I almost did D.H. Lawrence [poem]) but it seemed to me your intention was to be hazy-sloppy (as in Fidel Castro poem[100]) and so no point detailing what you know already, since you did not mean for each line to be perfect poesy, or try to be at least.

What occurs to me is that you're more perfect as poet when you're nearer the bone pessimistic, than when you are being wiggy and hopeful and social-anarchist-revolutionary-lyrical-optimistic. So maybe you should write now some strictly private and anti-social melancholy poems. Anyway that always struck me as your natural vein, that and a kind of empathy-nakedness which is rare.

The solidest element I always thought was apt precise images like the classical butterfly in and out of open boxcar door or the naked objects at the end of the Lawrence poem — rather than puns or ironic references to [John Foster] Dulles. And that the pattern of the lines should be arranging themselves into intuitive shapes, as end of DH Lawrence poem. Well anyway. This is all opium — diarrhea. Glad you got the statues. You want more? They're only three or four dollars each and another two bucks to ship. For twenty or forty dollars I could get you some big snazzy Kalis or Yab-Yums.

I'll work on "Aether" and send it in a week. Yes, *Bunch of Poems*, *Hiccup*, all too flat. I don't dig *Alba* either, because one little stinky poem is "Alba" the whole book isn't. It's actually a decade of poems. I'll come up with something yet. I wish it was *Red Cats*, like that.

Peter doesn't think of you like that, re the 8¢ edition, he wasn't talking about you, was he? You're getting (very gently and tenderly) paranoiac just like you said. It's only he has this ice cream cone price on his mind for years, so I guess it must be that way and it's obviously

---

100 A reference to Ferlinghetti's poem "1000 Fearful Words for Fidel Castro."

got no shade of bug at you since you physically can't print an 8¢ book any moron knows that. [. . .]

That's that. But aside from that, since I turned down Knopf and Penguin offers, you can't entertain the thought that I (and Peter) think of you as $ pimping poesy! Banish the thought, Chairman of the Board, and full speed ahead! San Francisco must really be bugging you. Or is it babyshit all over your living room floor? What's baby doing? Is it any good?

> Enough, enough,
> goodnight, love
> always
> Allen

July 17, 1962: Lawrence Ferlinghetti in San Francisco to Allen Ginsberg and Peter Orlovsky in Calcutta, India

Dear Peter and Allen . . . .
Got all your letters . . . . Wonderful letters . . . . First I've got some unusual recent happenings here to report: Kirby just gave birth to a 6-lb (8 ¼ month) bow-legged baby boy; it turns out his name is Lorenzo. (First thing he say upon coming out is, "Tell them poets in India." I say, "Would he like to send a card back to where he came from to tell he arrive here OK." He say, "That's all taken care of." He look very serious, hasn't smiled yet; seems to be considering the existential situation; and will let me know his conclusions.) Mother-in-law arrive same day as baby. In a few days I'm going to Bix Sur cabin with Lew Welch to get out of sight for a couple of weeks [. . .]

Lowry and *Red Cats* books[101] will be here in three weeks or so, and I'll send them on to you . . . . Your new book manuscript was sent to Villiers by surface mail about one month ago, so he should have it just about now, and, since I wanted it to be same in appearance, feel-

---

101 These books were issued as *Selected Poems of Malcolm Lowry* (1962) and *Red Cats* (1962).

154

ing, type, etc., as other two books, I told them definitely to go ahead with job, with title and "Aether" poem to be sent later. I don't think it will come to 100 pages (probably 80 will do it, depending on length of "Aether") and I will make the price on it as low as possible, not more than $1, maybe 95¢. I would like to hear Indian prices for future use nevertheless. How 'bout some prose from your Indian travels, to be printed there for us? You design it, etc. . . . any way you like . . . . Advantage of doing third book with Villiers is that we can then put all three books together sometime, if you ever wanted to do that.

Penguin deal is all off, but have sent [Richard] Newnham packet of fifteen books as you suggested . . . . Hope Peter will go ahead and print up his book there, as a City Lights book or otherwise, and I would be happy to send you loot to cover printing, etc, make whatever arrangements you want, and send me lots of the books. Why not now? . . . . I'll let you know Villiers price on your book anyway. Very nice of you to say you would take less royalties if I'm not getting my share, but don't worry about that, will continue as-is; since our publishing is tied to bookstore, and I draw $200 a month from the bookstore regularly to live on, I suppose I am getting something from the poetry, and I got an elegant Victorian bourgeois palace on Potrero [Hill] as you know, and a jeep and a cabin and a mother-in-law buying us things and so am far from shivering with hunger in Cuzco. [. . .]

Am glad to get your reassurances that you ain't considering me as poetry-pimpernel since I can see I have the usual poet's paranoia, and I guess my last letter was an offshoot of the draggy scene here which you also know too well, everything so petty and jealous and ingrown, and then Gregory bugging me on top of that. Well, Jack's new book is very sad, it makes you weep, when you see thru it; yes, it's out now, and there's probably a copy in the mails to you from him somewhere. (As you know? Jack has taken off for Europe.) And naturally I was paranoid about what he thought about me own poetry since I had never heard you say a word about it, which is a bad sign maybe, and so forth, well, OK, that's real good and true now, I know how you feel, and some real hard criticism is much better than the usual misleading hypocrisies or well-meaning compliments, as you know of course. I'm still working on the D.H. Lawrence poem. You've got to hear me read it aloud. You sure got the end straight: that "naked" statement is just what I was after. [. . .]

I finally chose the Shiva in the circle and gave Mike [McClure] the other. (I suppose I took the one which in India is like having Van Gogh's *Bridge at Arles* on the wall?) But it's beautiful crazy figure, I've got it on mantel. . . . I still like "Alba." Would it fit if "Aether" poem were left out of book? (But I really want that "Aether" poem!) But see what other title you can come with . . . . *Hiccup* is maybe best yet . . . . Egad I've really covered the wateryfront with this little note, so I'll see you in India one of these years. I'm figuring round world trip to France, maybe West from here next early Spring. Hope yer still there. Will leave note on kitchen table. Gone to India . . . .

> Green summer
> thoughts —
> Lawrence

At the last minute, when Ginsberg received the proofs, he thought of the title that would be used for his third City Lights book. In the meantime Penguin had now suggested Gregory Corso as one of the two poets to include with Ginsberg in their much-discussed anthology.

August 27, 1962: Allen Ginsberg in Calcutta, India, to Lawrence Ferlinghetti in San Francisco

Dear Larry:
Just a fast note. I received your long letter, also got the proofs and "Aether." I've finished proof corrections and am cutting down "Aether" a bit and should be finished by end of this week and will send it all together.

"Aether" is title of the poem but it's spelt properly ether the gas used medically in the poem. Whole title of book is now definitely *Reality Sandwiches*, from one of the poems, and says what the book is, not a full dinner and it's funny. Enough. "Alba" is too serious and others too too silly. *Tasty Scribbles* was a nice one, but I used the word scribbles too oft in the book already. *Vomit* is another title I'm saving for long politics book. Oral poesy with oral titles. Tasty vomit sandwiches. [. . .]

Penguin offer sounds good, I try contact Gregory see if he free to come in, if not mebbe [Philip] Lamantia or McClure who aren't much circulated in England. I just hope he not use any bad English imitation beatnik poesy, I'll write him and when plans made resume contact thru you. What English poet is good? Are those Denise Levertov recommends in *Kulchur* readable??? No?

I'm having good time with proofs, the book more pleasing than I remembered it. OK I'll send rest later this week.

As ever,
Allen

Among other publication projects, Ferlinghetti began working on the manuscript of Neal Cassady's autobiography, The First Third. *It would not be published in Neal's lifetime. At the time of this letter, Neal was working as an automotive tire recapper, a job that made Lawrence think of Vulcan at his forge.*

September 5, 1962: Lawrence Ferlinghetti in San Francisco to Allen Ginsberg in Calcutta, India

Dear Allen . . . .
[. . .] I got original *First Third* manuscript from Neal [Cassady] in Los Gatos after [Philip] Whalen found it in trunk and gave it back to him. I went, found Neal Vulcan at work in steaming recapping plant striding around like Bunyan in a forge of fireworks, and so now I'll publish it in toto if he'll let me . . . . Also Burroughs says OK for *Yage Letters* only having trouble finding copies of letters in *Floating Bear* and *Kulchur* (Have *Big Table* with letter) but will write New York soon for other . . . . Also have Jack Hirschman editing big Artaud book

and heard from [Paule] Thévenin who was rather upset by your letter thinking she wanted money for job, etc. She says she has "nothing to do" with permissions. Am also considering Michaux' *Miserable Miracle* (Mescaline) translation by Louise Varèse and may do it jointly with New Directions (Anaïs Nin sent it to me); Also maybe McClure's *Meat Science Essays* which he wrote you about; Also maybe reprint of Pound-Fenellosa *Essay on Chinese Written Character* maybe together with an attack on it by Yale sinolog. Also some kind of small edition of Kay Johnson's *Human Songs*; also maybe Hemingway's *Spanish Civil War Dispatches* out of print since 1930's, <u>if</u> I can get permission, tho I'm sure some New York publisher will steal idea (Hirschman found dispatches in *Kenyon Review* mags of 1938). So those are the books, along with yours, for next year — by next year this time, by which time I hope to be in Europe for some time . . . . Whew.

Later and Later
— L

September 19, 1962: Allen Ginsberg in Calcutta, India, to Lawrence Ferlinghetti in San Francisco

Dear Larry:
[. . .] Re Neal's *First Third*. See that piece that Whalen had in deposit, was the first scratchy writings, the real explosion was huge letter he sent to Kerouac which continued the story in personal exposition that turned Jack Kerouac on to his own possibilities of writing feverish personal narrative. The letter was lost by Gerd Stern the hipcat from across the bay[102] — I gave him once Jack's *Visions of Neal*, Neal's manuscript Burroughs South American letters and *Empty Mirror* because he said he was reading manuscript for a KPFA magazine. Well he put down everything but Neal's manuscript. And when he returned everything, Neal's manuscript was missing and he said he don't know what happened to it. What does remaining manuscript look like, is it

---

102 See earlier footnote (pg. 62) on the "Joan Anderson Letter."

interesting reading? If it is by all means publish it and is Neal in any state or mood to continue or edit — a lot of it was in handwrit notes and fragments, what? Jack would likely write preface. [. . .]

I hope it is feasible to do *Miserable Miracle*, I think it's great reading. Say have you been smoking pot? I get that impression from your book *Starting from San Francisco* — well there's a surprising underlying empty disillusion death angst, with horses fur windows and vomit, landscapes, that kind of drugged horrors, vibration that's been killing people the last couple years, certainly brought me down, surprising to find in your otherwise formerly optimistical work, seems in fact the main theme comes thru underneath San Francisco book that makes it serious if its got YOU too help! Yet it's inevitable step forward thru Blake's Gates of Wrath:

> To find the western path
> Right thru the gates of wrath
> I urge my way
> Sweet morning leads me on
> With soft repentant moan
> I see the break of day
> The war of sign and spears
> Melted by dewy tears
> Exhales on high
> And with soft grateful tears
> The sun is freed from fears
> Ascends the sky[103]

Or something like that. The clouds seem to have gone from over my own head of last year and half, partly it was working on the proofs and getting back to poetry again that did it, partly seeing in aether that I had been straining my brain beyond its capacity, to include blackout-death-unconsciousness, the brain is not built to function in. Said Carl Solomon: "I have a small mind and mean to use it."

---

103 Quoted from "Daybreak, " a poem by William Blake.

159

The poetry in *Starting From San Francisco* is still I say too loose, what you are best is:

> One telephone wire
> And one single iron road
> Hung to the tracks as by magnets
> Attached to a single endless fence, etc.

With its concrete visual detail, but not:

> Onward?
> Back and forth across the continent
> Bang bang
> By any wheel or horse
> Any rail
> By car
> By buggy

etc. There are seven lines where the bang bang tricks are minor and there's no poesy picture composition and I read most of your lines are loose like that — relaxed yes like speech, but that's not enough to make someone come back in 100 years to look thru your optics see what you saw — it's editorial prose "back in the beginning again, no people yet," lines like that aren't dense enough, despite their goodwill. Well sure I do that myself too much, that's what's wrong with me when I write. Only when the editorial prosaic is a sudden dramatic emergency statement can it serve as an image but half the book is editorial prosaic. One way out of that trap, what I am doing now, is blue penciling the fat, prosaic, articles, preposition, and so forths, and superimposing the different thin lines on one another so the key words at least make a poetry — i.e. "His dream was a mouthful of white prick that trembled in his head" is superimposed to "dream mouthfuls of white prick trembling in his head" and that's more Shakespearean. Kerouackian, too.

God forgotten Hudson burns
Indian autumn Saugerties Cocksackie
Trees fall leaves turning loam
Yellow god multitudes
Wood rake the streets
Leaves curl eternity
The same leaves burn again
White stallion pees in a red field

Well, that's superimposing a bit too far, yet you see, you can ex-
tract the vital words or phrases from the composition and combine
them to higher intensity somehow — this is not CUT UP so much
as it is normal concentration — I learnt it from Gregory tho it's what
I did to get hydrogen jukeboxes in *Howl* — origin was something
like: "Listening to the roar of hydrogen bombs | In their heads, while
the jukebox blasted its crack doom." Or something longwinded, boilt
down to: "Listening to the crack of doom on the hydrogen jukebox."
Though after some practice the mind automatically composes at first
draft with such shorthand. That's what Bill has learnt from cut-ups, to
compose with new concentrate strange ear. But requires to be merci-
less to own writings.

As I approach the state of pure Euphoria
Large size typewriter cases carry my underwear
...
moon hides in the rice of Chinese Painting
afternoon thunder can't sleep??
Summer attempts to play saxophone

Well, I'm only making hints to concentration, it loses some of the
relaxed sense but gains a little urgency, *but* it is the main problem of
your poetry, isn't it?

Peter not done nothing on his book yet, the lazy bastard smokes
opium and dreams instead. Soon maybe.

Hastily,
Allen

P.S.: Yes, certainly I'll write note preface anything for McClure if he thinks I'm competent to, send me a copy of *Meat Science*, I think he's further out courage guts than I am in his psychophysical COLD COLD COLD universes — I'm back in human body writing verse this month — so it may be presumptuous of me to write prefaces for his explosions — But if he thinks it makes sense I'll be glad.

September 27, 1962: Lawrence Ferlinghetti in San Francisco to Allen Ginsberg in Calcutta, India

Chers copains . . .

[. . .] Everything you say about my poetry is true altho you must realize that in my broadsides I was not trying to write the same kind of poetry you have in mind nor the same kind as I tried to write in "Hidden Door" (which somewhat employs the technique and method you describe.) And that long poem "Starting From San Francisco" was also not supposed to be anything but long relaxed line, tho I do agree I've overdone that by now and have already turned to more surreal compression actually somewhat like I was writing in prose years ago before *Her* (which is old spew book writ in 1948-49) . . . . Yes, and that "Big Fat Hairy Vision of Evil" was written on horrible pot-hangover in the Village last year. And after that once I had strange pot look at [Michael] McClure and Joanna [McClure][104] as beautiful reptilian animals posed together but I never got a poem out of that. I think also in my "Euphoria" poem, by the way, some of that same New York pot vision crept in and I certainly have surreal juxtaposition there. So these poems aren't to be compared in the same class with the admittedly propaganda scenes at end of book etc . . . . Now I'm on nothing but plays, have written five since last October: *Soldiers of No Country, Three Thousand Red Ants, The Alligation [sic], Light Bulbs,* and *Motherlode* . . . . in the last one, everything happens on a nude leg.

---

104 Joanna McClure (b. 1930), a poet who was at one time married to poet Michael McClure.

October 8, 1962: Allen Ginsberg in Calcutta, India, to Lawrence
Ferlinghetti in San Francisco

Dear Larry:

Speaking of big fat hairy visions, this weekend is Kali worship holi-
days, big paper mache statues of Durga a ten armed beauty (one version of Kali who kills the big bad buffalo demon) all over Calcutta in
big tents, in the evening people come out and make noise and bang
gongs and worship her, it's their Xmas, everybody gets presents — last
night I went out to the Kali temple burning ghats and sat around
with saffron robed sadhus smoking ganja in their private pipes in the
alcoves of the temple, and lazed around in nearby park looking at stars
and they singing bajans (classical holy songs to Kali and Durga and
Maya) and then I got up and like in big teahead dream walked thru
the ghats to see piles of logs burning new-dead corpses — attendants
pushing the shoulder and head bust part of an elderly businessman
who wasn't completely burned yet, pushing his bust over dripping with
fat into the center of the fire, I saw, anyway, there wasn't anybody inside
that head, nothing but an empty bottle or a sofa or a pillow as Ra-
makrishna 19th century saint remarked — very beautiful scene, young
teenagers in new pajamas or western pants strolling hand in hand thru
the temple past the funerary pyres and smoke of their grandfathers
wafting into the trees and they walking by solemn but unperturbed —
in fact the duty of eldest son here is to see his father's corpse is properly
laid out in woodpile and apply the first burning coals to the lips of the
corpsed loved-one. Anyway it's a really crazy place to get high, and
strangely it's the classical social place to get high — gangs of friends
come out regularly Tuesday and Saturday evenings with leaves full of
flowers and incense and special ganja and sit on ground lifting pipes
to sky shouting "Boom Boom Mahadeva!" before taking great cloudy
draughts of cannabis — all the while smoke of corpses rolling over
their heads at Ganges side and they laughing and playing drums and
serenading Maya illusion. Going out again tonight second nite Durga

Puja[105] see the ghats on other side of town where a lot of red robed tantrik practitioners hang out.

Enclosed another poem ["The Names"] to be put in 1957 place in *Reality Sandwiches*, I'm also sending copy to Neal and others in New York as I need permission to print as such, so don't send it to Villiers until I write you OK, yes? If it makes the book too long, can remove some short no account poems like "Squeal" and "Wrote This Last Nite," etc. This poem posed so many personal difficulties with people's names I never published it but anyhoo I changed some names and scenes in it now so may pass, but have to hear OK first. As usual, justify align right-hand margin, aligned (align is the right word) (finally). I had hid this, but Frank O'Hara saw and said to publish why not?

Re: Neal's manuscript. We tried to get him to write more years ago, maybe now. However the tortuous later style I did find interesting — don't remember the passage you object to but worried maybe you throw out some interesting prose twists? See he may not be sure. The Jack letter was very complicated sentences, that's what was so innaresting. Can't say at this distance. [. . .]

Love,
Allen

In October, Penguin's editor Anthony Godwin visited Ferlinghetti in San Francisco to continue discussing which three poets should make up the Penguin anthology. Suggestions multiplied. Ferlinghetti thought that combining a single British poet with Ginsberg and Corso would not make a balanced book, and he suggested Philip Lamantia as the third. Godwin believed that Ferlinghetti himself would be a better choice. Ginsberg did not think much of that idea and suggested that they include Kerouac's poetry instead.

---

105 Durga Puja, a Hindu festival in honor of the goddess Durga.

October 16, 1962: Lawrence Ferlinghetti in San Francisco to Allen
Ginsberg in Calcutta, India

Dear Allen —
[. . .] By all means, write direct to Anthony Godwin; Chief Editor
of Penguin in England, and persuade him to take Jack. I suggested
Jack after I suggested Lamantia — trust you got my note on it by
now — (You got to read Lamantia's new *Destroyed Works* to see why
I think he should be in there). [Richard] Newnham is only a leg man
for Godwin, so write to the Chief. He didn't dig Lamantia at all and
didn't go for Jack either, but you can persuade him. I'd rather make my
own scene anyway, as I mostly have in the past. I don't like anthologies
anyway. Tell Godwin all this, if you like. I'll be writing him anyway
. . . . OK?

xxx
— Larry

November 2, 1962: Allen Ginsberg in Calcutta, India, to Lawrence
Ferlinghetti in San Francisco

Dear Larry:
Got all your letters. First, Penguin. While Godwin was with you in
San Francisco, I was involved in three-way correspondence with Kerouac and [Richard] Newnham, which appeared to be going OK. Then,
simultaneously, Gregory wrote a Gregory letter to Newnham (not having heard from them only from me) saying they should print Ferlinghetti Ginsberg Kerouac or Ginsberg Jarrell Corso or not print Corso,
or something. I don't know what he wrote (he must have been very
flowery). Newnham instantly wrote him, Fine, Ferlinghetti Ginsberg
Kerouac. Gregory apparently opened his mouth and put his asshole in
it again. So he now writing me complaining letters saying don't be mad
at him he goofed, and anyway Kerouac is prose writer not poet, and
anyway he really wants to be in book, and he only wrote them because
he didn't hear from them, and why they hate him? etc. I finally wrote

Newnham/Godwin an airletter last week, saying, my own preference was for Corso, me and Kerouac; gave reasons for re-including Corso — mainly the "high quality" of his poetry; explained the whole business of personal relations made it difficult to judge and assert preferences, but I was interested in putting up a solid wall of spontaneous modern non-transient poesy, that much of your work (as 1000 Castros) ["One Thousand Fearful Words for Fidel Castro"] was deliberately statement with some sacrifice of Tinkle Poesy. Then I left decision up to them and said I'd go along whatever. I also quoted your letter saying it would be alright by you if I objected. So now it's in their lap. Unseemly mess, me screaming for months like prima donna who should be in book, Gregory yakking and yakking. Anyway I said what I thought had to be said and now let them worry, I've already written about fifteen letters hither and thither trying to arrange things right by my lights, I won't intrude no more. I'm waiting to hear from them. [. . .]

OK — later
Allen

November 15, 1962: Lawrence Ferlinghetti in San Francisco to Allen Ginsberg in Calcutta, India

Dear Allen
[. . .] Well, anyway, being a publishing genius and the ghost of Maxwell Perkins to boot, I have just been prodded by your India description to start another *Journal* which I have been considering for a long time, (and publish your description in it, along with anything else you send, and also publish that beautiful Weekly Manifesto of Hungry Generation of India[106] which you enclosed in letter — Can I publish yours and will Chatterjee give me permission to publish his?) and this here new *Journal* would be a big annual and be called *City Lights' Journal* or rather:

---

106 The Hungry Generation was the Indian equivalent of the American Beat Generation group.

and I will be sole editor since to work with any others never works out for lone dog me (like with Meltzer and McClure it was a continual hassle over every object and I ended up doing all the "production" anyway) and it won't have any connection with *Journal for the Protection of All Beans* but I've been on the verge of this for some time since now there is <u>simply nowhere</u> to publish except little magazines (which this won't be) (and *Evergreen* is soul-less — that slick hard format with those brittle subscription cards always bound in, etc.) and there's still a real place for a big review with very wide catholic tastes (small c) as you know, and you can send me big scenes from Indian poets and hairy descriptions of India and I've already got a crazy collection for first issue, taking chapters from new books we're going to publish, for instance from *The First Third,* and from McClure's *Meat Science Essays* which we are going ahead with. (He decided, by the way, not to have any other poets' comments or intros in book, altho we will include "editor's note" from me saying I violently disagree with practically everything he says in essays). And also a chapter from Michaux' *Miserable Miracle* which I've finally gotten the rights to (received some goofy little notes from Michaux in the course of all that) and so pass the word around and get poets to send stuff and not just poetry (in fact I figure *Journal* will be only one fourth poetry) and I'll plan to get first issue out this Spring before I take off for East, maybe around May . . . .

So I am sending you by boat the photocopy of *First Third* for you to go over and let me know what you think can be done with it — Neal has sent me signed contract, but something or other has to be done to [at] least pages 82 to 118 — you'll see what I mean when you get copy — will send it out today — I don't think anybody here can ever get Neal to do anything with it anymore but maybe you or Jack still can . . . . This copy cost $20 to make so guard with care and return — Maybe I can get it out next winter . . . . You will note also that in 99% of the handwritten corrections to manuscript he has made the passage worse, and the original is better in practically every case [. . .]

So I too am not writing Penguin anymore — let them make up their own minders — (Funny, you mention "1000 Words for Fidel," and this is the one poem they said they wanted me to be sure to include! Otherwise I wouldn't put it in.) Anyway, as long as we've got them to make it non-British book, let them take it from there, and who cares . . . . No word from Villiers on your new *Reality* proofs but they should be along soon . . . .

Larry

An annual devoted to
journals, letters, graffiti,For
feverish personal narratives,
true poems and prose blasts, manifestos, signs and
drawings, strange thoughts and curious perceptions, visions and other realities
Number One: 1963

◄ 1963 ►

January 10, 1963: Allen Ginsberg in Benares, India, to Lawrence
Ferlinghetti in San Francisco

Dear Larry:

[. . .] Howrah Bridge in Calcutta, over Ganges, one of world's great
bridges — as you can see in photo Chaucerian masses of folk passing
over, and the whole way by the rails lined with beggars, lepers, toy
peddlers, magicians, monkey pipers, fortune tellers, dying septuage-
narians, card players, astrologers, glassware salesmen and loungers all
sitting squatted waiting waving their balloons, coolies with bales of
merchandise balanced on their heads trotting along — on the roadway,
trams, buses, bullock carts, herds of goats on way to slaughterhouse,
trucks, autos, rickshaws, stray cows, taxis, all the horns bleeping with
cow-sounds-honks — and underneath the bridge temples and bathing
ghats and a strange plaza where sadhus encamp in burlap tents, sing
and smoke ganja and meet devotees and meditate — also some in dirt
wrestlers platforms, bodybuilders in g-strings working out ancient Indian yoga bodybuilding — further on a little tree-landscaped concrete
promontory over the water for cross-legged sitting meditation listening to the vast OM roar overhead on the steel bridge — and a dirt path
for massage boys and midnite sleepers under the bridge roof — walk a
mile up river and then come the burning ghats. We took those photos
at dawn, coming back from Howrah Railroad Station, just got off train
from two week trip to Konarak and Bubanishwar temples 300 miles
south, walking back into city across bridge. [. . .]

I still not started typing *South American Journals* for Auerhahn,
it's a fucking cross on my back. Hope to begin here. I suppose it's only
a few weeks steady work once I settle down. Don't want to start any
other projects till I finish Auerhahn book; will send you page of that
when I have them. Dunno when. Not yet received *First Third*, that's
normal, takes two months, received Creeley's *For Love*, Lamantia *De-*

stroyed Works, McClure *Dark Brown* and Corso *Selected Poems* from England — great harvest. Lamantia still has more poems even than *Destroyed Works*, I've seen manuscript. Could you get book from him? [. . .]

Later,
Allen

P.S. Moved here to Benares a month ago, settled in great room with nine French doors overlooking market and Ganges bank bathing ghat, balconies we can stare down on cows fighting with vegetable women, cows rush up to baskets of spinach and radishes and sneak a mouthful of greens, women squatting on street with their baskets chase cows away with stick — cows attack old ladies garlanded with flowers coming from temple, grab the flowers to munch — same cows and same ladies morning after morning like a repeated comedy — nobody gets mad for more than a minute — cows put heads together and plan new attack on baskets every ten minutes — Anyway, we settled here, and then with air mattresses and blankets took off overnight train ride to Agra for Xmas — Spent Xmas eve and day and nite and next days inside Taj Mahal — death anniversary of the Lady of the Taj wife of great Emperor Shahjehan 17th century. Those two nites the hereditary Moslem caretakers leave the doors open and invite friends to sleep over and hold big Kawali (poetry singing, improvised) contest under the great arch to the tomb — Moslems in fur caps cross-legged on rugs singing into microphone, capping and cutting each other with big dirty rose-pun lyrics in Urdu — slapping each other's thighs to mark the beat — we slept inside the Taj, most perfect hotel in universe — The place is sublime — I was amazed like a heavenly de Chirico painting — worth coming to India to see just that — I hadn't realized and thought it was just a picture postcard — Turns out it's a giant Martian Vibration Eternity Dome — The greatest human creation on the planet — We lived in it and stared at it for days — plenty ganja also improves the sensation — The place is mysterious — so vast in perfect symmetry it's like seeing two halves of mirror image from afar — up close each detail jeweled and perfect so any way you approach it you see something intelligent — The man who dreamt it up and got it put down in matter and stone must've been a great soul — He also planned a mirror image of Taj in <u>black</u> marble on the other side of the river — connected by a golden bridge — They locked him up in booby hatch finally — but that he got so far and got the Taj built's a miracle. Then, we went lived in abandoned Mogul City Fathepur Sikri 23 miles away — then a week in Mathura and Brindeban, home place of Krishna, center of Bhakti (love devotion) yoga cults in India — met some saints — came back here and found a month's mail — but as I say no proofs, of *Reality Sandwiches.*

January 24, 1963: Allen Ginsberg in Benares, India, to Lawrence Ferlinghetti In San Francisco

Dear Larry:
[. . .] Received Neal's manuscript and Peter and I read it. I'm in favor [of] publishing it too; at least the evidence of his kind of thinking process and prose (which he later developed more naturally in long letter to Jack sequel to *First Third* which is lost) is there. The thing I'm thinking about especially begins in the long sentence on p. 56 ending in total recall of the Daniels and Fischer clock face — that's where the style's discovered. The whole manuscript really begins to swing on page 50 where he begins with himself "For a long time I held a unique position," etc. [. . .]

The part that bothers me is the beginning, pre-history of family until page 50. Part about Neal's father and barber Schwartz is OK, and some ship jumping anecdotes are interesting — tho not as naturally written as later personal recollections — but the opening pages of family detail are tedious and stiffly written. Book could begin on page 50. Or could include the best of preliminary long family anecdotes.

I don't see any way I could edit it here much less rewrite it, partly because inability to tackle such job (as same inability to jobs my own journals). Still I'd try, for love of Neal; but I still can't read all the scrawls in this copy anyway. Carolyn [Cassady][107] could possibly retype manuscript to include the penciled additions; that might not be hard. The job of editing out the early (and later boring) family statistics is I guess something I might try, but I don't think I could do it here. [. . .]

OK, love
Allen

February 17, 1963: Lawrence Ferlinghetti in San Francisco to Allen Ginsberg in Benares, India

Dear Allen . . . .

New set of page proofs sent airmail first class to you from here on the 13th of February You'll have to work without manuscript, but all should be straight by this stage. Villiers hung up waiting for them now with slack press, so the sooner the better. Send them airmail first class via me. Or if everything is straight without much correction, why don't you send them direct to John Sankey, Villiers Publications, London, England . . . .

Always got so much business business to settle with youse that I never have time to tell you things like how when Nanda [Pivano] was here we worked on her *Howl* translations and I insisted on all words being translated without watering-down. (She actually was going to leave out certain four-letters words, and I think I persuaded her they had to be in there, but you'd better tell her too.) Also I think I helped in getting her to directly transcribe/translate telegraphic sentences where words are strung together without connectives, etc: she was adding "of" and "and" and so forth between them, saying that that just wasn't done in Italian, and I told her it just wasn't done in English either, etc, etc . . . . She now writes upset about dirty article published in Feltrinelli magazine, *Il Verri*, in which they used complete "Supermarket in California" without permission, and I just wrote her that Mondadori, not Feltrinelli, has all your Italian rights, for both *Howl*

---

107 Carolyn Cassady (1923–2013), Neal Cassady's wife for many years.

and *Kaddish*, and so maybe she can get you some loot for Feltrinelli use, etc. etc . . . . From what I can read in the Italian article it's a pretty shitty put-down from the usual square grounds: a little like Lawrence Durrell's put-down of Beats . . . . only much stronger . . . . Who cares, at this stage of existence [. . .]

Re. Cassady and *Foist Turd*:::: My objection to last part was that the prose got more and more complicated and the whole things seemed to bog down more and more as he began to draw closer to the present. It just became harder to follow (for an "outsider" to follow anyway.) And I don't see that last part, after page 80 something, as becoming more like that feverish personal narrative poured out which you hint it is . . . . If you could get him to take the pages that do exist, and "read" it into a tape recorder with his own new additions or corrections, (natural in speech as he went along) you might be able to get the whole end juiced up in just the way you conceive of it . . . . Or get him just to talk about that same period into the recorder, and completely throw out the written part for that period. And also get him to come up closer to the present?

Cookoo. What next? Mass of letters from you. Will make up *Journal* next week and use "Fragments of Letters from Allen Ginsberg" with Gary's letter plus his photos of all of you, plus all kinds of other great stuff, including new *Yage* pages from Burroughs, ("I Am Dying Meester?") stuff from Paris, Mexico, Morocco; much better than *Journal for the Protection of All Beings*. Going to be fantastic, I think [. . .] Damn if that don't cover the works . . . Kirby sends love . . . .

BOW TIE
—Lawrence

February 28, 1963: Lawrence Ferlinghetti in San Francisco to Allen Ginsberg in Benares, India

Dear Allen . . . .
[. . .] I've just had big hassle here with printer I'd picked to do new *Journal*. Son-of-a-beach won't set and print the word Fuck or Fucking,

much less no assholes or shits. So took the whole job away and will take it to England with me and produce it at Villiers in person this Spring-Summer. Not only that, but the prices for anything on a press here are outrageous, considering the shitty aesthetic they work by and the soulless paper and cold type. So fuckem. If it weren't for having that there City Light Book rack, Kirby and I would live out of the country permanently. We both have had enough of "the whole evil" government scene and of provincial petty back-biting San Francisco especially. A real hick town, North Beach flooded with tourists brought there by the Beats with the local Chamberpot of Commerce running ads in the *New Yorker* showing picturesque Beatnik leaning on Grant Avenue lamppost; while at the same time San Francisco fuzz and local press (including Rex who is no longer wroth) spitting on same with sneers. And the original excitement of "San Francisco Renaissance" brought here by a bunch of New York carpetbaggers anyway. What I continue to hang around for, I'll never fathom. Maybe I'll move City Lights publishing to Paris and make like Girodias print-wise. And foist the bookstore on Shig for good. (The nut doesn't want to own anything. Nevertheless, last year I made him partner, and eventually he'll have all the bookstore part.) Well, what do you think of all that? Or am I to be stuck here forever, to carry on this here "institution"? [. . .]

Larry

March 15, 1963: Allen Ginsberg in Benares, India, to Lawrence Ferlinghetti in San Francisco

Dear Larry:
[. . .] Not wrote songs of India egad. I've written a lot; publishing ten pages of scattered journal writing with Bengali Hungry Gents; *Esquire* lady editor here to do story on me and Peter in Benares saw same and asked for it but I said no. I manage to get time to scribble, but not to sit down quietly thoughtfully to type and edit if necessary. Writings piled up beyond my capacity to deal with; and am fucked up by letter answering in what leisure [. . .]

I'm sort of comfortable in City Lights womb so hate to think of inevitable changes if you flee to Turkistan. Haven't been in U.S. so long I seem to be out of touch with worst bring-downs, as per your disgust with hollow San Francisco.

Well, according to [Robert] Creeley, I'm due to teach three weeks in Vancouver in late June or July I forget; in return get round the world plane ticket — so I'll stop awhile in San Francisco and see who's there — then I guess New York see my family and Jack and Gregory there; then after I dunno months, go to Europe on same ticket — I'll find you where you wherever are — then go see Germany, Poland, Russia and back to Orient, on to maybe Japan.

So I'll see you in Europe if you do leave San Francisco this Spring. Maybe Winter in London we'll meet in Soho, I want to go there and spend a month reading up on Blake in British Museum. Yogis and holymen here tell me, lately "Poetry is your Sadhana" (sadhana is path, discipline, yoga) and "Take Blake for your Guru." Old lady bhakti (love-faith) saint in Brindaban (little holy town Krishna's birthplace center of Indian Bhakti Cults) told me stop looking for "human guru" and take Blake. I never read Blake thru, studied him, I'm getting interested in doing it finally.

Hoped to make Moscow, but latest news sounds like close-in of the Poetry Shoppe where [Yevgeny] Yevtushenko's[108] mistake was to "speak for" Mother Russia instead of speaking for own odd self. Now he's stuck with a public position he claimed. [. . .]

Love
Allen

Due to the responsibilities of having a family and running a bookstore, Ferlinghetti never made good on his threat to leave the country permanently. He did make frequent trips abroad, but always with a return ticket in his pocket.

---

108 Yevgeny Yevtushenko (b. 1932), a Russian poet.

June 10, 1963: Lawrence Ferlinghetti in Périgord, France, to Allen
Ginsberg in Kyoto, Japan

Dear Allen —
Am in Perigord but will be back in Paris for mail by end of month, and
want to find out from you if you remember the long letter you wrote
[William] Burroughs from Pucallpa in 1960 about <u>ayahuasca</u>,[109] and if
you will allow it to be printed in the *Yage Letters* now at the press. Bill
thinks it's a good idea, being a kind of seven-years-delayed answer to
<u>his</u> yage letters — I saw him in Paris last week and he said OK — By
a real stroke of luck I came on this letter at Melville Hardiment's[110] in
London, and he made me a copy of the original, and it is great. (There
are a few words undecipherable which I may have to get you to clarify.)
In the meantime, please write me in Paris (where I will be until July 3)
and let me know if OK on using letter, so I can get it [to] Villiers Press
right away. Love to all there. See you in San Francisco in August too.

xxx

Lawrence

June 14, 1963: Allen Ginsberg in Kyoto, Japan, to Lawrence Ferlinghetti
in France

Dear Larry:
Glad you're back in France. I just arrived here yesterday — week in
Bangkok eating pork and playing with Chinese boys, week in Saigon
paranoid capitalist war and week in Ankor Wat ruins Cambodia —
then space cut-ups by jet, now here sitting in Japanese house all of a
sudden.
    I remember Burroughs' letter, in fact I thought he'd done lost it,
and was piqued thinking ugh is that how much he cares now, but got

---

109 Ayahuasca is another name for yagé, the hallucinogenic drug found in the South
American jungles.
110 Melville Hardiment, a British writer and editor who was also a friend of Burroughs.

176

resigned. Yes, OK to publish that. The only hitch is, any mention (if any, I don't remember) of Lucien [Carr] got to be deleted or made completely unrecognizable, and of Francesca his wife. Please look over letter carefully to see if I tread on any other living toes. Experience being while I can spill my own guts gush, talking about other people in print gets them into trouble or annoys them. If we had time I'd ask to see letter, but since you say fast Villiers, please dig letter carefully to see I'm not intruding on anyone else's privacy.

Received *City Lights Journal* in India. Better not describe me as greatest living poet anymore. I have to go [to] Vancouver face Duncan, Levertov and they'll honk at me for that. And Jack'll get mad, etc., you know. Too much serpents roused by that kindliness, I was very touched and sad when I saw you'd written that. Feel too washed out to be "greatest" or even great, also, really, any more.

Has a copy of *Reality Sandwiches* come off press yet? Send here. Gary-Joanne [Snyder-Kyger] house very Japanese, like modern dream world after India slop. Peter still sunk in slum alley in Benares, studying music with shaved head, he'll travel this way soon I think. Same address Benares, please send him new City Lights books, etc., so he can keep in touch. See you in two months so will write, I mean talk, then. Just arrived and not yet been out of house for twenty hours sleeping and resting.

Send me Bill's address and give him my regards. Viet Nam war really shitty and now Buddhists protesting against government and U.S. officials in quandary at last. Love to Bill. Love to you. Boy, Japan is neat. Real keen here. Tho I not left house.

OK, Love
Allen

The June 6, 1963, issue of the New York Times *reported that Ginsberg had been suspected of spying by the Vietnamese Buddhists during his visit to South Vietnam. The story was not true; Allen would later insist that it was merely a prank invented by a bored reporter.*

June 28, 1963: Lawrence Ferlinghetti in Paris, France, to Allen Ginsberg in Kyoto, Japan

Cher Allen —
Have been in Maroc (Tangier, Marrakech), Algeria, Tunisia, Italy, and now back to France and found your Japan letter. (Someone told me there was some crap about you and Buddhists and Commies in *Time*, but I didn't see it.) [...]

Sorry you were bugged by "greatest living American poet" but <u>no one</u> had yet said same straight, and I just thought I'd say it straight face to see who would say what about it. In as much as <u>it's true</u>. Naturally all the little cliques of friend poets would be upset or sneer over it or honk at you but you can't help it if some publisher says square things about you while you're not looking. Fuck 'em. I wanted to say same for the record; will then keep silent; for who cares for "Great"? True.

Love
Laurent

After Japan, Ginsberg went straight to Vancouver to teach for a few weeks at the Vancouver Poetry Conference with Robert Creeley and others. In the end he succumbed to the pull of North America, discarding his plan to travel round the world back to Asia.

August 5, 1963: Allen Ginsberg in Vancouver, Canada, to Lawrence Ferlinghetti in San Francisco

Dear Larry:
All well here. Everybody down happy in heaven on earth. Don't worry about nothing no more. Everything's coming true. All wars over and all hells vanished — how's your lovely old belly?? I got the proofs and will read and correct them proper. There are a few references that have to be deleted — for love of peace, please don't give order for presses to roll till I finish. I'll write you within a week. See you in two weeks

about, in any case. You and wifey and babies all O.K.? I guess I'll get married and have little Ginsbergs, too. Find me a nice girl (tee-hee). Anyway — teaching here going fine — all the students feeling me up and me feeling them up and crying all over. I'll write.

Love
Allen

P.S. I got huge new book just about ready. God!!!

◀ 1964 ▶

The two poets exchanged no letters during the rest of 1963 because Ginsberg was in San Francisco, working with Ferlinghetti on projects and trying to help Neal Cassady with The First Third. *In January 1964, Allen returned to New York to reunite with Peter Orlovsky, who had just come back after traveling overland from India to Europe. Once again they set up house in the city, and Allen dove into a wide variety of political and literary issues.*

January 13, 1964: Allen Ginsberg in New York to Lawrence Ferlinghetti in San Francisco

Dear Larry:

[. . .] Working every day with Robert Frank — I now've learned to write filmscripts.[111] We've finished blocking out and extending details and descriptions of all Naomi-*Kaddish* scenes from poem, and are halfway thru writing scenes on present man who has finally turned out to be me anyway — the only good scenes I could write were from life, so that made the decision.

The Lower East Side movie world here is really thrilling like a poetry renaissance excitement parties tragedies, masterpieces in lofts, etc. Best thing in New York — take a look at Jonas Mekas'[112] *Film Culture* magazine to see, that's the best record.

Experience been handy — I was commissioned to write a ten minute filmscript for some uptown producers who promised $3000 if accepted — I wrote a fast skit about Buddha flying like superman with 3rd eye Zap-ray in Birmingham and around UN building to strains of Internationale — they gave me 200 bucks and said they'd sign contract and give me the rest of the loot this year. They asked Lenny Bruce to

---

111 Ginsberg was working with photographer and filmmaker Robert Frank on a screenplay of "Kaddish," but the project was never completed.
112 Jonas Mekas (b. 1922), a Lithuanian filmmaker and writer working in New York City.

do one too, and Jack. I suggested they look at *Unfair Arguments* and contact you. If you have any ten minute film ideas — maybe a visual sequence like your politics collage — theme they ask for is what's wrong with USA — send them *Unfair Arguments* and if you have any ideas or time try movie. George Foster and Bob Booker, they said they would be interested, and they know your poesy well.[113]

We took a cheap apartment $35 per month Lower East Side, Peter's painting it now. All my time now on *Kaddish* movie for another two weeks till finished script and then I go back to my papers and answer letters, etc. — everything else sliding behind — where's Neal? — not had time to write him — he around? Some new scenes for *Kaddish* we send you in a few weeks for *City Lights Journal* — I wrote up "Sunflower Sutra" as visual city dump scene, with entirely different words, not using poem, and dialogue. Kerouac saying "O go bite your lip" in the graveyard — everybody sitting around on busted sofa thrones in the dump beside a locomotive with Wine Sire, on a broken down table in sunset.

Love to Kirby. Lucien [Carr] still drinking, more miserable here than San Francisco. Peter fine, walks around in summer jacket in the snow and says he's not cold. Today huge overwhelming snowfall covered the city, so everything looks like transparent white overexposed photograph.

Love
Allen

---

113 Although the film was never made, Foster and Booker published many of the scripts they had commissioned in the book *Pardon Me, Sir, But Is My Eye Hurting Your Elbow?* in 1968.

February 6, 1964: Allen Ginsberg in New York to Lawrence Ferlinghetti in San Francisco

Dear Larry:

Interrupted two days ago — all sorts horrors in New York — [Herbert] Huncke in jail a year for a needle — I got his manuscript. Living Theatre Becks[114] going on trial for thirty-three year charge — Coffeehouses (Le Metro) told to quit poetry — pawnshop fingerprint crackdowns — new Rockefeller arrest laws — [Lee Harvey] Oswald was probably a CIA employee who flipped — Peter vacuum cleaning the apartment.

We got a cheap apartment 35 dollars month rent in bad junky street Lower East Side, I'll move there in a few days.

Finished 100 page *Kaddish* script with Robert Frank, but now he has no backer, has to look.

[Ed] Sanders and I designed nice *Roosevelt Inauguration* pamphlet,[115] it's printed, we have to collate and staple it tomorrow. Send you how many? 3 by 5 or 4 by 5 mimeo job. Sunil Ganguly[116] visiting here — Ahmed Yacoubi here also — such busyness, plenty fun — [Timothy] Leary in and out — I go visit Elizabeth Gurley Flynn Communist cocktail this Saturday. [. . .] Boy I'm running round like a butterfly — not much poetry (except two I wrote in new scenes for *Kaddish*). Peter fine, painting apartment, we all went out madhouse visit his brothers and Carl [Solomon] in Long Island last weekend looking at locations for *Kaddish* bughouse scenes — gotta find an actor. *Kaddish* "Man" wound up me after all. Gregory gave obnoxious-funny lively yak at Poetry Center symposium, put everybody down but made sense, wild nite. [. . .]

---

114 Julian Beck (1925–1985) and his wife Judith Malina (1926–2015), founders of the Living Theatre, an avant-garde theater troupe.

115 *Roosevelt After Inauguration* was a routine that William Burroughs had written earlier, but it had not yet been published.

116 Sunil Ganguly, *aka* Gangopadhyay (1934–2012), an Indian poet and writer that Allen met on his travels to India.

I'll write soon. Going to dentist today for more laughing gas, cheerio.

Regards to Kirby
Allen

February 8, 1964: Lawrence Ferlinghetti in San Francisco to Allen Ginsberg in New York

Dear Allen . . . .

[. . .] Will keep [Jonas] Mekas in mind for *City Lights Journal* article and write him . . . . I should have your copy for same by end of February if possible. If not, mid-March will do, at latest . . . . Yes, hope to have some Elise Cowen[117] in *Journal* . . . . Using part of Irving's [Rosenthal] *Sheeper* too . . . . Pound . . . Céline . . . . going to be great . . . .

Happy to hear you and Sanders did *Roosevelt After Inauguration*. That should be wild . . . . Send 100 to begin with . . . . or more [. . .]

Ain't heard from Neal. Nor his manuscreed . . . . ('cept first chapter you left with me . . . .) [. . .]

What is not nice is latest scenes you report happening everywhere in Lower New York, with Becks going jail, the snatch on everywhere . . . . At least here things are quiet. Not a low mumble anywhere since you left. A real dull season . . . 'Cept [Bob] Kaufman got busted week before Xmas for amphetamine and is in rehabilitation farm in Santa Clara and Eileen [Kaufman][118] got thrown out of North Beach apartment "by police."

Bye now. Rushed
. . . .
Larry

---

117 Elise Cowen (1933–1962), a poet and friend of Allen Ginsberg who had committed suicide.
118 Eileen Kaufman (1922–2015), Bob Kaufman's wife.

February 10, 1964: Allen Ginsberg in New York to Lawrence Ferlinghetti in San Francisco

Dear Larry:

[. . .] Robert Frank has *Kaddish* script 100 pages now, but no producer anymore and going out hustle for money. I think he'll want to try print scenes in *Show* or *Esquire* and use that loot for finance shooting the film, so I let him have free hand. I'll send you other material. Actually the script is interesting but not well written literarily as my preoccupation was giving prosaic detail descriptions and instructions for camera and the script was pasted together from pieces of scenes and people-descriptions, and it's too long to sit down and "polish" so it reads interesting on its own, as a poetical form. If he sells individual scenes to *Show* I'll have to revise those for "reading," but wouldn't bother otherwise as its meant as blueprint for practical shooting not for page literature, it's hackwork prose. Also done with eye to what he could film, so it don't represent my own personal free ideas, only just what he could work with with his limitations or his characters and film limitations. That's the trouble with movies it involves too many people so unless you're Chaplin there's not the same unlimited freedom as poesy. [. . .]

Gregory now in fine shape also and Sally's[119] baby nine days overdue. Possibly Santa Clara [prison] be good for Kaufman as that amphetamine really doing him in like Zombie. Metro Cafe got summons for poetry readings they'll fight and I suspect Mekas filmmakers next in line for police trouble. OK — later — Gary [Snyder] get there yet?

Love
Allen

---

119 Gregory Corso had married Sally November and together they had a baby girl they named Miranda.

March 14, 1964: Allen Ginsberg in New York to Lawrence Ferlinghetti in San Francisco

Dear Larry:
[. . .] All hell breaking loose in New York — I'm in middle of struggle with License Department on poetry reading in coffeehouses, now Jonas Mekas been arrested twice once for showing *Flaming Creatures*[120] film and once for showing Genet film[121] which is of prisoners and guards jacking off. Crackdowns and summonses on other small film clubs for showing unlicensed files. [Charles] Plymell[122] reports *Now* was "banned in Wichita" which is funny footnote. I up to ears in work appointments telephonings politics get no writing done, maybe an other month of this. [. . .]

OK
Allen

ca. April 15, 1964: Allen Ginsberg in New York to Lawrence Ferlinghetti in San Francisco

Dear Larry:
Enclosed several poems by one Alden Van Buskirk, who died in San Francisco sometime in 1962, blood disease, age 22 or 23. He must have been a real poet, to judge from the mood-music-rhythm of Spent Low section enclosed, and the clarity of his imagery and natural unforced person in his voice, very tender, no frantic obscurity of his feelings. "Lami in Oakland" also very generous-natured — elements of [John] Wieners lyricism and Burroughs' robot imagery but primarily a young humane sacredness, what he thinks walking thru Oakland markets seeing fellow selves.

I wrote several paragraphs for another section of his poetry

---

120 *Flaming Creatures* (1963), an underground film by Jack Smith. The New York City police seized the film because of its graphic sexuality.
121 Jean Genet's film *Un Chant d'Amour* (1950).
122 Charles Plymell (b. 1935), writer, editor, and poet.

185

for *Second Coming*; and will send some other to *Paris Review* and *Evergreen*. The enclosed for *City Lights Journal* if you have room. The quality of the poesy worth it. A whole book exists, young friends of his have got money together to have it printed by Auerhahn and [Dave] Haselwood accepted two weeks ago. Well treat it tender. [...]

Allen

August 12, 1964: Allen Ginsberg in New York to Lawrence Ferlinghetti in San Francisco

Dear Larry:

I been hustling all month, huge correspondence with [Nanda] Pivano correcting Italian works, arranging Congress Cultural Freedom circulate petition for Olympia [Press], wrote a bunch of new poems and sent them out to lil mags, annotated "The Change" poem, with T.S. Eliot notes, rounding up coffeeshop info for new law here, helped bounce the local DA for bugging Mekas and [Lenny] Bruce, worked on *Kaddish* movie, wrote article for *London Times*, working on Peter's brother Julius twelve years in loony bin silent as Bartleby now talks blue streak, orgying with nineteen year old girl, (me, not Julius, I mean me and Peter), and putting up Gregorio [Gregory Corso] who's writing mad desperate fast poetry book for New Directions deadline, registered to vote, made Pacifica tape with my father and TV tape with Selden Rodman ("I love obscenity, etc."), made good revision Lebel *Howl* with Robert Cordier[123] here, got Huncke outa jail, saw American Civil Liberties Union for Ray Bremser, wrote my congressman complaining about everything, saw Buster Keaton and [Samuel] Beckett under the Brooklyn Bridge, read at Le Metro, went to Indian and Negro parties, cleaned house, did laundry, am broke, [Robert] LaVigne found himself a place to live/work and a gallery, Peter hung with mad

---

123 Jean-Jacques Lebel (b. 1936) and Robert Cordier (b. 1933), French poets and translators.

brothers. Muggy here like Calcutta, not had chance to leave town. How's Frisco? Regards to Gary, Kirby and Co. When's *City Lights* magazine out?

Love,
Allen

Ferlinghetti had decided to print a few postcards of Ginsberg to sell in the City Lights store, so he asked Allen for suggestions.

September 30, 1964: Allen Ginsberg in New York to Lawrence Ferlinghetti in San Francisco

Dear Larry:

Yeh postcard OK by me though Fred McDarrah[124] might object or want a cut. Long as I don't have to send them myself like valentine, I'll look see if I can find a good picture. City Lights one be OK too. Tangier one be OK too. What do you think best? [. . .]

Say, for postcard — Richard Avedon[125] six months ago took a really *great* photo of me and Peter mellow naked (cropped around halfway down P's pecker and one fourth of mine) — one of the best classic photos he ever took says Robert Frank — he was too chicken to put it in book he's making, he has one of me alone naked holding hand in front of my loins. But *that* suppressed one would be great card, except can't probably send it thru mail — or could one?? I dunno.

Later,
Allen

---

124 Fred McDarrah (1921–2007) was the photographer who took the iconic photograph of Allen Ginsberg wearing an Uncle Sam hat.
125 Richard Avedon (1923–2004), an important portrait, art, and fashion photographer.

October 20, 1964: Lawrence Ferlinghetti in San Francisco to Allen
Ginsberg in New York

Dear Allen:
Still waiting for *City Lights Journal* to show up in bulk from England.
Have advance copy and your stuff looks fine . . . . Have two notes of
yours here unanswered: Re. photo of you nekkid by Avedon, hope you
can send me glossy copy (you and Peter in photo). Have not done
anything about postcard of you, tho I got snapshot duplicates I sent
you. Maybe some year we'll put out a whole row of postcards of poets. So save any great pictures, group shots or otherwise . . . . Fuck
Carnegie Steel Foundation, Fuck Ford Ball Bearing Turret Foundation, Fuck Who's Who, Fuck Fidel Fuck Mao for TO FUCK IS TO
LOVE AGAIN. (Hope [Ed] Sanders showed you my new poesy on
the subject.)[126]
    Must be nice in New York this Fall. Wish I were there. Collect
me an autumn leaf.

                                        love
                                        [unsigned]

December 3, 1964: Allen Ginsberg in New York to Lawrence Ferlinghetti
in San Francisco

Dear Larry:
Peter and I back after three weeks at Cambridge [Harvard Univer-
sity] — we gave four readings (also at Brandeis [University]) — had
wild nights and slept with lots of folks and got banished from Lowell
House our hosts and then redeemed ourselves by weepy poesy. Also we
sang as part of our readings — carry harmonium music box and chant
mantras to that.
    I have one man typing up Indian notebooks now. I promised long,

---

126 Ferlinghetti had sent a poem he titled "To Fuck Is to Love Again" to Ed Sanders for
his magazine *Fuck You: A Magazine of the Arts.*

long ago a book to Auerhahn Press so will send in about 100 pages when ready. There's lots more left after that, just a question of typing and editing and time. My handwriting is so bad that I have to be near the typist. Thank Mary [Beach].[127] If I move to San Francisco ever, I'll ask her help.

Apartment broken into while gone and the meth-freaks got all our Tibetan paintings, etc. Maybe later recover.

We gave a reading here last nite with a gang of new negro poets from Lower East Side, read with them up at Columbia. Peter stripped down to his bikini to read *Fuck You* sex experiment writing.

Love

Allen

December 9, 1964: Lawrence Ferlinghetti in San Francisco to Allen Ginsberg in New York

Dear Allen:
[. . .] Berkeley Free Speech Movement great scene here. Everybody in town getting in act, [Ralph] Gleason quoting from my routine "Servants of the People" with graduate student's speeches . . . . etc. etc . . . Sorry you won't let me do *India Journals* in same format as *Yage Letters*. I thought you'd promised Auerhahn *South American Journals*. Oh well, skip it. Am taking off for a whole year this February and don't expect to publish much.

love . . .

LF

---

127 Artist, publisher and translator Mary Beach had offered to be Ginsberg's typist.

◀ 1965 ▶

Dear Allen . . . .
Hear from your card to Pelieu-Beach[128] that you are going to "Cuba and Czechoslovakia". If you have a chance, will you drop me a card and let me know how you arranged this? I am going (with Kirby and kids) to Europe on February 14th, by plane, and will stay at least a year over there. Had invite to Czechoslovakia last year, thru Union of Writers, and may try to get that again . . . . On your travels, send me any manuscript you can, by anyone you dig en route, including yourself . . . . mail to City Lights will be forwarded pronto. Mary Beach will be handling editorial correspondence for me, etc . . . .

love
larry

Querido Allen . . . .
encantado que tu es en ruta a Cuba . . . espero que todo ira muy buen . . . . (Vencer-who-mos? Who will win?) [. . .] As I wrote before, Kirby and Lorenzo and Julie and I are leaving here February 14 for Europe, mostly France, though may go to Spain specifically to find Spanish lost poets in jail, or their manuscripts . . . for next *City Lights Journal* (Spring 1966).

Do you get to stay in Europe as long as you want, once you get to Czechoslovakia on free ride from Cuba? Or do you have to return di-

---

128 Claude Pelieu (1934–2002), a French poet and translator, was married to Mary Beach.

rect to New York from Prague? I sure would like to do same and meet Kirby in France afterward . . . . Anyway if you get to France, you can reach me thru Jean Jacques Lebel. [. . .]

I want to go back to Cuba and realize I could get invited by Casa de las Americas probably but am afraid of getting into it right now since I might get hung up and not be able to make rendezvous with Kirby in Europe, etc. etc., all too complicated, so I guess I'll probably go on under my own steam, as I usually do . . . . unless you can cue me into facts on getting to and from Czechoslovakia, etc . . . . Never mind, you too busy [. . .]

love

larry

ca. March 1965: Allen Ginsberg in Prague, Czechoslovakia, to Lawrence Ferlinghetti

Larry:

I'm here in Prague till about March 15 or 20. Also am guest of Writers Union — fine Ambassador Hotel and they gave me spending money two weeks.

I got kicked out of Cuba by Cuban Immigration. All told Cuba a hysterical drag. Long story, I kept hundreds of pages of notes. I have enough $ here to pay in crowns for train ride and return from Moscow — so I'll go there next, on my own. Had enough of the constraints of being a state guest, it's like a bribe to keep your mouth shut.

Prague lovelier in miniature than Paris almost. Have you arrived? They expect you here. Pujman[129] says he's waiting to hear from you, when you'll come, as guest. Jan Zabrana is a very nice man, real friend and intelligent and himself a good poet. OK, I'll write when I have more time.

Love,

Allen

---

129 Petr Pujman, acting head of the Czechoslovakian Writers Union.

I'll see you on my way back Prague — Moscow — Warsaw? — Prague — London. Can make side trip to Paris before fly home from London where I'll stay a month. Lots to say — later. Love to Kirby

In June, Lawrence and Allen saw each other in London, where they both participated in a massive reading at the Royal Albert Hall. Shortly after this, Ferlinghetti read at the prestigious Festival of Two Worlds in Spoleto, Italy. The high point of the event for him was hearing Ezra Pound read, which he described in a prose-poem called "Pound at Spoleto."

July 5, 1965: Lawrence Ferlinghetti in Venice, Italy, to Allen Ginsberg in San Francisco

Querido Allen . . . .

I am here for a few days with Jean-Jacques [Lebel] and his Denise, on the way back from Spoleto to Paris and then London again for a little while . . . .

I am still more or less in the same state I was in in London . . . I have written no one at City Lights or in San Francisco about all this . . . . It's a blind condition . . . . I keep forgetting I am not thirty . . . . Nothing to be done, nothing to be done! (Sous le pont mirabeau coule la vie, et il y a trop de ponts sous lesquels la vie coule.)

I imagine I shall turn up at City Lights in mid-August, and hope to see you. Leave your address. [. . .]

Spoleto was a week of luxurious living and drinking, and I shook some fruit, and read a new long poemblast on Vietnam to disturb the dreamy surroundings . . . . But don't believe what *Newsweek* and *Time* said about [Yevgeny] Yevtushenko [being] a Discus Thrower (referring to his melodramatic delivery). They made up a lot of lies and put them in my mouth. (If you read same, you'll be unable to imagine me saying them.) If you write or see Yev tell him I am sorry about the Discus Thrower . . . .

I am sitting here looking across the water at St. Marco, from Giudecca island where I have a room over the quai. Wonderful. People beside me are leaning out the window and sending you their love

Larry

◄ 1966 ►

By 1966 Ferlinghetti was editing the manuscript of Ginsberg's next book,
Planet News, *which would be published in 1968. The other books he mentions as being in the works also came to fruition with City Lights.*

March 11, 1966: Lawrence Ferlinghetti in San Francisco to Allen
Ginsberg in New York [?]

Querido Ginzap:
I have copy-read the enclosed for the printer, and copy-questions are
noted for your decisions. I think the cuts you made are fine. "West of
Chicago" you might make still more, but it's great and true. Mainly
typo questions, though I have dared to suggest a text-change or two.
[. . .]
    We are taking on newer dimensions in the City Lights publishing: Colin Wilson was here and gave me *The Outsider* for a paperback!
(If his agent doesn't get in the way.) And I've written Olson loving
to do his *Call Me Ishmael*. Don Allen says Grove gave it up. So. And
probably Rexroth's *Beyond the Mountains Greeks*. And we now have an
international distributor traveling the books all the way around the
world. [. . .]

                                             "Larry"
                                             Love to all

*From time to time New York publishers still asked Ginsberg to allow them
to print a large hardback edition of his collected poems.*

March 15, 1966: Allen Ginsberg in New York to Lawrence Ferlinghetti in San Francisco

Quieredo Lornzap:

OK, fine, I notated and took most suggestions and also eliminated a few more dead lines, descriptions of terrain that aren't so sharp-imaged. If you see anymore that looks dead, well cut it. I know it's too long, just don't know — so soon — where to cut. I'd know better after a year's distance, ripening.

Al Grossman, Dylan's manager's office, called this morn and said they had Town Hall free Saturday nite and nobody to fill it, some other plan fell through, would I like to read there? I said fine, benefit Leary Defense Fund,[130] and by this evening they had [an] ad in the *Times*. Professional.

I finally figured out how to handle U.S. hardcover edition. I don't want to separate from City Lights really, but I want to take advantage of established mass distribution of big New York publisher. Talked with some people and they said it's possible to have combine imprint Doubleday/City Lights or Grove/City Lights, etc. but City Lights would get percentage of publisher's profits and credit. I don't know the details of how that would break down and if it could be worked out and with who, but I'll slowly investigate in the next months and report back, if this scheme sounds possible and satisfactory to you. I would give the book to City Lights to do hard cover but having been in Lincoln, Nebraska, and Wichita, etc., I don't think it's possible in the next few years for City Lights alone to compete with Grove, etc. for distribution. I wanna get big mass distribution if I can. Maybe we can also retain soft cover reprint rights for some similar deal with NAL [New American Library] or Signet? I'll find out. In any case will work it slowly and ask publisher friends in New York for technical suggestions and do it right. Does this sound OK as a resolution of the problem? I think it's possible. I have offers of $10,000 advance from

---

130 Timothy Leary had been arrested on drug charges and a fund had been set up to help pay his mounting legal fees.

Seymour Lawrence for hardcover rights, so if it's worth that much, and [if] I forego an advance, it would make it possible to make a deal for New York publisher to share profits with you and imprint, and they wouldn't be risking an unprofitable investment that way. Please say OK. Unless you have groovier alternative.

Enclosed OK notice from Penguin. All's well. [Tom] Maschler[131] probably waiting for me to deliver manuscript before he sends contract. He's advertised the book already. God knows when I'll have it with all the work at hand. Trying not to get too time-involved with [Timothy] Leary, but want to help where I can. Wrote Fugs record-jacket prose.

[. . .] Maybe soon get together a book of Interviews Explanations Manifestos. Huge one [interview] in May *Paris Review* I'm reading proof of now, and [Ed] Sanders publishing shorter one I made at BBC with Eric Mottram in next *Fuck You*. Shit I didn't get to see the TV program we were on, don't have TV and didn't notice it was playing till too late. Heard it was humane. I like Charlie Rose. Wrote some tape poems, one I gave to *Life* and they may publish with the story ([Michael] McClure has a copy) and one yet untyped I want to rush into print in newspaper form in *Voice* or *New York Review of Books*. "Wichita Vortex Mantra," announcing termination of Vietnam War. I'll read it at Town Hall. Gad what activity, and *Playboy* rejected marijuana [article] so we sent it on to *Esquire*. [. . .] Can you try to get some coherent narrative of [Ken] Kesey's activities for *City Lights Journal*? That would be a great document, too. Huncke gave his book to Grove Press to look at. He gave lovely 3 1/2 hour reading at Buffalo University, had me in tears. Everybody sitting on floor of a student coffee room in compassionate silence, listening. Irving Rosenthal has book at Grove they'll take it. Kirby Doyle novel *Angel Faint*? Diane Di Prima will print — ask her to see? — for *City Lights Journal*? Rosenthal starting printing press in N.Y.C.

OK, Love
Allen

---

131 Tom Maschler, a British publisher and editor of Jonathan Cape books.

March 22, 1966: Lawrence Ferlinghetti in San Francisco to Allen
Ginsberg in New York

Cher Ginzap:

Saw you on TV "Poetry USA" with Peter, Julius [Orlovsky] and [Robert] LaVigne. You were <u>beautiful</u>, so were everyone. LaVigne painting scene fine. I followed with Homer and Chinese Fisherman in Adler Alley and in my attic . . . . (They didn't tell me they were putting our two films together. Not my idea!) . . . (Who wants to follow you on-stage?)*

    * I followed [Louis] Simpson at Reed College Read-in last weekend and demolished the scene, seven hundred crazy students and townspeople fell apart. But like Jack say, "That ain't no competition."

Will follow your final corrections in "New York to San Francisco" — OK. Thanks again. It'll be out this summer . . . . Worked with Charley (Ply [Plymell]) on "Rose"[132] and will use it, too: much improved, I feel, he happy to have my critickwork . . . . Well, I'm to be dug as an editor, anyway.

Natch, we City Lights can't compete with big commercial scenes like Grove — and of course if you can work out any joint publication schemes for hardcovers, still leaving us with rights to distribute our own paperback original editions, OK natch. Isn't New Directions big enough for you? Guess not. Though they did OK by Gregory, treated him nice, etc. And my *Coney Island* now above 165,000 with them, They could do beautiful black hardcover like Pound *Cantos*. [. . .]

OK — Love —
to you and Peter
—
Lorenzo

---

132 Dave Haselwood published Charles Plymell's *Apocalypse Rose* in 1966.

March 26, 1966: Lawrence Ferlinghetti in San Francisco to Allen
Ginsberg in New York

Dear Allen:
[. . .] Read your "Kral Majales" in *Evergreen* [*Review*] and must admit I was presumptuous in saying it was a little loose in spots; it isn't;
which proves your ear is better than mine (Mine's good but you're a
fuckin genius, as usual). Your crosscunt trek wiped us out and we're
now reprinting all three of your books, rushing *Kaddish* and *Reality*
from England. Sent your "SF-NY" to printer; out late August or sooner. Will send proofs if you want'em. Gregory is kicking cold in Athens,
wrote for moneyhelp and I sent 100 (for nursing home) in case you
haven't heard. [. . .]

love,
LF

April 17, 1966: Allen Ginsberg in New York to Lawrence Ferlinghetti in
San Francisco

Dear Larry:
Shit's hit fan on [Timothy] Leary and LSD in New York and phones
ringing in every direction; also enclosed latest municipal yakkings see
East Village Other and *Village Voice* for more. [. . .]
Desk piled with mail. I don't know when the *Life* article will come
out if it isn't killed maybe in a month now delayed, but if it does please
have several thousand copies of all books ready for sale I guess. I'll be
touring reading more intensively this year so they'll be heavier sales.
So completely wrapped up with politics telephone all last two weeks
unable to start work on book for you, poems to 1966.
Have nice time with Voznesensky??[133] Saw him here, we went
to Fugs together and I got shut out of all official parties and readings

---

133 Russian poet Andrei Voznesensky was visiting San Francisco at the time to give a
series of readings.

with him. Didn't even get a chance to turn him on. But I saw all his readings and taxied around a bit.

Grove offers to do collected works of mine with your collaborative imprint.

Allen

In this letter Ferlinghetti describes the suppression of Michael McClure's play The Beard. *The police continually arrested the cast for obscenity whenever it was performed.*

August 24, 1966: Lawrence Ferlinghetti in San Francisco to Allen Ginsberg in New York

Dear Allen . . . .

[. . .] I'm thinking of using photo of poets at City Lights taken last December 5, with you in middle, Himalayan umbrella, etc, on cover of *City Lights Journal* 3. If you think it is a bum idea, please advise. Otherwise I may go ahead and use it.

You remember all the ruckus about the Mayor's Committee on the Arts here which the Artists Liberation Front was formed to raise voice against, etc? Well, surprise, I just got a letter from the Mayor asking me to join the Committee (Rexroth behind this I think) . . . . Now, as the major tactician of the Movement, what would you advise me?? Join or refuse. I'm sure if it was you, you'd accept; but I am not Allen Ginsberger, nor was meant to be . . . . though I did jump up and make extempore speech at McClure *Beard* performance in Berkeley the other night — he had first five rows stocked with people like Mark Schorer, Al Bendich, etc. etc. ACLU on stage beforehand, etc. It was a beautiful performance and the whole evening a gas. The fuzz filmed and took film back to show to Daddy D.A. to decide whether or not to make bust. So far no noise, tho trial for original bust at The Committee, two weeks ago, still not resolved . . . Grove has evidently given Mike a contract to publish *Beard* . . . (I had my chance at it, but was writing my own full length play and didn't wish to be hung up on trial or otherwise distracted right in middle of it.) Artists Liberation Front, by the way, has yet to take a stand on *Beard* (which is precisely what it should be in existence for) . . . . Anyway, shall I now play cultural commissar or still leave the field to Waxroth [Rexroth]? I rather think I will refuse on the grounds of Mayor's administration allowing police harassment of *Beard*, Mime Troupe, and etc . . . . in a public letter . . . .? [. . .]

My only achievement is lying naked on the beach at Bixby . . . .

luf
Larry

When Lawrence gave a reading at the St. Mark's Church Poetry Project in New York City in the fall of 1966, he was disappointed not to see Allen there. But as Ginsberg explains, his continued domestic problems with Peter Orlovsky had prevented him from attending.

October 26, 1966: Lawrence Ferlinghetti in San Francisco to Allen Ginsberg in New York

Cher Maître —
Just back to San Francisco — [. . .] Only disappointment of whole trip was your absence at my reading at St. Mark's. Had hoped to persuade you I was saying a sound worth listening to. Well, maybe some year I'll reach you. (Peter said it "was not very exciting"!)

Love —
Larry

October 29, 1966: Allen Ginsberg In New York to Lawrence Ferlinghetti in San Francisco

Dear Larry:

Sorry I missed the reading it wasn't my wish — had been at Goddard and Franconia College after Dartmouth giving two readings and ended three in morn sleeping in cabin in fields — expecting early start back to city — but Peter was mad at me and suddenly got up left me Barbara [Rubin][134] and Lafcadio [Orlovsky] there and drove back to New York — so had to scout up a ride home the next day — stopped in Massachusetts bughouse to see Maretta Greer who was to be released next day and's now here with me in bed — so arrived in New York 3AM, too late. All news of the reading was very satisfactory — warm atmosphere everyone friendly and big crowd and good reading — Peter was probably still irritable. Julius [Orlovsky] now returned home — found by friends after nineteen days standing in clean old overcoat labeled Paterson N.J., clean shaven and silent in front of Lincoln Bus Terminal 41st Street near Times Square never said where or what he'd done. [. . .] I still have to look over Grove, etc. He wants me to set a date for the manuscript and I've been putting it off a year, I'll try get that done soon.

Gary be here in a week — Creeley and Wieners passed thru — answered ten letters today — enclosed Paterson comedy. Don't know how that'll work out.

Ok, ok oke
Allen

---

134 Barbara Rubin was a filmmaker and friend of Ginsberg's who had encouraged him to buy a farm in Cherry Valley, New York.

◄ 1967 ►

*During the winter of 1967, Ferlinghetti visited Berlin and then the Soviet
Union, finally taking the Transsiberian Railroad all the way to Russia's
eastern shore. It wasn't quite the* Doctor Zhivago *experience he had hoped
for. After being denied passage on a ship to Japan, he fell sick and had to
spend several days in the hospital before flying back to Moscow. By this
time, Lawrence and Kirby were having marital problems, and he laments
the fact that he and Allen narrowly missed being able to talk about personal
issues together in San Francisco.*

March 25, 1967: Lawrence Ferlinghetti in San Francisco to Allen
Ginsberg in New York

Dear Allen:
I am back from the Wilderness, having got sick in Siberia and spent
some sad time in a hospital in Nakhodka, miserable place, joyless
country . . . . I have been trying to change my life but find myself
back at the same stand. Too bad we didn't get a chance to talk when
you were here this last trip. There was a lot I wanted to tell you about
personally, but not a moment to do it, it seemed . . . .
   Anyway, the scene in Berlin was a big success as far as the big
reading with Voz [Andrei Voznesensky] was concerned, and I found
out a lot about the German publishing scene which will help in the
future. For instance, I learned that Limes Verlag, our publisher there,
is really a two-bit publisher with no circulation or advertising or anything, and we goofed to go with them, though I suppose it was better
than nothing, and we had no other offers for your books from anyone
else at the time, and they are good-looking editions. The thing is that
a big and most important publisher there got interested at the reading,
especially after I told the professor chief of the fucking foundation that
it was shocking they had not invited you sometime during the winter

202

program, what with Olson, Creeley, me, etc. . . . . Anyway you will see by the enclosed letters what is up now. It is Reinhard Lettau who is my good friend there, and he's the one responsible for getting Hanser off the pot and onto the Ginsberger autobahn. If you will give me the info in answer to the questions asked in the second Hanser letter, I will answer them: (1) Auerhahn *Journals* (2) prose books being done by ? Random House? Harcourt? Or you can answer him direct; but please return these letters to me . . . . Lettau is probably the brightest and hippest editor in Berlin now, in addition to being a good novelist and poet hisself. And Hanser Verlag is one of the best [publishers] in Germany — maybe the best for the avant-garde and Group 47 etc. [. . .]

We flew to Moscow, where I met Frieda Lurie and Ylena Romanova and Andrei [Sergeiev] your translator and mine, at the Writers Union, etc . . . . Zoja Voznesensky took us around to other scenes, including the Drama Theatre where John Reed's *Ten Days That Shook The World* was being "dramatized" . . . . Then off on the Transsiberian, world's longest and most boring train ride. Kept a big journal (which doesn't seem very interesting to me now). Also got one long poem, "Moscow in the Wilderness, Segovia in the Snow" which I will send you . . . . More later . . . .

Love to youse

. . . .

larry

April 2, 1967: Allen Ginsberg in New York to Lawrence Ferlinghetti in San Francisco

Dear Larry:

I didn't write much poetry poetry in Russia either, tho I did instead take down everything everyone said like a spy. Still I'm glad you got to do the Transsiberian and saw Moscow, and Red Square? That gave me a thrill, like Asia space station. [. . .]

I'm off on big reading tour — Boston, Nashville and Johnson City, Tennessee, Baltimore, Oberlin, L.A., Boulder — stopping off in

San Francisco on April 16 to rendezvous with Peter who'll drive out to pick Julius up for he's in Napa in durance — we'll stay in San Francisco a couple days, then drive down to Santa Monica for a reading with the Fugs on April 21 — maybe spend a day at Big Sur on way down? So see you then. Maybe if Shig bear with us we'll stay with him. Then drive out near Albuquerque spend two weeks nearby with Larry Bird, McClure-Snyder Pueblo Indian friend, on his territory and learn Amerindian chants — then I continue reading in L.I., Kenyon, Columbia Missouri, Iowa City for SDS, end at Madison — and somewhere a stopover in Columbus, Ohio help busted d.a. levy[135] — then May 15 to July 4 do nothing but assemble manuscript once and for all deliver *Planet News*. Then to England poets conference July 12, mind benders conference July 20, then rest, then August 15 my seventy-two year old poppa gonna visit Europe first time, so I'll spend three weeks London, Paris, Rome with him, then fuck off for a few weeks, come back to U.S. for another reading tour and then — disappear into East. [. . .]

Other books are: *Indian Journals* (manuscript finally delivered to Auerhahn but still to be edited down by Haselwood): I think I retained foreign rights to that or made arrangement similar to City Lights. [. . .]

Have you recovered from Siberial Shits? What illness did you have? Send Xerox of "Segovia," when you have time. Or, I'll see it in two weeks, see you in two weeks. Maybe we all spend day at Sur? I'm working hard but much distracted — still it's all coming along.

As ever
Allen

---

135 d.a. levy was a Cleveland poet and underground press publisher who was arrested twice on obscenity charges and committed suicide in 1968.

Dear Larry:

[. . .] Been here in Milan working on Italian translation of poems
with Nanda [Pivano] and editing *Planet News* which still hope to get
ready and done with by return. Best one book regular poems with
pieces of Vietnam poem and second book later with entire two years
war poem. That should simplify the work. [. . .]

Drove with Nanda to her mama at seaside near Genoa, and spent
Saturday with [Ezra] Pound at last and Olga Rudge.[136] Lunch, he was
silent, she asked if you were publishing, I think Creeley, or whoever,
so they're friendly aware of City Lights, I gave him your respects. He
asked me if I wanted to wash hands before lunch (at her prompting),
but almost dead silent like Julius [Orlovsky] was, the rest of day. I
sang Hari Krishna and Prajnaparamita (Nanda said he looked startled
and a little scared when I began singing vigorous loud ooom oooms)
but Olga said he enjoyed it or he wouldn't have stayed in room. Then
Nanda and Ettore[137] and I took him out for drive alone to Portofino,
sat an hour, had tea walked around, he said "No" to various inquiries
(like, had he ever smoked pot, or want more iced tea?), but nothing
else. Though completely clear in head, talking about Céline at lunch
I said Céline recommended Paul Morand prose, Olga Rudge asked
what was name of his book that once Pound had liked and he said in
crisp French "*Ouvert à la Nuit.*" So he's there, yogi silent. Rapallo area
like Big Sur but crowded with sea-edge stone villas and orange walled
houses, hundreds of miles of property built up. Pound lives in relative
penury — small apartment; in house overlooking bay from mountain
height — not much luxury at all; a maid to cook tho; but very simple
small rooms. Great views and blue light.

My father's trip over, he had ball: we met [Giuseppe] Ungaretti[138]

---

136 Olga Rudge (1895–1996), Ezra Pound's longtime mistress and the mother of his
daughter.
137 Ettore Sottsass (1917–2007), a designer for Olivetti and Nanda Pivano's husband.
138 Giuseppe Ungaretti (1888–1970), a prominent Italian poet.

in Venice, saw Rome, Paris (stayed at Hotel Madison by Diderot's statue across from Notre Dame on St. Michel Blvd: Gave George Whitman a poem for his French magazine just out.) My father got two offers for books in England — thank god he's safely berthed now and happy.

OK — I'll be here couple weeks — don't know where next maybe home as money low. Hope you're happy, Big Sur is Paradise. Love to Shig and love to you as ever. Nanda says hello and Ettore too.

Allen

After his father and stepmother returned to the U.S., Ginsberg went back to Venice. He spent several weeks visiting Ezra Pound and wrote down every utterance the nearly silent old poet made. In the end Allen felt that he had made a real connection with Pound, and it became an important event in his life. Meanwhile, Peter Orlovsky had remained in the United States and was indulging in drugs, especially amphetamines.

The offhand remark that Ginsberg will phone Ferlinghetti once he gets home marks a fundamental shift in their correspondence. Over the coming years the two would rely less and less on the mail and more on the telephone, thanks to lower long-distance phone rates.

November 11, 1967: Allen Ginsberg in Milan, Italy to Lawrence Ferlinghetti and Shig Murao in San Francisco

Dear Larry (or Shig):
Peter writes that he's driving Irving Rosenthal out to San Francisco and should be there any day now, if not already. He's broke, so please advance him any money he needs. I don't know how much I have there, if he needs more than $500.00 let me know. I already owe you $100.00 on bounced check.

Saw Pound several weeks on and off in Venice. He said "Cantos a mess spoiled by stupid suburban anti-Semitic prejudice." I gave him Beatles records and [Bob] Dylan, sang Hari Krishna on his 82nd birthday by fireside and wrote huge poems on Venice — putting my own mind thru his condensation and image focus — light "crooked-mirror'd on the glassy water" of Grand Canal. Returning to New York in a few days. I'll phone.

OK, love
Allen

[P.S.] I kept complete record of conversations and his few comments.

November 15, 1967: Lawrence Ferlinghetti in San Francisco to Allen Ginsberg in New York

Cher Allen:
[. . .] Peter is here, having arrived last week in VW bus from New York with Irving (Rosenthal) and he is very Speedy; and has had trouble with VW bus. There is a $450 estimate for repairs on it, new transmission, etc. and we will pay it so that he can get the car out tomorrow. I hope this won't upset you, but I imagine it's still your car, and we'll charge it against your royalties . . . .

Just a quick note . . . . Thanks for laying my "Segovia" poem on Nanda. Love to her and Ettore and you . . .

Larry

[P.S.] (Kind of worried about Peter. Any words of advice?)

Dear Allen

Got the word from Shig you were back and that phone was discon-
nected, etc. Peter should be arriving in New York City about the time
of this letter. I wrote you in Milan the day he left to tell you we'd ad-
vanced him $450 for you for VW repairs here. OK. He was out here
just long enough to shine up our shop (I never seen him so Speedy)
and take off again . . . .

Got your letter about conversations with Pound in Venice and
singing for his birthday Rama Krishna. Beautiful. Note you say you
kept full notes on same. *Ramparts* is eager to get these notes and publish them, since I told Scheer[139] about them yesterday, having your
letter in hand. Will you send to me to lay on them for an early issue?
(I would also like to put them out in a separate little book, if there is
enough, but you probably have plans for it in some hardcover?) Anyway, send them for *Ramparts* if you can. (Send the handwritten notes
if you want to, and I'll have them typed up.)

Shig says you are going to concentrate on getting *Planet News*
manuscript rounded up. So hope to have it before Xmas . . . Book in
the Spring. Am putting Artaud's complete, definitive *To Have Done
With Judgment of God* in the Pocket Poets Series, with original French
en face, in a new translation by Beach-Pelieu. (Guy Wernham's is really
very bad.) . . . . So this should come out about this Spring too . . . . I remember you once had corrected copy of Edition K, with handwritten
corrections by Paule Thévenin, and Irving Rosenthal had it and refused
to let me borrow it at one point when we were working on Artaud
Anthology. I asked Irving about this copy when he was here last week
but he says he doesn't have it and doesn't know where it is unless you
have it. If it is at all possible, could you possibly find it and send it? I
know you're swamped with mail and chores and correspondence, but

---

139 Robert Scheer (b. 1936), a journalist who was the editor of *Ramparts* magazine.

if you can think to find this, it might make a big difference in the final definitive edition in English and French [. . .]

I just got back from Southwest tour last week, Tucson, Albuquerque, Taos, Santa Fe, El Rito, Placitas Drop City . . . . Saw lotsa your friends . . . . There was one Indian in a cultural pocket north of Cameron, Arizona, who had never heard of you. But then he was deaf and had his head buried up his ass in a kiva fourteen feet underground.

Love

Larry

Although Ginsberg says that Peter is in "fine shape" in the following letter, that was far from the truth and typical of Ginsberg's ability to delude himself when it came to unpleasant matters. In fact, Peter's drug problems and mental health would be a major concern for the rest of their lives.

November 22, 1967: Allen Ginsberg in New York to Lawrence Ferlinghetti in San Francisco

Dear Larry:

Got back, cleared mail off desk, typing poems for book, cut off phone and all other activities. Books as I left them in shelves in house a little disordered tho all there but I don't remember where I put the Artaud Dieu — it may be in Paterson, but I'll have to look carefully thru books here, I'm not sure I can find it tho — just looked and couldn't locate — I managed to hang on to it keeping track after loaning it out for on and off ten years, but now when crucial I dunno. Dammit. I'll keep trying.

Peter arrived back here fine shape no speed and calm. Thanks for putting out money. I must already have 700 or 800 in advances now.

I kept thirty or so pages notes description and conversations (Pound only said a half page in all three weeks) but it's in notebook journal I'm using — can't send it and don't want to distract from main work — it'll hold. Tell Scheer a recent Pound biographer Michael Reck (just put out book *Ezra Pound a Close-Up*) was present at conversation about anti-Semitism and took notes and checked them with me and said he would write an article so perhaps he already has if they contact him. (There's enough for a little pamphlet someday that I got but it's as much work as I can do to keep my head above water on poems right now). [. . .]

Went over "Segovia" in detail explication du Americains with Nanda, she says fine and's translating it. Fret, dig, gut, pick, bridge as puns with literal double use impossible to duplicate in Italian, posed problems, as you can imagine when you realize the musical terms are different in Italian, and the streetwork terms also different. I dunno how she solved it. I spent weeks with her translating "TV Baby" line by line, word by word, in effect rewrote the poem in Italian listening for sonorities and figuring out best values for puns and logopoeias. It took weeks for twelve pages of syntax and probably wrote a new wild Italian language solidity.

Can't figure out politics at all these days. Tho if it costs $20,000 to kill one Vietcong, Who gets that $20,000? might be an interesting angle, *à la* Pound, so I've started reading *New York Times* financial page. Pound's usura idea very simple and real: all money made by manipulating money is, like, unproductive and therefore a kind of conman robbery deal, taking a mafia cut of what us workmen produce. Banks are built on this con, and banks should be run for service by state not for skimming off profits by private fat cats. OK.

Love to Shig and
Kirby
Allen

November 27, 1967: Lawrence Ferlinghetti in San Francisco to Allen
Ginsberg in New York

Dere Al:

Got your V-Letter and will tell Scheer about Michael Reck re: Pound,
OK. I sure appreciate your having gone over my "Segovia" with Nanda
so carefully: yeah those double word plays are impossible in translation, unfortunately . . . .

Pound's usury still true and his message so simple and so long ago
now and all ignored of course since the steamroller bank-business-
military mobster rolls right on over such nuts and bolts as Pound, flat-
tening them out so flat on the pavement that they cannot be seen even
from the curb (much less the Stock Exchange itself), but the whole
thing grown so much more complicated than when Ezra Pound first
freaked it that no one even considers it the same thing anymore. [. . .]

Glad to hear you're working on book and that Peter and Gregory
are in such good shapes . . . . Nothing to answer in this letter, so, OK,
press on —

xxx —
larry

◀ 1968 ▶

Both Ferlinghetti and Ginsberg were highly active against the Vietnam War and both were arrested during civil protests. In January 1968, Lawrence spent ten days in Santa Rita Prison, while Ginsberg was brought to court in New York. Meanwhile, LeRoi Jones had also been arrested and put on trial, being prosecuted by the Newark police on charges of gun possession.

January 21, 1968: Lawrence Ferlinghetti in San Francisco to Allen Ginsberg in New York

Cher Allen:

I am loose and back at the ole horn editing Carl Solomon's next book[140] with your paragraph blurb, thank you . . . . Perhaps you will be sending the completed manuscript for *Planet News* soon? I am ready . . . . Prison wasn't so bad: got sprung after ten days by lawyer [Robert] Treuhaft; kept journal which will be in *Ramparts* (March issue, probably) . . . . I will be coming East in April: reading tour of about six highspots (one arranged thru your man [Charles] Rothschild;[141] all paying at least $750) . . . .

Haven't heard of your sentence for anti-war bust . . . . hope not much . . . .

Am happy you signed my name to C.O.P.[142] proclaim on LeRoi Jones. Use my name anytime you want for him. (I wrote his judge before sentencing; tho no result.) Hope he can keep out . . .

[Robert] Scheer and [Saul] Landau and others in Cuba for Culture Congress in early January and they asked them where was I, claiming I'd been invited. Never got the word here, tho was ready and

---

140 A reference to *More Mishaps*, published by City Lights in 1968.
141 Ginsberg's agent for his public appearances was Charles Rothschild.
142 Ginsberg created and funded a foundation called the Committee On Poetry (C.O.P.) to support poets and activists.

primed to go . . . . Maybe will go to Theatre Conference there in Fall
. . . .

I have been thinking it would be nice to put a square spine on *Howl*, made possible by using slightly thicker text paper, and raise price to $1, on next printing. What do you think of that? All the other books in Pocket Poets Series are a buck or more . . . . We would also then be able to put lettering on spine, so that book can be spotted on shelves. What you think, what you desire? [. . .]

Larry

January 24, 1968: Allen Ginsberg in New York to Lawrence Ferlinghetti in San Francisco

Dear Larry:
Glad you're out of clink. Bulk of manuscript, *Planet News* finished, I'm manicuring a few poems, I wound up revising a lot, the texts look slightly leaner but nothing's missing much, but buts, ands, ors, alsos, thoughs, ifs, etc. Fat out. Gave poem speech in court and got unconditional discharge no fine no jail like rest of arrestees *sans* record. Signed up subsequently on aid and abet draft-dodge scroll so if military state gets hairier guess I'll be open for prosecution. [. . .]

Lowell (Robert) said he wanted to go to Cuba but got stymied by State Department and at the time didn't know how to get around it. Contact Ed de Grazia[143] lawyer before you go if State Department doesn't give you validation for visit as journalist/publisher/writer. They have to, will save legal expenses of later passport fight.

Yes square spine and $1 *Howl* is fine for next editions. Do with other books what you think practical. [. . .]

Reading up on Military-Industrial Complex: it's the largest single business in U.S. (Defense Department Octopus) and trying to work with Underground Press Liberation News Service to get a sort of mandala-map-poster-centerfold articulation of the whole set-up.

---

143 Edward de Grazia (1927–2013), an activist lawyer and friend of Ginsberg's.

Then can zap others than Dow with specific jujitsu insteada butting head against whole Wall Street.

LeRoi however won't talk to me tho I been phoning and writing him, his secretary says, "Kiss my ass," and "Mr. Jones too busy." Wella-day. Spoke to his wife and father and am sure he was framed on guns.

OK, jail must've been fun, "Peanuts," said Baez charmingly.[144] Hope it stays that way but general sense of things — maybe much worse police state to come. Seems inevitable tho nightmarish.

OK. Love
Allen

On February 4, 1968, Neal Cassady died in San Miguel de Allende, Mexico. Allen sent a note as follows in the form of a poem to Lawrence.

February 13, 1968: Allen Ginsberg in New York to Lawrence Ferlinghetti in San Francisco

Dear Larry:

> [. . .]
> Alas Neal —
> Love to you, while we're alive, and Kirby —
> Jack on phone said "felt like the bottom dropped out"
> and Peter said "ooh" on phone hearing
> and I thought Sir Spirit's now home in Spirit.
> [. . .]

Love
Allen

---

144 Singer and activist Joan Baez (b. 1941) had been arrested at the same time as Lawrence Ferlinghetti.

March 15, 1968: Lawrence Ferlinghetti in San Francisco to Allen
Ginsberg in New York

Dear Allen:
Called you last night and left word with Peter that your final [version
of] "Wales [Visitation]" arrived, etc. Have now airmailed the whole
manuscript off to Villiers in England, and figure to print 5000 let-
terpress over there, and leave most of it over there for sale, and do a
20,000 offset edition here right away. [. . .]

The "Wales" poem is really beautiful, one of the greatest you have
ever written. (Janine [Pommy Vega] was here and read it yesterday and
said the same.) And it's not like any poem you've ever written before.
It's like the English Romantic poets strained thru the Lake Country
into Wales and you . . . . the gravity and the beauty of Old Word-
iesworth and Keatsniff . . . . only without Wordsworth's late draggy
keening . . . . Closer to Dylan (Thomas) of course . . . Scooped everybody again, you bum . . . . And of course you really sound like nobody
but yourself. . . . At a great distance from you, poetically, as usual, I
enclose my "Pentagon" poem, which I hope may somehow delect you
anyway.[145]

Back to the manuscript of *Planet News*, I left in "Stotras To Kali",
and hope you will be persuaded to leave it in, though you can remove
it in the proof-stage if you want to. You say it's too much a "Beatnik
poem," but I never thought of that reading it now, and anyway, who
didn't pass that way? It's got a lot more in it than that aspect, and it fits
in the book, I think . . . .

I note you have another book with "Long Poem to These States"
coming up,[146] and of course I'll be glad to have it for Pocket Poets
again, whenever you're ready. End of this year would be fine. [. . .]

Oh yes: while I'm away in April, if you want to use Bixby cabin,
please get keys from Kirby, since she won't be using it while kids are

---

145 Ferlinghetti's poem "White House Automat" was included in this letter.
146 *The Fall of America* would be published in 1972, but several other Ginsberg titles
would be issued before then.

in school. I've just gotten electricity down there. Which will make it easier for you to work there, if you want. Maybe when your father comes with you this summer, we can all go down for a while . . . Looking forward to Big Sur this summer . . . .

Love . . . .
Lawrence

Early in December 1968, Ferlinghetti stopped to visit Ginsberg on his new farm in Cherry Valley, New York. Peter Orlovsky and Allen drove Lawrence to the airport afterwards so that he could fly to Paris, but immediately after seeing him off they met with an accident.

December 7, 1968: Allen Ginsberg in Albany, New York, to Lawrence Ferlinghetti in San Francisco

Dear Larry:
[. . .] As you can see I'm still in Albany, I never did get back to the farm from the airport — just after we left you, we took off for downtown Albany and as we were leaving the blue-lit field area we ran into another car in the night rain. Terrific nauseating thud — ugh bump in hip and ribs, and car stopped and I lay back on seat saying "Ooh Jesus, how'd I get stuck in this body-stump again, and what kind of mortification got to pass to get out of this fix?"

So I've been in Albany Hospital with fractured hip and four cracked ribs, pain all gone now, I'll be here a week, and then a couple months in bed and crutches on the farm. It's been a sort of pleasure to go thru — I never had a broken bone before in forty-two years. Nobody else was hurt bad except for a few scratches. [. . .]

I been lying in bed writing postcards and reading newspapers and some [William] Blake and feel pretty good — perfect excuse to be lazy, stay in bed all day. Apparently the insurance company pays. We lost that station wagon tho, complete wreck. My bowels were paralyzed ("ileus") for almost a week and I kept floating back to hospital bed in Demerol dreams on great bags of flatulence. Wrote one poem about the "body-stump" and made a weird TV interview from hospital bed raving about body-stumps being collapsible traps.

OK, I'll write again, just to get this off to you.

Love,
Allen

◀ 1969 ▶

Ginsberg's Indian Journals *became bogged down in production with Dave Haselwood and the Auerhahn Press, and Ferlinghetti decided to take over its publication. It was a tangled situation to deal with, but eventually Lawrence was able to shepherd the book through the final stages of publication. Lawrence also comments here on a major project Ginsberg undertook, which was to set all of Blake's poems to music. Blake's poems had originally been composed as songs, but the music had been lost, and Allen did his best to tune dozens of them to a modern ear. Lawrence's advice that Ginsberg not sink too much money into the project was not heeded.*

July 7, 1969: Lawrence Ferlinghetti in San Francisco to Allen Ginsberg in New York

Cher Allen:

I. Re. *Indian Journals*. Finally got to Haselwood, and we agreed to do a joint contract with you, using our standard forms, and I've just made one out and sent it to Dave. He'll send it to you. We'll co-publish it, splitting all costs and so-called profits, if any. (He's several thousand in the hole on the job already, evidently, and we will split that with him, too.) Hopefully the book can be gotten out by late this Fall, at the latest. He says that all that remains to be done is to paste in the captions on the photos, the page-proofs having been corrected already. If he does the remaining work soon, we could get it in our late Fall catalogue.

II. Can you tell me anything about the Cassady manuscripts which I hear from Ann Charters[147] are at the University of Texas library? She says there are 106 pages prose plus poetry (probably by him?). I wrote to Carolyn (Cassady) but she doesn't know where this

---

147 Ann Charters (b. 1936), a Beat scholar and the first Kerouac biographer.

material came from. I've written University of Texas to see if they will send me Zerox of everything. Otherwise I'll have to take a special trip down there to see it. We were in the final stages of putting his *First Third* to the press, after the editing I did of all the manuscript in San Miguel this Spring, and having just conferred with John Bryan who had photos and other manuscript pages which he had published once in his *Notes from the Underground*. In fact, John was about to type the final version for camera on his IBM Selectric. Now we are holding off until the Texas material is checked out. I may also go to Florida in late July to see Jack (K) who says he will write Introduction to *First Third* if I will show him or make him cognizant of contents. (He seems in a good mood at the moment, and said he'd welcome a visit.)

Who else might still have relevant material for *First Third*, [Ken] Kesey? If so, do you have his address? I have never been in any contact with him, except passing by in his Wayoutward Bus . . . .

I hope you are not getting in too deep on the recording costs of Blake! (Strange that the angel can't otherwise be heard, sweet bird . . . .)

Luf,
Lawrence

Another large Allen Ginsberg project that was being put together by City Lights turned out to be fraught with problems. George Dowden had compiled an extensive bibliography on Ginsberg's writings, which City Lights agreed to publish. Unfortunately, Dowden had not used a standard bibliographical format. Although Lawrence writes about putting the book to press in January 1970, it would take far longer to get the book into publishable form.

January 9, 1970: Lawrence Ferlinghetti in San Francisco to Allen Ginsberg in New York

Allen

I would like to use two full-page photos of you on inside front and back covers of your big *Bibliography*. The ones with the most "historical" importance, in line with bibliography, I suppose are the Uncle Sam one and the Richard Avedon one of you naked. How would those do for inside front and backcovers, full page bleed? And if OK how do we get the permissions to use them? [. . .]

I am still counting on you being here in April to have a final go on the Cassady manuscript for *First Third*. Please save a few solid days to work on it in Big Sur; yes?

Gregory still here, and back on the jalopie, but talking about going back to Santa Fe if Belle[148] will have im . . . .

luv,
LF

---

148 Belle Carpenter was Corso's wife at the time; she lived in Santa Fe.

Jan. 24, 1970: Allen Ginsberg in Cherry Valley, New York, to Lawrence Ferlinghetti in San Francisco

Dear Larry:
Enclosed some notes on the *Bibliography* I sent to George Dowden —
I didn't have a chance to read it thru till this week (read it thru except index I didn't read). George asked me not to make any changes till he arranged them as he'll send you the suggested corrections. [. . .]

Pallbore at [Charles] Olson's funeral last week in Boston, John Wieners, [Ed] Dorn, [Ed] Sanders, Harvey Brown and professors, [Robert] Creeley disappeared to Caribbean whence I'd just come. OK, Love

Allen

May 29, 1970: Lawrence Ferlinghetti in San Francisco to Allen Ginsberg in New York

Allen —
Re: "The Neal Cassady Legend" can you tell me if you think we should include photos of Neal with Ann Murphy, Stella [Levy], and others — ? — How does/did Carolyn Cassady feel about them? We have some great shots, but I imagine we'll have to leave them out, won't we? As well as things like that final love note from Neal to that chick in New York [J.B. Brown]   ? — What's your advice — ? — And could you write a few pages on Neal for the book — I've asked [Ken] Kesey for same — OK? —

Just received Miles'[149] letter about Dowden's *Bibliography*, which is really <u>upsetting</u>, for I am afraid Miles is completely right and I think we are going to have to <u>reset</u> the whole book — even though we've already spent exactly $500 on composition. Enclosed is a letter for

---

149 Barry Miles (b. 1943), a British writer and the first Ginsberg biographer.

Miles on the subject. We'll see what Dowden's response is. We'll delay publication now, anyway. (It was already to go to press) [. . .]
— Larry

June 6, 1970: Allen Ginsberg in Cherry Valley, New York, to Lawrence Ferlinghetti in San Francisco

Dear Larry:

Answering on the run. I don't think Carolyn [Cassady] cares about suppressing other chicks' photos, I mean, I think she'll be amenable to reality — she's writing a book of memoir herself. So if you use photos, use any you think appropriate. Yes, I'll write source memoir I guess. I haven't been able to do anything but answer mail, read proofs and sign contracts all month tho.

I think Miles is right too, re: *Bibliography*.

Gotham Book Mart with Ann Charters put together one photo book [*Scenes Along the Road*] involving Jack [Kerouac], Bill [Burroughs], and others and myself so I'm afraid there be a glut of picture books involving me. I don't object to your project as photo book, I guess, if it would help pay for the *Bibliography*, but are you sure it's cheap to produce? Title *Allen Ginsberg: Literary Photographs* might give it some class instead of being a personality poster yearbook. (Still I wonder whether Gotham book and this would be redundant?) Also can you use same photo plates for *Bibliography*?? My father's getting the World's Fair photo, someone borrowed it, it turns out.

If money is needed to finance re-processing of bibliography let me know and I'll help pay for it — either out of pocket cash or advance on City Lights royalties used for that. Whatever is necessary.
Allen

Sadly, although Ferlinghetti had hoped to visit Jack Kerouac in Florida, Jack had died the previous October before Lawrence could make it there.

July 14, 1970: Lawrence Ferlinghetti in San Francisco to Allen Ginsberg in Cherry Valley, New York

Dear Allen —
Down here on lake in Central Florida at mother in law's fishing camp — houseshack like on some banana plantation; wearing pith helmet; recouping from hepatitis . . . If it were last summer, I'd be seeing Jack [Kerouac] — I was going to see him about Neal's book, but due to family trouble never made it . . . . Reading all of *Indian Journals* here again now, since to read same in proof stage in a hurry is like reading Angkor Wat up close with a magnifying glass and missing the whole of it — a tit or cock sticking out here and there all that was left in memory of proof-reader's Braille . . . .

It leads me naturally to remind you I hope you will get back to *South American Journal* soon, so that it could be put out in matching format — all your journals maybe in matching identical volumes. Which also reminds me that just before I left San Francisco I had a call from Simon and Schuster editor who said they were interested in doing a mass market paperback edition of *Indian Journals* and I told him please to write us a letter about it and I would show it to you. (When I said I didn't realize Simon and Schuster did "mass market" paperbacks, he said he meant Pocket Books, Inc., which was part of the same corporate conglomerate now.)

So I'll let you know about that when I get back to the scene, about August first at the latest . . . Also, the latest offer for a *Selected Ginsberg* is from New American Library who offers $50,000 advance to you! I've not answered that but figured your attitude was still the same, not wanting to get into that sort of Establishment yet? (Let me know if you want me to send you their letter.) Perhaps you might want to consider making up some sort of "selection" which would not include poem *Howl* nor main part of *Kaddish* — since those big publishers act now as if they'd take just about anything they could get — but the trouble is, even a selection without the above might knock huge holes in our sales of your separate volumes to colleges, where we sell enormous amounts, perhaps amounting to as much as half of your

City Lights royalties. (We've really got the country covered now with wholesalers and actual traveling bookmen in every region — as you can see list in back of our new booklist.)

Anyway, speaking of Jack [Kerouac], that also reminds me that I've written Sterling Lord since Jack's death, asking for *Visions of Neal* and *Some of the Dharma* but I never get the time of night from him — like we're not worth his trouble for the big money, etc. Maybe you could tell him we complained and push him a bit to send same — We could pay as good royalties as anyone, though of course not with those huge stock and bond corporate aggregate advances. (Jack called me once and offered *Visions* and I said send it, but he never did . . .)

Seems like getting out of town allows me to remember all these important matters I am too busy to write about when home. —

Well, I hope you are having a groovy summer up there on the farm — Looks like, given Dowden's somewhat hysterical reaction, we are going to have to go ahead with your *Bibliography* as-is — and catch all hell from the professors and librarians — I did tell Dowden very explicitly from the very beginning of our correspondence that it <u>had</u> to be in "standard bibliographical form" — he seems to have a short memory on the subject — I had my doubts that he was qualified to do a standard bibliography but I encouraged him since it was an important thing to be done and no one else was doing it. It <u>will</u> have great value in its present form — though it's practically impenetrable to the casual peruser — (I didn't appreciate much all those paranoid threats he made to me in his last long tirade rundown, all about "exposing" our correspondence on the *Bibliography* to the literary world so that everyone could see what a first class shit I was. I never wrote him much but the briefest notes).

Ah well — love
—
"Larry"

Dere Allen . . . .

[. . .] Re: Dowden's *Bibliography*: OK, so it's agreed, we'll go ahead with his version as-is. I think that's the only solution at this point. (Another semi-hysteric semi-paranoid billet-amer has just come in from him, and I can sympathize with his reaction to Miles' having thrown a monkey into his gears. Who wouldn't flip, after the amount of work and personal wear and tear he threw into it?). So I'll try to get it to the press later this month, soon as I get caught up around here — stuff is piled up all over the place — I been knocked out for months with hep . . . .

Feeling pretty good now: got lots of sun in Florida (where the natives are all either half-dead-half-alive, or half-asleep) . . . . Guess you got my epistle from down there. [. . .]

Love . . . .

LF

◄ 1972 ►

Although Allen and Lawrence wrote quite frequently during the 1970s, their correspondence was usually little more than postcards or notes. Travel had become easier so they saw each other more frequently, and they used the telephone for communications that once would have been done via mail. After the seventies the quality and importance of letters they wrote continued to drop, so only random samplings of those items have been included. The age of great letter-writing was drawing to a close.

In 1972, Ferlinghetti and Ginsberg traveled to Australia together to give a series of readings around the country. Lawrence took his son Lorenzo along and they went off alone for some side trips.

March 26, 1972: Lawrence Ferlinghetti in New Zealand to Allen Ginsberg in Australia

Dear Allen —
This is to save you a trip to New Zealand. West 150 miles to Rotorua the supposedly Maori town. (It looks a bit like Monterey, California). I did see the volcanic geysers but was hard put to find a Maori not fully assimilated into the WASP culture and living in a semi-tract house. The Maoris seem to be, on the <u>North</u> Island at least, completely ingested. The "Institute of Maori Arts and Crafts in Rotorua" had hardly anything in it except <u>contemporary</u> wood sculpture being done in a workshop there — I think all the authentic original Maori art must be in big museums in other countries, certainly not here. The other postcard does depict an authentic legend of the princess who swam to the island in Lake Rotorua but it was the only "real" thing I found. There are a few unassimilated tribesmen on the South Island but that would take more time than you'll have this trip — For the rest, it's a great place for sheepskin rugs and meat pies. The country-side on

the North Island doesn't look English — the houses look like Pacific Grove California — Just forget all about it, will you?

Love —
Larry

Back in San Francisco Ferlinghetti continued work on the fifth book of Ginsberg's poetry, The Fall of America, *which eventually won the National Book Award in poetry.*

July 6, 1972: Lawrence Ferlinghetti in San Francisco to Allen Ginsberg in New York

Allen —
The copy questions are not so extensive — and you could run through the works in an hour — The rest — the forming of the "Long Poem" — I hope you will take a good deal of time to do up on the farm the last half of this month — I hope you will just take off up there <u>by yourself</u> for three or four days, and do nothing else — It won't take that long, if you get to it — As I said on the phone, I hear your voice sounding in every line, and when I do that, every line and every poem makes it — of course — It would take an editor who had never heard your actual voice to make any suggestions for omissions, i.e. poems that should be left out . . . . but then <u>his</u> criteria would be arbitrary too — like whose rules to follow? — So in the end it's your voice sounding through every syllable which is the only thing that counts and your "mind" or consciousness itself — (Just so, when imitators of your style — or others who follow the "graph of consciousness" formula for a poem — try the same thing, they fall flat — or theirs is just not interesting great poetry — because their minds and consciousnesses are just not so interesting — their "graphs of consciousness" may put me to sleep half the time — Never yours)

love —
Larry

◀ 1973 ▶

The idea of publishing a large book of Ginsberg's collected poems continued to recur, though Lawrence seemed reluctant to give up control of Ginsberg's poetry to a large New York publisher and Ginsberg seemed to have little time for the necessary editorial and collating work. In the letter below, Lawrence also makes a rare indirect comment about domestic problems.

July 24, 1973: Lawrence Ferlinghetti in San Francisco to Allen Ginsberg in London

Dear Allen . . . .
[. . .] Working things out with New Directions [James] Laughlin on your *Assembled Poetries*, though the costs of producing the enormous book seem to be enormous; but it will all work out. At the moment, we're a long way from a working agreement or contract with them, but we won't do anything without your approval, needless to say, New Directions is hot to do it. [. . .]

Well, Kirby took Julie and Lorenzo to Florida to live and go to school this year (Gainesville), and I'm going to move back in my house at 706 Wisconsin on September 1 . . . . During the second half of August I may go visit Laughlin on his ranch in Wyoming . . . .

Larry

◀ 1976 ▶

In 1975, the manager of the City Lights Bookstore, Shig Murao, suffered a severe stroke. While he was recuperating, Lawrence hired another store manager, and that act insulted Shig, who felt that Lawrence was trying to force him out of the business. Such a great rift was created between the two partners that they never spoke to one another again. Lawrence wrote the following letter to Allen on a photocopy of the letter to Shig reproduced below it.

May 12, 1976: Lawrence Ferlinghetti in San Francisco to Allen Ginsberg in New York

Dear Allen —
This I proposed to Shig. He has just refused! So I'm doing a two-year "lease" arrangement with Craig [Broadley] and Joe [Wolberg].[150] I need a two-year leave of absence, to do my own work! But everything will remain the same and I'll still edit a book or two a year — Can we get to your new one now? *Mind Breath?*

Love —
Larry

May 11, 1976

Dear Shig . . .
I know Bob Briggs has worked out a buy-sell agreement which you approve, but this is one last attempt to persuade you not to sell out.

Since this seems a bad time to try to sell the whole of City Lights to someone else — due to the fairly poor balance sheets for the past

---

150 Craig Broadley and Joe Wolberg were two employees of City Lights.

five years, in both publishing and bookstore — but since I still want to get out from under, especially since you're not going to be there — I am therefore going to lease-out the whole operation, as outlined in the attached. (This was dreamed up by Craig; Joe is in the East); but I still wish you'd stay in and be a part of it — See the enclosed provision for you to get 50% of what I get per year under the lease arrangement — ½ of $6000 . . . . if you don't sell out.

So — please consider it again! — and call Bob Briggs or me if you want to stop the proceedings . . . .

lawrence

Shig did not change his mind, and he sold his interest in the bookstore back to Ferlinghetti. The two years that Lawrence hoped to take off from the business, like so many other plans to get away, never materialized. On July 8, 1976, Ginsberg's father died, and Lawrence, who was on a vacation with his son, sent this note of sympathy.

July 14, 1976: Lawrence Ferlinghetti in Seattle to Allen Ginsberg in New York

Dear Allen —
Nancy [Peters][151] told me on phone yesterday of Louis' passing (into some other form) and it was good to hear he did it without prolonged pain. Please tell Edith I'm thinking of her and wishing her the best. Anything I can do, let me know. (Back in San Francisco by July 25; with Lorenzo on those islands sailing up here.)

Love —
Larry

---

151 Nancy Peters (b.1936), a poet and editor who became managing director and co-owner of City Lights Books, now retired.

‹ 1977 ›

In response to Ferlinghetti's complaint that Ginsberg never said anything about his poetry, Allen makes an effort here to give his opinion on Lawrence's poem "The Old Italians Dying."

January 5, 1977: Allen Ginsberg in New York to Lawrence Ferlinghetti in San Francisco

Happy New Year
Dear Larry:
I enjoyed the poem, subject is close to you so details are possible and poem's an opportunity to remember actual perceptions playfully. It's a good poem, good moment.

Despite usefulness of repetition for building mournful/doleful humoresque style, some of the repetition seems excessive especially in opening page. I tried cutting to see what effect: as follows (just p. 1)

> For years the old Italians have been dying
> all over North Beach San Francisco
> For years old Italians in faded felt hats
> sun themselves dying on the benches in Washington Square
> The old Italians in their black high button shoes
> men in old felt fedoras with stained hatbands
> dying day by day the slow bell
> tolls ten in the morning in the Church of St. Peter and Paul
> marzipan church on the plaza
> and the old men still alive sit
> sunning themselves in a row
> on wood benches in the park.

Twenty lines reduced to twelve, with basically same movement, but more condensed or concentrated, leaving out no detail. Just a thought.

Working on my own book, returning to anonymous Baltimore for two weeks. Gordon Ball[152] here, with five hundred page manuscript of my early journals finished for Grove.

Love
Allen

January 7, 1977: Lawrence Ferlinghetti in San Francisco to Allen Ginsberg in New York

Dear Allen —
[. . .] Re: my "Old Italians Dying." You've made that passage into a good poem in your own voice, but you've got to hear me read this aloud. I read it slowly, gravely, and there is nothing "humoresque" about it (except of course for "They enter the true church for the first time/ in many years". But this is immediately followed by "in these carved black boats / ready to be ferried over". . . . I've cut lines in earlier poems — especially derivative literary lines — at your suggestion — But this time it's different. This is no "Tentative Description of a Dinner to Impeach President Eisenhower" — and I feel you're hearing that old voice rather than the new (I'm just getting started. I was just warming up, back then!) . . . . In the first line of the passage you've rewritten, you deleted "the" in "the old Italians have been dying" — But this is not just "old Italians" in general, in the abstract; it is the old Italians of North Beach San Francisco, the specific ones you've seen here for years. (You always said the concrete is the most poetic.) And in this case there's much detail in "the". . . .

And when you hear this poem aloud, the repetitions make it — it builds and keeps building —

---

152 Gordon Ball is a professor of English literature and the editor of several of Ginsberg's books and journals.

Glad to hear you're really working on your own book — we're ready for it, whenever — soon I hope!

Larry

June 29, 1977: Lawrence Ferlinghetti in San Francisco to Allen Ginsberg in New York

Dear Allen —

City Lights' Fall Announcement will be out in two days, with your book [*Mind Breaths*] and Peter's [*Clean Asshole Poems and Smiling Vegetable Songs*] announced for early Fall, so we need final manuscript from both of you very soon. Please put "all else" aside and concentrate on it for twenty-four hours and send same! (Peter too) The time is ripe and the ripe is ripe. The future is not a faded rose. Life is a one-wheeled cycle on the roof of Starship Enterprise. Pooch is my keeper and I shall not weep . . . . (Send manuscript now).

Enclosed is a letter from [James] Laughlin re: two matters

1. "Assembled Poetries" I'd asked him if New Directions was now ready to proceed with book. He wants multiple-volume edition, but I don't see that (bookstores hate them — volumes sell or disappear unevenly, leaving many incomplete sets) — And anyway we already <u>have</u> separate volumes —

2. Following paragraph about New Directions books not being available in New York City bookshops — I had written him about people who could not find *Coney Island* "anywhere in New York" — and see his reply — "Bookstores won't order the <u>backlist</u> books — only the new ones" — I'm beginning to think New Directions distribution, even through Lippincott, isn't any better than our own — perhaps not as good — Ours is really better than it appears to you except in New York City area — and we are going to do something about that.

Love to you and
Peter —
"Larry"

August 23, 1977: Allen Ginsberg in Farasita, Colorado, to Lawrence
Ferlinghetti and Nancy Peters in San Francisco

Dear Larry and Nancy:
Finally having finished the book to the last corrections, I can take care
of contract business with easy heart. Art first, business next. [. . .]
    Since I'm staying faithfully with main poetry and other books
with you as personal decentralized publishing project mutual work,
and sacrificing maybe some money from Big City Big Time New York
books, I hope you think it's fair of me to make provision that the condition be that we stick to it together. OK? [. . .]
                                                    OK,
                                                    Allen

◀ 1978 ▶

March 14, 1978: Allen Ginsberg in New York to Lawrence Ferlinghetti in
San Francisco

Dear Larry:
I'd seen "Adieu A Charlot" — call for subjective state is right on. *Los
Angeles Times* Op-Ed is grand place, who's the man there? How rec-
oncile subjective state (of poets) and ecologic bodhisattva politics? Big
questions — nice poem raising them.

Allen

*In this letter, Ferlinghetti mentions a book of Ginsberg's collected interviews.
This project would not be realized for nearly two decades. Ginsberg had also
proposed several younger poets for publication, and Ferlinghetti suggested
that a volume of three of Allen's favorites — Antler, David Cope, and Andy
Clausen — might be a good way to introduce the poets to a wider readership.*

November 1, 1978: Lawrence Ferlinghetti in San Francisco to Allen
Ginsberg in New York

Dear Allen . . .
[. . .] What about the Antler-Cope-Clausen 3-in-1 volume for us?
We will need the manuscript this month if we are to get it out this
Spring. Otherwise, we will schedule it for the Fall. It's OK if you want
to delay it til then, but we have to know now, since I've got to do the
blurbs for the catalog of forthcoming works . . . Just drop me a line
right away now to let me know when exactly we might expect the
finished manuscript . . .

What have you been up to? I hope you're getting up to the farm
for Thanksgiving, the best time of the year in that country. I wish I
could be there to rustle among the autumn leaves.

After the Antler-Cope-Clausen, will you be ready with your new one? You said last Spring you had enough. We've gotten nowhere with Harper and Row on your Historic Interviews. I rather think they don't know what to make of it. We'll see. At present it's way beyond our finances. Depression-Inflation, y'know . . . .

> Love to youse
>
> guys,
>
> LF

Around this time, Allen's meditation teacher, Chögyam Trungpa, became entangled in a controversy. A few years earlier, Trungpa had forcibly stripped the poet W.S. Merwin and his girlfriend after they had refused to attend a party Trungpa was giving. This incident gave birth to a scandal that came to be known as the Naropa Poetry Wars. Allen did his best to keep out of the fray, but he was gradually drawn in. Ferlinghetti was not as sympathetic toward Trungpa as Allen was.

November 6, 1978: Lawrence Ferlinghetti in San Francisco to Allen Ginsberg in New York

Allen —

Big poetry weekend here — Big crowd at bookstore for Bill [Burroughs] and we're going to do a quickie edition of *Roosevelt After Inauguration* which he read at Festival, plus new "The Whole Tamale" anti-Briggs castigation, etc. . . . He's at UC tonight . . . Had lunch with Anne Waldman[153] at Tivoli today and she says you wondering if I was going to publish or spread the Ed Sanders Merwin Report, thinking I'd gotten a copy. Don't worry, I never got a copy and anyway

---

153 In addition to being a poet, Anne Waldman was the co-director with Ginsberg of the Jack Kerouac School of Disembodied Poetics at the Naropa Institute in Boulder, Colorado. Naropa was founded by the Tibetan lama Chögyam Trungpa as the first Buddhist college in America.

you know I wouldn't publish such without checking with you first. (I'm not Captain Bly.)

Re. Naropa/Trungpa, we laid off the question mostly in *Co-Evolution Quarterly*, except for a few glancing shots for the hell of it. The questions you objected to in my interview with [Jack] Kornfield[154] were Dragon's Advocate asking questions that should be brought up or at least was in a lot of people's minds, and the answers were excellent. You know I'd written the VP (Jeremy Hayward)[155] asking for articulation of Buddhist approach to nuclear politics, and got no response whatever. Hence Kornfield —

Anne filled me in on a lot of Merwin background, and I told her about my meeting with him in Maui, including the Trungpa haiku formulation and his response.

Whatever anyone says I can see that never in history has there been such a Poetics Institute as you have started at Naropa . . . Proving again you're a fucking genius   Peter's book [*Clean Asshole Poems And Smiling Vegetable Songs*] should be ready in a couple more weeks

love —

Larry

Negotiating with the poet Antler was not always easy. He refused to be part of a three-in-one volume and Ferlinghetti was reluctant to dedicate a single volume to his work alone. Ginsberg kept trying to persuade Lawrence to go ahead with the publication.

---

154 The interview was published as "Buddhism and Nuclear Politics" in the *Journal for the Protection of All Beings*, no. 4 / *Co-Evolution Quarterly*, no. 19 (September 21, 1978).
155 Jeremy Hayward, a trained physicist and biologist, helped establish the Shambhala training program in Buddhism during the 1970s.

November 12, 1978: Allen Ginsberg in New York to Lawrence Ferlinghetti in San Francisco

Dear Larry:

[. . .] I still think you oughta do Antler's book. Where you gonna find more solid poetry and ideas and expansiveness? McClure thinks it's an imitation of me; but it didn't prevent you from printing *Howl* which was imitation of Whitman. You gotta be influenced by somebody. My first impression (you remember? back in early 1970s) was that it was taken off from Gregory's one word concept poems ("Bomb", "Death", etc. "Last Words", "Factory", etc.) not so much me. And Gary [Snyder] doesn't own the Antler'd dancer (dancer — the Antler'd dancer of "prehistoric" caves) anyway Antler's probably spent more time alone in wilderness than Gary the last few years. I'll bet it's true! But actually the name didn't come from an intellectual pose. It was his high school nickname anyway! Long before books of poesy. Everybody's so humorless.

One reason I'm so strongly dogging you on this is, I want City Lights to make money! You'll make it up on Peter's book. But you gotta have some new classic poetry, not just new mumble mumble poetry, or OK poetry. All my instincts say that you (we) have a chance with someone real, some real expansive solid rock like "Last Words" poem and "Factory" and the cluster of poems around it, things that can go into anthologies and affect thinking and style. I'm willing to put $1,000 out helping subsidize it even. It's poetry. I don't fuck Antler, I have no special reason to talk like this except amazement at his poetry. Ron Padgett, Ted Berrigan and others also are looking for publishers, it's the same thing as 15-20 years ago when there were books and no publishers!

Also dig Michael Lally. There's also someone young and interesting. As well as [David] Cope, and Andy Clausen poor guy moved to Austin in despair. I'm going down there to do a reading with him and share the $ in the Armadillo rock club in the Spring. Poesy must go on! There's geniuses around! We got genius young poets all around and nobody's picking up! It's not a repeat "renaissance," it's just a natural ripening.

I know there's money problems, but the cash spent on Antler and others — poets' poets — will always bring return for more.

Send Peter's book, well you'll do that I know, soon as can — send him a copy extra in Cherry Valley, he may be up there in next weeks. Can we have traditional party for him at Gotham Bookmart? He'll bring his momma and all his mad brothers, Lafcadio and Julius and Marie! I'll split costs if it's too expensive (or three-way dual City Lights/me/Gotham fund it). Berrigan talked to Nancy [Peters] about it, it was his inspiration.

We all played CBGB's[156] last week. I had four-piece band with electric bass — went terrific. [Andrei] Voznesensky read there too, powerful. My musicians — Arthur Russell,[157] Stephen Taylor,[158] and one Stephen Hall (Naropa '75) all played together the last three years so everybody was totally clear with the music. Voznesensky will take a tape back to Russia, maybe I'll go to Russia a year from now with a musician. I'm taking Steve Taylor (lives next door) with us (Peter [Orlovsky]) to England in June.

Hokay!
Onward!
Allen

Late November 1978: Lawrence Ferlinghetti in San Francisco to Allen Ginsberg in New York

Dear Allen and Peter —
I hope you are up in the country enjoying the annual turkey trot. I've been eating Antler instead of that fucken bird. I've reread all of Antler's "Factory" poems and others, including your masterly introduction,

---

156 CBGB's was a legendary punk nightclub on New York City's Bowery. Ginsberg enjoyed performing and felt that through song he could reach even more people; venues like CBGB's offered him that opportunity.

157 Arthur Russell (1951–1992), composer and musician.

158 Steven Taylor (b. 1955) would be Ginsberg's musical accompanist for more than twenty years.

with which I very faintly agree. I've been wrong before, as I know all too well (but not too often). Still I don't really think Antler's anywhere near the Great Poet you seem to think he is, and I'm somehow unimpressed with him as the Great Original thinker you make him out to be. He's very good when he's good, but surely no huge universal Genius, give or take a Wauwatosa or two.

To get down to the texts, I would say the main "Factory" is heavily over-written and should be cut (*à la* Pound cutting *The Wasteland*) by at least a half a dozen pages. The heavy over-use of rhetorical questions is especially notable in the main poem and in several lesser poems. This device must be used sparingly, as you know from your own practice. (In his case, the rhetorical questions are often neither funny enough nor profound enough to carry the weight.) If Antler would allow you to cut the poem, I'd welcome it.

Finally, the use of his high school nickname, Antler, is touching, but still has that corny 1960s connotation of a Wasp hippy passing himself off as some sort of Wawa Indian. When I was in the Boy Scouts I was called Moose, but I wouldn't want it to get around now, having I hope happily outgrown my juvenile horns, even though they might still be an ecological or tribal asset in some retarded circles. [. . .]

love and kisses —

L

December 7, 1978: Allen Ginsberg in New York to Lawrence Ferlinghetti in San Francisco

Dear Larry:
[. . .] Well now, Antler — re: your letter. As I said "Do what thous wilst is the whole of the law." I already sat down two years ago and went over 7/8 of it line by line, mostly for repetition and condensation within lines. You might suggest to him, as you have with me, general or specific cuts to bring down the size, if you do bring out three poets book. Get three great poets and it's ok. If one is weak,

the project's not so hot idea. I'll try sending his whole book to Fred Jordan,[159] meanwhile.

Peter's book is marvel. Glad Gotham Book Mart party's coming off, be a gala crowd, dopes and geniuses all mixed up giggling.

"Scavengers in Truck"[160] is genuine moment of eternity with red light for an instant. Switch to democracy generalization tapers off the intensity of the "observed moment." Wish you'd keep watching adding details instead of going off in editorial.

"Sign Painters" the same. There's actuality in the details you describe and you have Chaplinesque clarity of eyesight which I think becomes fogged and lax by diverting mind from central idea. Though in this case the picture within picture is fine.

"Dispel Gloom Elegy" — The hush sections OK especially "at a hot potato stand on Pier 20" followed by People's Temple. Hot potato stand is a tiny accurate particularity, and it's that particularity I dig. Otherwise things is just idears.

I'll probably be ready with another small book of poems in about a year, "Plutonian Ode," etc. That'll maybe be printed in *Voice*.

Merry Xmas
Allen

---

159 An editor at Grove Press.
160 This is a reference to Ferlinghetti's poem "Two Scavengers in a Truck, Two Beautiful People in a Mercedes."

◀ **1979** ▶

Gregory Corso was living in San Francisco at this time and began caus-
ing some financial problems for City Lights. He broke into the store several
times with a stolen key and took money from the cash register, but when they
changed the lock, he broke the window in the door to burglarize the store.

April 25, 1979: Lawrence Ferlinghetti in San Francisco to Allen Ginsberg
in New York

Dear Allen —
I am at Art Institute drawing model (one day a week). Gregory has
broken into City Lights at night and stolen about $400 — At least
three witnesses saw him do it — We think he has set of keys to the
store, and we had changed locks — Hence, he broke in this time —
Almost $3000 has disappeared during the past year — $300 or $400
hundred every few weeks — Always at night after the store was closed.
I am not reporting him to police, and I am not bringing charges against
him, but the police have the goods on him — witnesses and fingerprints — and I advised him today that he'd better get out of town fast
before one of his enemies squeals on him and gets him busted.
     We are in terrible financial shape, partly on account of the Corso
robberies, and Nancy [Peters] has had to cut her salary in half! Therefore we are not going to be able to send you the full $8000 we still
owe you. I believe Nancy is planning to send you $5000 next week —
which will mean we will still owe you $3000 to be paid whenever it's
possible.
     More later! Got to draw —

Love
LF

May 14, 1979: Allen Ginsberg in New York to Lawrence Ferlinghetti and
Nancy Peters in San Francisco

Dear Larry and Nancy:

Saw Harrisburg poem[161] in the *Times*, I like the white snowjob, and
what element of visual can be seen from above small plane. Tho it be
difficult to translate the puns, as ever — but the white imagery seemed
good equivalent to radiation.

Gregory is here, was outrageous the first few days then settled
down sober writing. From conversation with Lisa [Brinker],[162] him and
Raymond Foye[163] I gather, or guess, that he's responsible for breaking
the window, but was unharmed or un-cut and didn't rob the register,
but is responsible for the money stolen that night since he broke the
window. Lisa and Raymond say he didn't have a key previous, so there's
no reason to assume he is responsible for previous losses. Besides, it
doesn't make sense. If he kicked in window in order to rob money, why
would he have to do that if he already had a key?

I would bill him for window he wrecked and losses consequent
on that — from what I gather from your letter, and casual talk with
Gregory, Lisa, and Raymond, it doesn't make sense to assume he was
stealing from the store with a key before that. [. . .]

Love
Allen

May 19, 1979: Lawrence Ferlinghetti in San Francisco to Allen Ginsberg
in New York

Dear Allen —

I'm glad you're so fair-minded about Gregory, though I can't resist
straightening you out on the facts of what actually happened, even

---

161 A reference to Ferlinghetti's poem "A Nation of Sheep" which appeared in the *New
York Times*.
162 Lisa Brinker was Gregory Corso's wife at the time.
163 Raymond Foye (b. 1957), editor of *The Unknown Poe* (San Francisco: City Lights, 1980).

though at this point I don't know what's the point in proving it. You got your information from Lisa and Raymond Foye, and I really feel sorry for Lisa if she is that naive — (and I fear for what Gregory will eventually do to her in general — I'm sure she's suffered a lot with Gregory already, and is going to suffer even worse, no doubt). [. . .] You evidently have no idea how Gregory upset the people working at City Lights or the store in general — the operation of it — over the past six months or so. And it wasn't just the missing money every three weeks or so — He browbeat everyone who worked there — or at least those he dared to — and you can't imagine the language he used on Nancy and other women — etc. — a stone drag, to say the least. (While the eternal sycophants — stood around snickering.) You say, why did Gregory break the glass to get in, if he had a key? Because we had changed the lock the day before, and the old key wouldn't work. Well, there are at least three witnesses to the actual break-in. One was standing with Gregory across the street from the store at midnight or later, when he said "I'm going into City Lights and get some money." Then he saw Gregory break the window and go in, and he <u>saw</u> Gregory stuff a bunch of money (bills) into his pocket and split.

It's a good thing I hate cops or he would be behind bars right now. (Not only were there witnesses, but the cops got fingerprints an hour later, etc. etc.) A fine friend he turned out to be after all these years. [. . .]

Love and kisses to
you and Peter and
Denise[164]
Larry

---

164 Denise Mercedes was Peter Orlovsky's girlfriend at the time.

◀ 1980 ▶

Lawrence continued to show reluctance to publish a single volume devoted to Antler, despite Ginsberg's firm support. In addition to Antler, this letter also mentions Allen's poor health. It was a premonition of the fact that his declining health would take up more and more of his time and energy until his death in 1997.

January 27, 1980: Allen Ginsberg in Boulder, Colorado, to Lawrence Ferlinghetti in San Francisco

Dear Larry:

I'm working on sorting thru and selecting from the mass of manuscript I have of Cope and Clausen.

I have high blood pressure from multiplicity of commitments and anxiety over doing them all. I just can't rush any more. Taking it easier and sleeping more and sitting more regularly and no salt and cut diet and so feeling better than New York.

Antler! It seems insoluble. His work is too good to miss! Should I try to find a patron to subsidize City Lights publication of his whole book? Is that reasonable? How much would *Last Words* cost? I think his poetry will gain many readers, already has made some big impression via *Co-Evolution*, which will publish "Enskyment" next. What can we do . . . . Also, substitute Bobby Meyers for Antler in 3-in-1 book. [. . .]

[Jean-Jacques] Lebel is already translating *Factory* and [Nanda] Pivano says she'll find an Italian publisher, so there must be an American publisher!

[unsigned]

245

Dear Larry:

Antler and I are re-circulating his book and he seems settled now not
to go any further with the 3-in-1 City Lights format since it would
require the odd sideways printing. It's really a shame there isn't enough
money in City Lights poetry sales to make it possible to publish his
book. But your estimate on that point seems definite so there's no use
scratching head further. I think he will find a publisher and it'll be a
literary event — as Stewart Brand[165] has figured too; Antler's "Enskyment" will be in this Spring issue, and Stuart writes he's considering
doing Antler's book himself when next *Whole Earth Catalogue* money
comes in, if book hasn't found publisher by next Spring. It's been rejected by a dozen publishers, I'm amazed at the tangle — it reminds
me of the days when Kerouac's *On the Road* and Bill's *Junkie* couldn't
find a publisher, I trudged from publishing house to house and editor
to editor and wrote letters and no luck! same as with this text.

Do you still want to go ahead with 3 in 1 book? I've gone over
Cope's work — hundreds of pages — and edited and selected a mass
of poems his best, and have a student working on getting it Xeroxed
chronologic and assembled. Another student's doing the same with
Clausen. I wrote Robert Meyers and asked him if he had a 48-page
manuscript for me to see, in place of Antler's. Let me know if you're
still game. If not, I think the texts are all good enough, once they're
together, to circulate as individual books. It may be plenty of trouble
finding publishers tho. Still I have faith in their writing, because every
time I go back and read it, it's still there, and still interesting. Cope
particularly, now that I've re-read nine long pamphlets 1974-79 and
reviewed all his little gems. Anyway I've been working like an editor
with fine tooth comb over the texts. [. . .]

Saw Tom Clark's *Poetry Wars* book.[166] His commentary is such a

---

165 Stewart Brand (b. 1938), a writer and the editor of the popular *Whole Earth Catalog*.
166 *The Great Naropa Poetry Wars*, Tom Clark (Cadmus, 1980).

tangle of mis-information and fibbing I don't know what to do — he's [criticizing?] me giving the Rome money to Trungpa for Trungpa, while I brought it back for the poetics school; he says I wanted the "original" tape of our interview back. While I've repeatedly asked for a copy only, so I could restore the prejudicial cuts he made, and he still hasn't had the fairness to even give me a copy. It's maddening, it's like dealing with my mother when she thought Aunt Elanor was conspiring against her. Nothing to do about it but forget it. At the end he even attacks Ron Padgett for being part of a totalitarian conspiracy to give more to Naro-poids like Carl Rakosi and Bobbie Louise Creeley. Ach! Check it out.

Love
Allen

February 24, 1980: Lawrence Ferlinghetti in San Francisco to Allen Ginsberg in New York

Dear Allen —

Reading your letter written 2:55 A.M. 13 February re: Antler: I don't think I've ever changed my mind about a manuscript — You know how stubborn I am (and, as [Michael] McClure would say, stupid!) — except Antler's — and I'm willing to change it now — I don't think he's as great a poet as you think he is (great poets aren't always the greatest critics) — some of your other greats leave me in doubt — for instance, e.e. cummings I think is a much greater poet than W. C. Williams, but where is he in your pantheon? And then a lot of other "graph-of-consciousness" poets you have promoted — (the "graph" is great when the poet has a great and/or interesting mind, so that what-ever comes out of it is interesting/unusual/great/comely — but how many of them have that kind of mind and consciousness? They just ain't got yours). Fortunately, Antler is not a graph-of-consciousness poet. (I've got a hundred notebooks filled with my graphs of con, but, as Picasso said, I don't exhibit my experiments!) Anyway, back to Ant-ler, you may be right in the end, particularly if he develops more on his own line. You've been right before, when I was wrong. So I am willing to go along with you on his *Factory*, if he can see his way to its being printed in our Pocket Poets format. He can have a volume to himself (the line can be set wider by cutting the margins to the very minimum). And we can do your selected 3-in-1 <u>after</u> Antler's volume (Cope — Meyers — Clausen). If you want to, send a Xerox of this letter to Antler, and ask him. If he says OK, ask him to return the 3-in-1 proposed contract to me, and I'll send him a single-volume contract. (I don't know where he is now, and anyway I don't feel very enthusiastic about writing him anymore since he makes Xeroxes of every word and seems to spread them around!) (Whole poetry wars built on them!) Well, even the greatest editors make mistakes! And of course I'm one of the greatest —

love —
"Larry"

February 24, 1980: Lawrence Ferlinghetti in San Francisco to Allen Ginsberg in New York

Cher Allen —
Other matters — Communiques to the Front — As I said on the phone — your letter to [W.S.] Merwin, reprinted in Tom Clark's book, is masterly — as are all your other ripostes to attacks at Boulder. However, basically, from <u>my</u> Herbert Read-Rexroth-anarchist point of view, you are-on-the-wrong-fuckin-side! No matter how great a casuist and master of eloquence you are, you are W-R-O-N-G to be defending an <u>oriental despot</u>, in the great aristocratic monarchic tradition of oriental despots — I agree with Merwin, I agree with Peter Marin, I agree with Gary [Snyder], I agree with Rexroth — what are you doing defending this petty dictator, and who needs experiments in monarchy at this point in the U.S.? (Isn't that what Nixon was?) So — the sooner you get on the "right" side, the better!

Love and Kisses
to all
Lawrence

March 20, 1980: Allen Ginsberg in Boulder, Colorado, to Lawrence
Ferlinghetti in San Francisco

Dear Larry: Don't forget the spirit of comedy!
[. . .] The local "Poetry War" (reminiscent of a little of old fashioned
San Francisco poesy wars of past) (and present) has taken a slight turn
for the better. Gordon Ball visited saw Stan Brakhage who was con-
vinced (possibly by rumor or Tom Clark's book or [Ed] Dorn's letter therein) that the "oriental despot" or yellow peril or me and Anne
Waldman or some "Machine" from Naropa under my direction was
"breathing heavy" on Clark's and Dorn's phone, following them, had Norman K.
been spying in their office to steal their manuscript (*Boulder Maga
zine*) and otherwise persecuting them. The whole scene reminds me
of the white-black paranoia promoted by Cointelpro-FBI in late 60s
— friends paranoid of each other, rumors that one or another party is
the CIA or FBI or an agent, escalation animosity between factions,
obnoxious or inflammatory pictures or statements repeated one to another, etc.

Brakhage and I talked, then he talked to Ed Dorn who told him,
no, nobody was following them and then Brakhage talked to Clark,
and Clark and Dorn came around to saying, well, no nobody was harassing them, at least not Naropa nor the Buddhists as far as they
knew; then I had lunch with Ed Dorn whom I hadn't seen since last
summer then Peter [Orlovsky] and I went over and saw Tom Clark at
Dorn's and stayed up talking till A.M. and they finally presented me
with a copy of my own taped interview with Clark. Clark's editing of
tape was much more considerable than I had remembered — sooner
or later I'll transcribe it and probably publish the parts he excised —
about two ten-minute sections, something like that.

Ted Berrigan is in town and is a sane friendly presence, talking to
everybody. Clark called several days ago saying he was getting so much
flak from the book his *Poetry Wars* — from Brakhage and others whom
he said were "paranoid" or "corrupt" that he wanted to de-escalate the
hostilities, which of course makes sense. I don't know if you've taken
into account how much "inflammatory" mis-information is contained

in his prefatory half of the book, and that has caused a great deal of paranoia in every direction. I've been trying to straighten it out, and Clark says he will try to — he says — tho half the time hinting more dire and bloody crimes hidden under the Vajrayana carpet. There is no end to downer gossip if he is obsessed in that direction. However he and Dorn now seem to be altering their stories slightly.

If the present month's anxiety for me in your mind has to do with Clark's book's presentation that the Buddhist, or Naropa, or me and Anne, etc., have been harassing them, please now check back with Clark or Dorn. If you'll look back in Clark's book: 1. Dorn's letter to Callahan "as in being tailed" p. 49. 2: Clark's comment par 1 sentence , page 39. 3: Callaghan's petition point 2 p. 51. 4: Par 38.49 Callaghan's comments on reaction. 5: "It became a poets' war" etc. paragraph 1 page 40. Please do take 5 minutes to check this out and you'll see folly.

I'll try to answer more fully later. Working on David Solomon[167] petition, teaching school, writing new poems, practicing meditation ten hours a day last weekend and this, and trying to work on PEN Club FBI report.

As ever
Allen

Larry: Please don't publish this letter. I'm trying to de-escalate the gossip and paranoia because I think it's strange folly. You wrote so strongly I thought I'd better let you know where things are at around here.

---

167 David Solomon (1925–2007), was an editor and psychedelic expert whose work to inform the public about marijuana use created difficulties for him.

April 7, 1980: Lawrence Ferlinghetti in San Francisco to Allen Ginsberg in New York

Dear Allen:

Don't worry I wouldn't publish your letters re: Poetry Wars without your permission.

Thanks for the detailed "explanation" (which I really don't need). You know I'm just against the whole idea of subjugation of one's mind and will and body to anyone who is considered to be on a higher level or authority or consciousness or whatever. (Or should I say "submission" rather than subjugation?) The anarchist in me just isn't interested! in fact, views it with aversion. (Even though I realize that never in the history of the world has there been such a poetics institute!) (There's a quote for you!)

So you're following Dylan: "You got to serve someone." Poor Dylan, I think he has lost his brains on this latest record of his (*Slow Train Coming*). Fer Christ's sake! I don't gotta serve nobody. You gotta serve someone, indeed. (King, guru, lama, führer, fucker, lover!)

See you in church —

love —

Daddy F

ca. April 1980: Allen Ginsberg in Durham, North Carolina, to Lawrence Ferlinghetti in San Francisco

Dear Larry:

[. . .] When I get to San Francisco let's try and figure out *Collected Poems*. Are you sure New Directions can't do it? [Tom] Maschler in London would fund most of the typesetting he says. Otherwise Joyce Johnson[168] at Dial would be willing to co-publish it with City Lights, as would others. So please check out New Directions once for all — *Collected Poems* and *Collected Interviews* and *Collected Essays* is slowly

---

168 Joyce Johnson (b. 1935), a writer and editor who once had dated Jack Kerouac.

in works. Otherwise Fred Jordan, Metheuen, Joyce, and others are interested, and I'm about ready to roll. [. . .]

OK, Love
Allen

September 8, 1980: Lawrence Ferlinghetti in San Francisco to Allen Ginsberg in New York

Dear Allen:
[. . .] Wrote a lot this summer in Europe — and will enclose my big Amsterdam poem "Endless Life" if I can find an extra copy — I'd like to know what you think of it — I never really get any comment from you!

Craig was here from Subterranean distributors and said we really need a book by you now — for the Spring list. Can you now get that *Plutonium Ode* book manuscript together now and send it soon? Let me know — Last winter you said it was ready.

Antler's book in page-proof stage, and he will see it soon. It should be out by November.

Due to money, I don't think we can do the 3-in-1 poets book in quite some time.[169] Three unknown poets in a book simply can't make it now. When I thought of the idea, the times seemed better for it. [. . .]

Sweet Dreams —
Lawrence

---

169 In fact this book never materialized.

◀ 1981 ▶

July 13, 1981: Allen Ginsberg in Boulder, Colorado, to Lawrence
Ferlinghetti in San Francisco

Dear Larry:

Here's signed contract for *Plutonian Ode*. I'd not wanted to send it in
till the product (book) was really completed. I'll send the book manuscript in in a week, it needs ten pages more retyped and a final look-
see. [. . .]

I received the *Endless Life* selected poems. I'll use it to select
which of the longer poems or manifestos to teach as part of my anthology, I hadn't yet made that selection.[170] I keep thinking of the "Wilfred
Funk" poem. I just typed up and revised a poem from Yugoslavia called
"Bird Brain" for *Plutonian Ode* book, similar in style to "Funk." ("Birdbrain wrote this poem.") "Dog" still looks good. I had included *Pictures
Gone World* #12 and #17 which you didn't include. I have to add in the
poem with butterfly going in and out of boxcar rolling on field, still.
"Golden Gate Park" and "Constantly Risking Absurdity" and "The cat
on counter moved among licorice sticks" are still memorable in 2nd
book *Coney Island*, or are my favorites. "Underwear" looks good and "I
Am Waiting," still OK. "Hidden Door" has lots of material but the re-
frain seems in the way. I'm glad you have notes to "Assassination Raga"
since both translators and 1980s students won't otherwise recognize
the references. I think "In Time of Revolution" poem itself makes a lot
of sense as a scene, but the point you make at end is irrelevant to the
scene you paint so accurately and has always unnerved me a little at the
end of otherwise perfect poem. (To be continued)

In haste

Allen Ginsberg

---

170 Ginsberg was teaching a course on the Literary History of the Beat Generation at
Naropa and put together an anthology of materials for his class.

◄ 1982 ►

Ginsberg's hopes of signing a contract for his collected poems continued to be foiled by difficulties, this time with Knopf.

March 29, 1982: Lawrence Ferlinghetti in San Francisco to Allen Ginsberg in New York

Dear Allen:

Long time no see or hear. Knopf has never answered or sent actual contract after telling us on phone "it's in the mail." So I have reopened talks with Dial, and just had a letter from Joyce Johnson saying they are delighted and will write soon about contractual details. So hope this OK with you. Knopf was insisting on a "Selected" paperback within two years and Dial has never mentioned such a thing. Since we now think that City Lights itself should do a "Selected" soon, naturally we want to go with Dial. (Joyce J. suggests Don Allen should be asked to edit "Assembled Poetries" and an Introduction. What do you think?) (I know you've already done most of the editing.) And: Is it OK if we schedule a "Selected Poems" for, say, a year from now? If so, would you be able to make the selection by this coming Fall? I think it is time to do it. (Include only one section or two sections of *Howl*, so that that book would continue to sell.)

> Hope you're fine
> and dandy —
> Love —
> Lawrence

For Ginsberg, most of 1982 was taken up with his work planning and hosting the 25th anniversary celebration for On the Road *at the Naropa Institute that summer in Boulder. On a shoestring budget, Allen managed to bring together nearly everyone connected with the Beat Generation, including Ferlinghetti.*

May 4, 1982: Allen Ginsberg in Boulder, Colorado, to Lawrence Ferlinghetti in San Francisco

Dear Larry:

[. . .] How are things with Knopf and Dial. Let me know the various propositions and progress, or ask Annie [Janowitz][171] to let me know.

Kerouac Festival looks better and better, tho shoestring finances limit our megalomaniac schemes. We haven't got a strong visual arts activist tho we have Gregory's pictures and seven by Karel Appel,[172] and are trying to organize someone to handle yours, [Jack] Micheline's, Kerouac's thru Sterling Lord, [Robert] Frank's photo, [Fred] McDarrah's collection, etc., all in due time. Jane Faigao's[173] working like ten people. Putting together posters, brochures, and prospective schedules this week. A million things to check out for accuracy.

OK

Allen

Despite pessimisms from various directions it seems to me a time of great poetry. Gregory's new book[174] is brilliant and his best, Antler's *Factory* is really remarkable and at least not boring, Nanao's [Sakaki] book is rare and permanent, *Plutonian Ode* is solid rock, your *Collected Poems* is very rich, David Cope tho unpublished is one of the century's best and most extensive epiphany vignette collections, and that's a lot going on at once. The move to public music is also a good sign — lots of heroic social electric word bands and art bands are emerging from New Wave and Old Punk and I bet that produces some new kind of

---

171 Annie Janowitz was working at City Lights at the time.
172 Karel Appel (1921–2006), a Dutch painter.
173 Jane Faigao (1943–2001), one of the organizers of the Jack Kerouac event at Naropa.
174 *Herald of the Autochthonic Spirit*, Gregory Corso (New Directions, 1981).

poetry. I'll be on next Clash album,[175] and my own double album from Hammond is due out late June, already in physical production. I did more club dates in Denver with Birdbrain "Gluon" band man Mike Chapelle, and we may have a good long (21 stanza) version of "Capitol Air."

One thing poetry can do is say what poet really thinks so it has more function than ever in U.S. drowned in hypocritical television. I was listening to tapes of Prague "Plastic People of Universe" poetry band — halfway new wave halfway Brecht-Weil and folk tradition — and see how crucial a catalyst they are tho half of them are in jail in Czechoslovakia by now.

---

175 *Combat Rock* (1982) by the Clash.

‹ 1983 ›

When a contract with Knopf for Ginsberg's Collected Poems *finally fell through, Allen's patience reached its end. He decided to hire an agent, Andrew Wylie, to negotiate on his behalf for all future books and contracts. It was the end of his twenty-five-year publishing partnership with Ferlinghetti, although Allen would continue to work with City Lights from time to time on various projects. Less dramatically, Allen's visit to the photographer Berenice Abbott in the letter below marks the beginning of a renewed interest in photography, something he would pursue for the rest of his life.*

September 28, 1983: Allen Ginsberg in Boulder, Colorado, to Lawrence Ferlinghetti and Nancy Peters in San Francisco

Dear Larry and Nancy:

[. . .] I hired Andrew Wylie to reconstruct my publishing life and get a New York publisher for *Collected Poems, Essays, Interviews, Mid-1950s Journals* that Gordon Ball is editing now in Japan, etc.

I woke up a month ago $6,600 in debt for the first time in my life that big. After twenty-seven years of publishing I'd like to make a living from writing, even if it is mostly poetry. I was spurred to action when Miles came to town and said he couldn't find a copy of *Kaddish* anywhere in Village or East Village or uptown. There must be some copies in New York, but he had trouble finding them. Maybe New York publishing house distribution would ease that situation for a collected poems and selected, etc. I'll leave it up to Andrew Wylie, who'll be in touch with you. I instructed him basically to make the best deal he could, at the same time preserving City Lights editions which are traditional and beautiful.

I'm back in Boulder, with Peter [Orlovsky] till December, then I'll be co-director *Emeritus* and move my goods here to New York — books and clothes — and come visit summers like I used to. Although

August trip to New York's poisonous smog heat made me wonder why live there. In Maine I saw Berenice Abbott and she said that after lung operation twenty years ago or so, her doctor told her she'd die within a few years if she stayed in New York. [. . .]

Love

Allen

P.S. I let matters lapse so badly, not taking care of business, that I could find neither *Collected Essays* manuscript nor *Howl* contract in my files. I do have the *Collected Interviews* that Don Allen edited, which I think you once had in safe. I can't remember where I last saw *Collected Interviews*. Did you ever have it? Any recollection of sending it to me or my taking it? We do have the index and can retrieve copies of the texts, but I hate to go thru re-editing.

◀ 1984 ▶

January 1, 1984: Allen Ginsberg in New York to Lawrence Ferlinghetti and Nancy Peters in San Francisco

Dear Larry and Nancy:
[. . .] I told Andy [Wylie] to figure out a way that will leave everybody feeling good and not feeling bad. That was the basis of my first rejection of the Harper contract in order to keep City Lights free to publish its editions. I was a little bewildered by your change of mind later. But whatever works out best for all of us will obviously be the best solution. I just want to make sure I have a permanent income after quarter century of publishing austerity on my part. So he'll get in touch with you. We got your letter.

As ever,
Allen

Through Andrew Wylie, Ginsberg secured a contract with Harper & Row to publish his next five books, including his Collected Poems *and* Selected Poems. *These were uncertain times for Ferlinghetti and City Lights, for although Allen wanted to protect them and make certain they could continue to publish Ginsberg's older titles, it remained uncertain what impact the move would make on City Lights.*

April 3, 1984: Allen Ginsberg in New York to Lawrence Ferlinghetti and Nancy Peters in San Francisco

Dear Larry and Nancy:
The difference between Knopf offer, and Harper is:
    1. Harper will publish the next five books of poetry, interviews, essays, journals, correspondence with an advance of around $25,000

each, as well as collected poetry. They do that whether the book sells well or not. They take on my books, on those terms. With Knopf, they did not want to talk to me about other books, when I asked them, in trying alone (without agent) for a month to work out contract with them. They didn't even answer an eight-page letter I wrote to editor Bob Gottlieb. So they would have had [*Collected*] *Poems* which is the choice book, without committing themselves to be my publisher.

Doesn't that make the decision wise, and inevitable, to go with Harper? What would you suggest otherwise, or have done yourself? You also advised me to get an agent, finally.

2. As to terms, Harper offered a shade higher advance — $26,300 [and] better percentages. [. . .] I have approval on binding, paper, design, etc. in Harper, and not in Knopf contract.

Knopf is part of Newhouse chain. Harper is independent, part employee owned. These were some of the considerations, not all. Further, I just need an agent to take care of all the correspondence and publishing of essays and poems.

I think it's clear that Wylie has done alright by me for the Harper contract. So please don't be so hard on him, he is doing his job, better than I imagined could be done. I didn't even know I had right to contract for approval of binding, paper, and type. This way I've been able to have Harry Smith[176] design a cover logo for all of the books. Please work the rest out with Wylie.

OK, love, toodle-oo till London

In haste
Allen

Even as his health declined, Ginsberg showed no signs of slowing down. He traveled more than ever, not only to give poetry readings, but to perform his music and exhibit his photography as well. Photography ate up a lot of the new money he was getting from his Harper & Row contract, in fact. In the

---

176 Harry Smith (1923–1991), an artist, filmmaker, and ethnomusicologist who lived in Ginsberg's New York apartment for a while.

*autumn of 1984 he visited China as part of a writer's delegation and then
stayed on alone for a few more months.*

October 28, 1984: Allen Ginsberg in Si-an, China, to Lawrence
Ferlinghetti, Nancy Peters, and Bob Sharrard[177] in San Francisco

Dear Larry and Nancy and Bob and all:
All well here, folk on street polite and friendly, I just walked down side
alley at nite and kicked over a couple glasses of beer, they were selling
on the ground next to a sliced pig liver stand lit by kerosene lamp in
the dark across from big department store in this old capital of Hun
and Tong Dynasties where Li Po and Po Chi[178] walked, and the beer
seller bowed said thank you, when I stopped in shame, and refused my
fistful of incomprehensible yuan $.

Been a week in Beijing, big reading at Foreign Language School,
400 English scholars crowded in auditorium, big hit, they (many of
the poets) knew *Howl* since 1963. Gary [Snyder] and Maxine Hong
Kingston[179] and ten others read ten minutes each. Spent today in Sian
(warrior army of clay) and now wandering around alone, the others at
expensive hotel, guests for supper. Banquets every nite. China's great!
New Socialist Free Enterprise!

Love
Allen

---

177 Bob Sharrard, an editor at City Lights.
178 Li Po (701–762) or Li Bai, and Po Chi (772–846) or Po Chu-i were ancient Chinese
poets.
179 Maxine Hong Kingston (b. 1940), an American writer.

◀ 1985 ▶

Dear Larry, Nancy and Bob:
Thanks for royalty check arrived in good time, I'd been low on money,
spending $800 a month on photography.

Did you receive the photos I took of you and printed, in the cafe
with mirror, Larry?

Peter [Orlovsky] is settling OK between here and Karmê Chöling
("Tail of the Tiger") Buddhist retreat center, his looks improved as the
alcohol's evaporated from his system, weight and appearance back to
normal.

I've been overwhelmed worse than ever with hyperactive zig-
zagging reading, teaching, photographing, interviewing New York,
Boston, Detroit, Chicago, Washington, L.A., San Francisco, London,
Vancouver — now have seven weeks home quiet working on *Deliberate
Prose* or some such prose essays book, next order for Harpers; a preface
to [John] Wieners' *Collected Poems* to do this week, and finished edit-
ing interview with *Aperture* magazine on photography. Been seeing
Robert Frank a lot, and Berenice Abbott one long afternoon here in
New York, old lady of photography, took her picture.

Dear Allen —
Got your letter of May 30, and, yes, I did receive your photos of me.
You evidently didn't receive the letter I wrote you about them in which
I asked if I could reproduce the one in the Puccini Café (with you in

mirror) on a postcard. Or will you do it on one of your commercially-marketed ones? I love the photo!

— xxx —

LF

Ginsberg's Collected Poems *was published by Harper and Row in 1985, and he spent a good deal of time traveling around the world to promote it along with various translations of his work. The following year, he spent much of his time working on the manuscript for an annotated edition of* Howl. *Allen was to dedicate that book to Ferlinghetti.*

◀ 1986 ▶

Dear Larry:

I've been amiss in not keeping in better touch on my plans, though I wanted a part of it to be surprise.

There was little about *Howl* trial and publication, and very few footnotes for *Howl*, because I planned to cover all that extensive in *Annotated Howl* which was one of the six books scheduled for Harpers in original contract arrangement.

Your letter April 27, 1986, came in time to include one paragraph re: prior contact with ACLU. Enclosed is the whole section dealing with the trial.

1. Excerpts from "Horn on Howl," in which I've integrated your paragraph from above. I've used these portions for inside factual account by you.

2. Shig's [Murao] account of his arrest.

3. Selections from excellent account of trial by David Perlman, *The Reporter*, December 12, 1957. This supplements and extends your account as I've edited it from "Horn on Howl."

4. Excerpts from the judge's decision.

"Horn on Howl" is well known from *Casebook*,[180] and recently reprinted in Lewis Hyde book.[181] Miles suggested we excerpt your account, and edit down *The Reporter* article which is otherwise lost to public view and forgotten, but which was a sympathetic account of the trial drama. I tried to avoid repetition of info between the two articles cross-referenced. I hope this seems balanced historical documentation.

The poem eliminated in your editing was "The Names" (*Collected*

---

180 *The Casebook on the Beat* edited by Thomas Parkinson (Thomas Y. Crowell, 1961).
181 *On the Poetry of Allen Ginsberg*, edited by Lewis Hyde (University of Michigan Press, 1985).

Poems) according to Miles and Cherkovski[182] (your biographer). I had remembered wanting to include "Green Automobile." That'll be covered in my preface (not yet written and I'm two months behind deadline) to the whole book.

In acknowledgements section, back of *Collected Poems* there's brief mention of City Lights and your help, with Nancy Peters and Annie Janowitz, though it may seem lost in the mass of material I had to compile remember — trying to account for everyone who'd put in work on that particular volume — it takes several pages. It's true, there is not enough description of your role editing and City Lights' long support of me and the poetry. Though the back cover photo told the story somewhat — I'm holding up all the City Lights books.

In any case what I hadn't wanted to tell you, till the *Howl* book was out, so it be a surprise, was that the entire *Annotated Howl* book is dedicated to you anyway and has been from the beginning of the work on it. So I hope this pleases you and assuages your irritation with me — partly my own negligence in keeping you abreast of progress of the *Howl* book.

The Six Gallery reading documents and your telegram is included in another section of the book. There's also correspondence with you back and forth in the "contemporary literary correspondence" section put together several months ago. The whole job has been vast and I'm up too late. One problem in editing was to keep it to the text of the "Howl" poem (facsimiles and all) rather than the whole pamphlet and so that eliminated some background. [. . .]

If you have further notes on editing the book, or the trial before and after, etc., that you still think should be included, either write them out or point them out. I want to keep as much as possible focused on the single poem though. [. . .]

Love As ever
Allen

---

182 Neeli Cherkovski (b. 1945), poet and author of *Ferlinghetti: A Biography* (Garden City, NY: Doubleday, 1979).

◀ 1987 ▶

February 18, 1987: Lawrence Ferlinghetti in San Francisco to Allen
Ginsberg in New York

Dear Allen . . . .
I hear your health is better these days — which makes all of us feel
better! Anyway, thanks for the beautiful *White Shroud* (and the dedication to the *Annotated Howl* . . . . Wrote you about it several weeks past).
You've done it all as no one else could!

Lawrence

March 9, 1987: Lawrence Ferlinghetti in San Francisco to Allen Ginsberg
in New York

Dear Allen . . .
I've now received all your latest books, *White Shroud*, *Annotated Howl*,
Collected Poems, with written dedications, for all of which I much thank
you, (as well as for the printed dedicate in *Howl*). [. . .]
 Shroud is bound to get a lot of really bad reviews, I figure. You
know, if you really want to get away from "hideous public karma" why
don't you consider the simplest practical solution — move out of New
York City permanently? — move West . . . Go West, Ole Man — like
you always said you were going to do after your father died. After all,
you do own a house up at Gary's [Snyder], don't you? Really retreat
this time! One has to be a masochist to live in the Lower East Side
these days. I can't stand New York City anymore at all and won't go
there for any reason this year or soon — "dirty little island" . . . Or is
that Literary Club[183] too much to leave behind? (I see you've just got-

---

183 A reference to the American Academy of Arts and Letters, which Ginsberg now
belonged to, and to which he had recently supported Snyder's nomination as well.
Ferlinghetti himself would also be inducted into the American Academy.

ten Gary into it — why not just change places with him for a year, to begin with!)

New Directions seems to be very much taking me for granted these days — rejected my last two offerings — my early (pre–*Gone World*) poems, as well as my new (French) novel. And they don't even manage to get my books listed correctly in *Books-in-Print* — Laughlin has retired to Norfolk with Shakespeare and Lear and Ezra Pound and it shows in the New York office . . . .

— Love —
Dad

◄ 1989 ►

After the publication of Barry Miles's biography of Allen Ginsberg, Ferlinghetti sent a note complaining about the treatment he had received at Miles's hands and accusing Allen of having "vetted" the book. Allen was quick to reply in his own defense.

September 7, 1989: Allen Ginsberg in New York to Lawrence Ferlinghetti in San Francisco

Dear Larry:
I didn't "carefully vet" Miles' book — Skimmed large parts of it, corrected things I spotted here and there, didn't read it all — got hung up on his English-leftist view that I was asking for trouble from noble Castro police state and in delicate Prague conditions, and that Chinese communists did Tibetans a favor by freeing them from Trungpa-style hierarchical serfdom — so went carefully over those sections, consulted others expect in Tibetan and Trungpa history said it would affect Naropa funds — That part I exhausted myself over — repulsed to interfere and that Miles had such heavy Marxist spin on his account — (such as, that 1973-1983 Naropa period my poetry declined and got better when I left — I pointed out that "Plutonian Ode", "Father Death Blues", "Capitol Air", "White Shroud" poems were all done at Naropa so he removed that sentence).

But I didn't read or "vet" the whole book — too neurotically repulsed by the task — couldn't face it — particularly his denigration of Kerouac's persona and Corso's — giving me (as in your case) a kind of Pyrrhic Victory. So didn't intrude much on those areas — I talked to hills.

Love
Allen

◀ 1991 ▶

One short exchange of postcards late in 1991 indicates that Ferlinghetti and Ginsberg were over their difficulties and on friendly terms.

November 22, 1991: Lawrence Ferlinghetti in San Francisco to Allen Ginsberg in New York

Allen —
I wanted to tell you what a fine performance you turned in at the Berkeley benefit last week, and I hear you said some wonderful things about City Lights at your Herbst Theater reading. You sure have developed your voice to its fullest. It keeps getting better and better — clearer, fine articulation, volume modulation, tenderness and power!

Love —
Lawrence

November 29, 1991: Allen Ginsberg in New York to Lawrence Ferlinghetti in San Francisco

Dear Larry:
Thanks for card. I've been giving so many poetry readings that I'm getting better at it. One main element added in last ten years is Shambhala or Bodhisattva "attitude" repeatedly encouraged (first by Trungpa) more recently by spiritual friend Ghelek Rimpoche[184] (I've been seeing) who says I shouldn't "doubt" what I'm doing giving readings because it does some good particularly for younger people to see someone sane with independent mind and background of meditative equanimity whether called dharmic" or just "poetic," (Ghelek says

---

184 Ghelek Rimpoche (b. 1939), the head of the Jewel Heart Buddhist group that Ginsberg joined after the death of Chögyam Trungpa.

269

take a courageous "doubtless" or doubt-free) attitude, lift head and shoulders, face the phenomenal world and proclaim subjective feeling insight and imagination freely, as good example, whether the "ideas" purveyed are valid or not, the open attitude is valid as model. So it's given me strength and encouragement to set forth thru the states and yawp. Thanks for tender card.

I'm working with Steve Taylor on book of songs for City Lights — have to pay him for rewriting all the lead sheets exact neat up-to-date. [. . .]

As ever,
Allen

◄ **1993** ►

In a postscript to a postcard that Ginsberg sent to Ferlinghetti on May 17, 1993, Allen had mentioned, "Also doing book with Eric Drooker[185] for Four Walls Four Windows Press."

May 21, 1993: Lawrence Ferlinghetti in San Francisco to Allen Ginsberg in New York

Cher Allen —
Got your epistle to my home address and I too am going to Europe this Fall — though only Spain — Alora, near Malaga — You be in Spain or Italy? Perhaps we meet up over there, as so many times in the past. [. . .] . . . . Anyway, since I've been heavy into studying Italian, I really can't appreciate "French" anymore . . . . Nancy [Peters] and I both highly surprised that you're doing a book with 4 Walls/4 Windows (what about the floor and the ceiling?) Press. We thought our/ your agreement with Harper and Row — for-your-life precluded any other press, but them. Why not us, then?

> Love and Kisseth
>
> —
>
> Lawrence

June 28, 1993: Allen Ginsberg in New York to Lawrence Ferlinghetti in San Francisco

Dear Larry:
I've been working nicely, hard, getting work done. [. . .]
    Eric Drooker (see enclosed sample) has been making Lynd Ward

---

185 Eric Drooker (b. 1958), an artist and illustrator whom Allen knew from the East Village.

— Franz Masereel-like expressionist posters for the Tompkins Square anarchists for five years and posters for [Steven] Taylor's ex-punk group False Prophets. He came to me a few years ago and we decided to do some kind of project together. This year he got a contract from 4 Walls 8 Windows Press to select a big bunch of my HarperCollins *Collected Poems* and some from *White Shroud* and make cartoons or illustrations of them — it's his own project — he got Harper's OK for printing his selection — and negotiated it all himself, so I have no active work there new, just encouraging him and OK'ing his work — a cartoon book of poems. So I'm not "doing a book" except remotely — it's Drooker's project. [. . .]

Love
Allen

July 1993: Lawrence Ferlinghetti in San Francisco to Allen Ginsberg in New York

Caro Allen —
[. . .] So you've got yourself a Masereel — that's a fine fit. Drooker's art and your voice — (only Masereel closer to Brecht-Beckett-Kafka, the young Werther . . . .) . Go for it. And yes, City Lights would certainly be interested in <u>your</u> Naropa lectures — Ask him to send us a list of possible subjects.

In the meantime we await Stephen Taylor's work . . . . for the songbook . . . .

Vado al campo per studiare italiano la settimana prossima. Io preferisco italiano al francese!

Ciao —
Lorenzo

◀ **1994** ▶

This is one of the last letters between the two old friends. After this they were still in touch, but only by telephone or through letters from their respective secretaries.

December 21, 1994: Allen Ginsberg in New York to Lawrence Ferlinghetti in San Francisco

3AM answering mail

Dear Larry:

Rhino made effort to put out the box set [of recordings] I never expected to see the light of day before I died.

They wanted to break into the chain market for distribution, otherwise they didn't think they'd sell enuf to get expensive project off the ground.

They're distributed by Warner Brothers, big brother.

I sent them *Poets and Writer's* guide to independent literary bookstores, with annotations and list of special stores I'd done book signings in and have been pushing them to deal as much as possible with them — Ingram distributes for them also. They'd been lame on that area.

I'll try to keep Harper's strict to deal with the independent stores in book signings, next book next April 29 *Journals 1954–1958* (filling in gap of previous journals).

Just back from Europe, did signing at George Whitman's — he did have City Lites Books, and we sold about 150 varied books, including English Penguin *Cosmopolitan Greetings*.

If I go to Tibet with Ghelek Rinpoche, my cardiologist Dr. Tallwin who wants to visit his mother in India says he'll go along to get me settled at 12,000 feet. If I go! It'll be June 15-August 15, 1995. Maybe not.

Gregory's just ill, physically and in pain all the time, and also short of breath.

In Paris, stayed at Ritz three nights with assistant Peter Hale who came along, helped carry bags, made travel easier — bills paid by *Nouvel Observateur*.

Saw painter George Condo, one nite at Maxim's and Ritz Club with Prince of Hannover via Condo who did two portraits. Rest of time with Lebel, Bourgois, Michel Bulteau, [George] Whitman on his birthday.

This first day back answering missives.

Love to all,
Allen

In late March 1997, Ginsberg's health took a turn for the worse and he went to the emergency room of New York's Beth Israel Hospital. The doctors found that he had undiagnosed and inoperable liver cancer and they gave him only six months to live. He returned to his apartment and called friends ,including Ferlinghetti, to tell them the bad news. The prognosis was overly optimistic, and within a week, on April 5, 1997, Ginsberg passed away. When Lawrence heard the news he wrote the following poem for his old friend.

Allen Ginsberg Dying

Allen Ginsberg is dying
It's in all the papers
It's on the evening news
A great poet is dying
But his voice
won't die
His voice is on the land
In Lower Manhattan
in his own bed
he is dying
There is nothing
to do about it
He is dying the death that everyone dies
He is dying the death of the poet
He has a telephone in his hand
and he calls everyone
from his bed in Lower Manhattan
All around the world
late at night
the telephone is ringing
This is Allen

the voice says
Allen Ginsberg calling
How many times have they heard it
over the long great years
He doesn't have to say Ginsberg
All around the world
in the world of poets
there is only one Allen
I wanted to tell you he says
He tells them what's happening
what's coming down
on him
Death the dark lover
going down on him
His voice goes by satellite
over the land
over the Sea of Japan
where he once stood naked
trident in hand
like a young Neptune
a young man with black beard
standing on a stone beach
It is high tide and the seabirds cry
The waves break over him now
and the seabirds cry
on the San Francisco waterfront
There is a high wind
There are great whitecaps
lashing the Embarcadero
Allen is on the telephone His voice is on the waves
I am reading Greek poetry
The sea is in it
Horses weep in it
The horses of Achilles
weep in it

here by the sea
in San Francisco
where the waves weep
They make a sibilant sound
a sibylline sound
Allen
they whisper
Allen

Index